Counterclaims in Investment Arbitration

International Litigation in Practice

VOLUME 13

The titles published in this series are listed at *brill.com/inli*

Counterclaims in Investment Arbitration

Holding Foreign Investors Accountable for Violations of International Law

By

Edward Guntrip

BRILL | NIJHOFF

LEIDEN | BOSTON

Library of Congress Cataloging-in-Publication Data

Names: Guntrip, Edward, author.
Title: Counterclaims in investment arbitration : holding foreign investors accountable for violations of international law / by Edward Guntrip.
Description: Leiden ; Boston : Brill/Nijhoff, 2024. | Series: International litigation in practice, 1874-0502 ; volume 13 | Includes bibliographical references and index. | Summary: "Foreign investors benefit from investment protection standards in international investment law that are enforceable in investment arbitration. However, international law does not directly bind foreign investors, and investment arbitration struggles to address foreign investor misconduct. Thus, host States cannot easily claim against foreign investors for breaches of international law in investment arbitration"– Provided by publisher.
Identifiers: LCCN 2024019617 (print) | LCCN 2024019618 (ebook) | ISBN 9789004420946 (hardback) | ISBN 9789004420953 (ebook)
Subjects: LCSH: Investments, Foreign (International law) | Investments, Foreign–Law and legislation | International commercial arbitration. | Set-off and counterclaim.
Classification: LCC K3830 .G86 2024 (print) | LCC K3830 (ebook) | DDC 346/.092–dc23/eng/20240511
LC record available at https://lccn.loc.gov/2024019617
LC ebook record available at https://lccn.loc.gov/2024019618

Typeface for the Latin, Greek, and Cyrillic scripts: "Brill". See and download: brill.com/brill-typeface.

ISSN 1874-0502
ISBN 978-90-04-42094-6 (hardback)
ISBN 978-90-04-42095-3 (e-book)
DOI 10.1163/9789004420953

Contents

Acknowledgements

This book has been influenced by numerous people from a range of research institutions. The idea for the book stems from the conclusions I drew in my PhD thesis undertaken at Brunel University, London. Although countless people provided me with support during this time, I would particularly like to thank my PhD examiners. They challenged me in a way that strengthened my convictions regarding the potential role that counterclaims could play in investment arbitration. During my time as an academic in Sussex Law School I have learnt how to become a better researcher through discussions with my colleagues and mentors. Thanks to those of you who have provided me with feedback on presentations or draft papers and those who have simply chatted about research with me in the corridors. I am also grateful that Sussex Law School fosters a conducive research environment and allowed me to take research leave so that I could start drafting the book. Part of this book was written when I undertook a Visiting Fellowship at The Human Rights Centre at the Faculty of Law and Criminology at Ghent University in 2019. I would like to thank everyone who contributed to the discussions about the book at my work in progress seminar.

Some people deserve to be mentioned individually. Thanks to Professor Chris Henderson and Dr Ahmad Ghouri who provided me with feedback on a draft version of this book. Thanks also go to the anonymous reviewer for their constructive criticism and suggestions for improvement. As always, all errors and omissions are mine. This book was written in challenging circumstances – a global pandemic, nearby construction work being undertaken seven days a week during a national lockdown, an incredibly stressful house move and other significant life changing events. Considering this context, I would like to thank my dog Emi for ensuring that I maintain a work-life balance. His ability to prevent me from working beyond normal hours by nuzzling my elbow when it is time to play or go for a walk has kept me grounded. I am incredibly grateful to Steph for supporting me and for listening to me talk about the book for years. Her achievements in this regard are even more impressive given that she is writing her own book. I am also grateful to my parents. It is a shame that Dad won't get to see the final book.

Abbreviations

AF	Additional Facility
ARSIWA	Articles on Responsibility of States for Internationally Wrongful Acts
BIT	Bilateral Investment Treaty
CCPR	Committee on Civil and Political Rights
CESCR	Committee on Economic, Social and Cultural Rights
COMESA	Common Market for Eastern and Southern Africa
DR-CAFTA	Free Trade Agreement between Central America, the Dominican Republic and the United States of America
ECOWAS	Economic Community of West African States
EFTA	European Free Trade Association
FTA	Free Trade Agreement
IBA	International Bar Association
ICCPR	International Covenant on Civil and Political Rights
ICESCR	International Covenant on Economic, Social and Cultural Rights
ICJ	International Court of Justice
ICSID	International Centre for the Settlement of Investment Disputes
IIA	International Investment Agreement
IIL	International Investment Law
ILC	International Law Commission
NAFTA	North American Free Trade Agreement
OIC	Organization of the Islamic Conference
PAIC	Pan-African Investment Code
SADC	Southern African Development Community
UDHR	Universal Declaration of Human Rights
UNCITRAL	United Nations Commission on International Trade Law
UNGPS	United Nations Guiding Principles on Business and Human Rights
VCLT	Vienna Convention on the Law of Treaties

Table of Treaties

Model Investment Agreements

African Union Commission, Draft Pan-African Investment Code, December 2016.
Belgium-Luxembourg Economic Union Model Bilateral Investment Treaty 2019.
Brazil Model Cooperation and Facilitation Investment Agreement 2015.
Draft India Model Bilateral Investment Treaty, March 2015.
Final India Model Bilateral Investment Treaty, December 2015.
Netherlands Model Bilateral Investment Treaty 2019.
Southern African Development Community Model Bilateral Investment Treaty Template.
Slovakia Model Bilateral Investment Treaty 2019.

Investment Agreements

Agreement on Promotion, Protection and Guarantee of Investments amongst the Member States of the Organization of the Islamic Conference (adopted 5 June 1981, entered into force February 1998).
Argentina-United Arab Emirates Bilateral Investment Treaty (adopted 16 April 2018, not yet in force).
Australia-Republic of Korea Free Trade Agreement 2014 (adopted 8 April 2014, entered into force 12 December 2014).
Belarus-India Bilateral Investment Treaty (adopted 24 September 2018, entered into force 5 March 2020).
Belgium-Luxembourg-Burundi Bilateral Investment Treaty (adopted 13 April 1989, entered into force 12 September 1993).
China-Colombia Bilateral Investment Treaty 2008 (adopted 22 November 2008, entered into force 2 July 2013).
China-Hungary Bilateral Investment Treaty (adopted 29 May 1991, entered into force 1 April 1993).
China-Mauritius Free Trade Agreement 2019 (adopted 17 October 2019, not yet in force).
Comprehensive and Progressive Agreement for Trans-Pacific Partnership 2018 (adopted 8 March 2018, entered into force 30 December 2018).

Economic Community of West African States Supplementary Act A/SA.3/12/08 Adopting Community Rules on Investment and the Modalities for their Implementation with Economic Community of West African States.
Energy Charter Treaty (adopted 17 December 1994, entered into force 16 April 1998) 2080 UNTS 95.
European Free Trade Association-Costa Rica-Panama Free Trade Agreement (adopted 24 June 2013, entered into force 19 August 2014).
Free Trade Agreement between Central America, the Dominican Republic and the United States of America (adopted 5 August 2004, entered into force 1 January 2009).
Investment Agreement for the Common Market for Eastern and Southern Africa Common Investment Area (adopted 23 May 2007, not yet in force).
Iran-Slovakia Bilateral Investment Treaty (adopted 19 January 2016, entered into force 30 August 2017).
Italy-Romania Bilateral Investment Treaty (adopted 29 May 1991, entered into force 1 April 1993).
Japan-Switzerland Free Trade and Economic Partnership Agrement 2009 (adopted 19 February 2009, entered into force 1 September 2009).
Japan-Uruguay Bilateral Investment Treaty 2015 (adopted 26 January 2015, entered into force 14 April 2017).
Morocco-Nigeria Bilateral Investment Treaty (adopted 3 December 2016, not yet in force).
Morocco-United States of America Free Trade Agreement 2004 (adopted 15 June 2004, entered into force 1 January 2006).
Nicaragua-Taiwan Province of China Free Trade Agreement 2006 (adopted 23 June 2006, entered into force 1 January 2008).
North American Free Trade Agreement (adopted 17 December 1992, entered into force 1 January 1994) 32 ILM 289.
Romania-Greece Bilateral Investment Treaty (adopted 23 May 1997, entered into force 11 June 1998).
United Arab Emirates-Slovakia Bilateral Investment Treaty (adopted 22 September 2016, entered into force 5 Febuary 2018).
United Kingdom-Venezuela, Bolivarian Republic Bilateral Investment Treaty (adopted 15 March 1995, entered into force 1 August 1996).

Treaties

Convention on the Recognition and Enforcement of Foreign Arbitral Awards (adopted 10 June 1958, entered into force 7 June 1959) 330 UNTS 3.

Convention on the Settlement of Investment Disputes Between States and Nationals of Other States (adopted 18 March 1965, entered into force 14 October 1966) 575 UNTS 171.
International Convention on the Elimination of All Forms of Racial Discrimination (adopted 21 December 1965, entered into force 4 January 1969) 660 UNTS 195.
International Covenant on Civil and Political Rights (adopted 16 December 1966, entered into force 23 March 1976) 999 UNTS 171.
International Covenant on Economic, Social and Cultural Rights (adopted 16 December 1966, entered into force 3 January 1976) 993 UNTS 3.
Rome Statute of the International Criminal Court (adopted 17 July 1998, entered into force 1 July 2002) 2187 UNTS 90.
Vienna Convention on the Law of Treaties (adopted 23 May 1969, entered into force 27 January 1980) 1155 UNTS 331.

Arbitration Rules

ICSID Additional Facility Arbitration Rules (2006).
ICSID Additional Facility Arbitration Rules (2022).
ICSID Additional Facility Rules (2006).
ICSID Additional Facility Rules (2022).
ICSID Arbitration Rules (2006).
ICSID Arbitration Rules (2022).
UNCITRAL Arbitration Rules (1976).
UNCITRAL Arbitration Rules (2010).

United Nations Documents

Committee on Civil and Political Rights, CCPR General Comment No. 25: Article 25 (Participation in Public Affairs and the Right to Vote), The Right to Participate in Public Affairs, Voting Rights and the Right of Equal Access to Public Service (12 July 1996) CCPR/C/21/Rev.1/Add.7.
Committee on Economic, Social and Cultural Rights, 'General Comment no 12' on 'The Right to Adequate Food' (12 May 1999) UN Doc E/C.12/1999/5.
Committee on Economic, Social and Cultural Rights, 'General Comment no 15' on 'The Right to Water (arts. 11 and 12 of the International Covenant on Economic, Social and Cultural Rights)' (20 January 2003) UN Doc E/C.12/2002/11.

Committee on Economic, Social and Cultural Rights, 'General Comment No. 26 (2022) on land and economic, social and cultural rights' (24 January 2023) UN Doc. No. E/C.12/GC/26.

Committee on the Elimination of All Forms of Racial Discrimination, General Recommendation 23 on the rights of indigenous peoples, 18 August 1997.

International Law Commission, Draft Articles on State Responsibility for Internationally Wrongful Acts in 'Report of the International Law Commission on the Work of its 53rd Session' (23 April – 1 June and 2 July – 10 August 2001) UN Doc. A/56/10.

International Law Commission, 'First Report on *jus cogens*' by Dire Tladi, Special Rapporteur' (8 March 2016) UN Doc A/CN4/693.

International Law Commission, 'Fragmentation of International Law: Difficulties Arising from the Diversification and Expansion of International Law' (13 April 2006) UN Doc A/CN4/L682.

Rio Declaration on Environment and Development (concluded 13 June 1992) UN Doc. A/CONF.151/26 (vol. I).

UNCITRAL Working Group III, 'Possible Reform of Investor-State Dispute Settlement (ISDS)' (5 September 2018) UN Doc A/CN.9/WG.III/ WP.149.

UNCITRAL Working Group III, 'Possible reform of investor-State dispute settlement (ISDS): Annotations to the draft provisions on procedural and cross-cutting issues' (31 July 2023) UN Doc No. A/CN.9/WG.III/WP.232.

UNCITRAL Working Group III, 'Possible reform of investor-State dispute settlement (ISDS): Draft provisions on procedural and cross-cutting issues' (26 July 2023) UN Doc No. A/CN.9/WG.III/WP.231.

UNCITRAL Working Group III, 'Report of Working Group III (Investor-State Dispute Settlement Reform) on the Work of Its Thirty-Fifth Session (New York, 23–27 April 2018)' (14 May 2018) UN Doc A/CN.9/935.

United Nations' General Assembly Resolution 64/292 (3 August 2010) A/RES/ 64/292.

Universal Declaration of Human Rights (adopted 10 December 1948) UNGA Res 217 A(III).

Other International Documents

IBA Guidelines on Conflicts of Interest in International Arbitration (2014).

IBA Rules on the Taking of Evidence in International Arbitration (2020).

ICSID, 'Report of the Executive Directors on the Convention on the Settlement of Investment Disputes Between States and Nationals of other States'

<https://icsid.worldbank.org/rules-regulations/convention/report/section-one> accessed 22 February 2023.

ICSID Arbitration Rule 40, Note B(a), 1 ICSID Reports 100.

International Court of Justice, Rules of Court (1978) (adopted 14 April 1978, entered into force 1 July 1978).

International Labor Office's Tripartite Declaration of Principles concerning Multilateral Enterprises and Social Policy (of 1977, as amended in 2006).

Iran-United States Claims Tribunal Claims Settlement Declaration (19 January 1981) 20 ILM 223.

UNCITRAL Notes on Organizing Arbitral Proceedings (2016).

United Nations, Statute of the International Court of Justice, 18 April 1946.

Domestic Law

Albanian Foreign Investment Law 1993.

Amended and Restated Concession Agreement between the Republic of Liberia and Firestone Liberia Inc.

Ecuadorian Constitution 2008.

Egypt Law No. 43 of 1974 concerning the Investment of Arab and Foreign Funds and the Free Zone.

Venezuelan Foreign Investment Law.

Table of Cases

ICSID Awards

Abaclat and Others (formerly Giovanna a Beccara and Others) v. Argentine Republic ICSID Case No ARB/07/5, Decision on Jurisdiction and Admissibility, 4 August 2011.

Abaclat and others (formerly Giovanna a Beccara and others) v. Argentine Republic ICSID Case No ARB/07/5, Procedural Order No 15, 20 November 2012.

Abaclat and others (formerly Giovanna a Beccara and others) v. Argentine Republic ICSID Case No ARB/07/5, Dissenting Opinion to Procedural Order No 15, 20 November 2012.

ADF Group Inc. v. United States of America ICSID Case No ARB(AF)/00/1, Award, 9 January 2003.

AES Corporation v. Argentine Republic ICSID Case No ARB/02/17, Decision on Jurisdiction, 26 April 2005.

Alex Genin, Eastern Credit Limited, INC. and A.S. Baltoil v. Republic of Estonia ICSID Case No ARB/99/2, Award, 25 June 2001.

Amco Asia Corporation v. Republic of Indonesia ICSID Case No ARB/81/1, Decision on Annulment, 16 May 1986.

Amco Asia Corporation and others v. Republic of Indonesia ICSID Case No ARB/81/1, Decision on Jurisdiction in Resubmitted Proceeding, 10 May 1988.

Antoine Goetz and others v. Republic of Burundi [II] ICSID Case No ARB/01/2, Award, 21 June 2012.

Azurix Corp v. The Argentine Republic ICSID Case No ARB/01/12, Award, 14 July 2006.

Bear Creek Mining Corporation v. Republic of Peru ICSID Case No ARB/14/21, Partial Dissenting Opinion of Professor Philippe Sands QC, 30 November 2017.

Burlington Resources Inc. v. Republic of Ecuador ICSID Case No ARB/08/5, Decision on Liability, 14 December 2012.

Burlington Resources Inc. v. Republic of Ecuador ICSID Case No ARB/08/5, Decision on Counterclaims, 7 February 2017.

Burlington Resources Inc. v. Republic of Ecuador ICSID Case No ARB/08/5, Decision on Reconsideration and Award, 7 February 2017.

CEMEX Caracas Investments B.V. and CEMEX Caracas II Investments B.V. v. Bolivarian Republic of Venezuela ICSID Case No ARB/08/15, Decision on Jurisdiction, 30 December 2010.

Ceskoslovenska obchodní banka, a.s. v. Slovak Republic ICSID Case No ARB/97/4, Decision of the Tribunal on Objections to Jurisdiction, 24 May 1999.

CMS Gas Transmission Company v. Republic of Argentina ICSID Case No ARB/01/8, Decision of the Tribunal on Objections to Jurisdiction, 17 July 2003.

CMS Gas Transmission Company v. Argentine Republic ICSID Case No ARB/01/8, Award, 12 May 2005.

Continental Casualty Company v. Argentine Republic ICSID Case No ARB/03/9, Award, 5 September 2008.

David R. Aven and others v. Republic of Costa Rica ICSID Case No UNCT/15/3, Final Award, 18 September 2018.

EDF International S.A., SAUR International S.A. and León Participaciones Argentinas S.A. v. Argentine Republic ICSID Case No ARB/03/23, Award, 11 June 2012.

Eli Lilly and Company v. Government of Canada ICSID Case No UNCT/14/2, Final Award, 16 March 2017.

Elsamex, S.A. v. Republic of Honduras ICSID Case No ARB/09/4, Award, 16 November 2012.

Emilio Agustín Maffezini v. Kingdom of Spain ICSID Case No ARB/97/7, Decision on Jurisdiction, 25 January 2000.

Enron Creditors Recovery Corporation (formerly Enron Corporation) and Ponderosa Assets, L.P. v. Argentine Republic ICSID Case No ARB/01/3, Decision on Jurisdiction, 14 January 2004.

Fedax N.V. v. The Republic of Venezuela ICSID Case No ARB/96/3, Decision of the Tribunal on Objections to Jurisdiction, 11 July 1997.

Fouad Alghanim & Sons Co. for General Trading & Contracting, W.L.L. and Fouad Mohammed Thunyan Alghanim v. Hashemite Kingdom of Jordan ICSID Case No ARB/13/38, Award, 14 December 2017.

Georg Gavrilovic and Gavrilovic d.o.o. v. Republic of Croatia ICSID Case No ARB/12/39, Award, 25 July 2018.

Grenada Private Power Limited and WRB Enterprises, Inc. v. Grenada ICSID Case No ARB/17/13, Award, 19 March 2020.

Gustav F W Hamester GmbH & Co KG v. Republic of Ghana ICSID Case No ARB/07/24, Award, 18 June 2010.

Helnan International Hotels A/S v. Arab Republic of Egypt ICSID Case No ARB 05/19, Decision on Jurisdiction, 17 October 2006.

Helnan International Hotels A/S v. Arab Republic of Egypt ICSID Case No ARB/05/19, Award, 7 June 2008.

Ioan Micula and others v. Romania II ICSID Case No ARB/14/29, Award, 5 March 2020.

Industria Nacional de Alimentos, S.A. and Indalsa Perú, S.A. (formerly Empresas Lucchetti, S.A. and Lucchetti Perú, S.A.) v. Republic of Peru ICSID Case No ARB/03/4, Award, 7 February 2005.

Industria Nacional de Alimentos, S.A. and Indalsa Perú, S.A. v. Republic of Peru ICSID Case No ARB/03/4, Decision on Annulment, 5 September 2007.
Inmaris Perestroika Sailing Maritime Services GmbH and others v. Ukraine ICSID Case No ARB/08/8, Excerpts of Award, 1 March 2012.
Karkey Karadeniz Elektrik Uretim A.S. v. Islamic Republic of Pakistan ICSID Case No ARB/13/1, Award, 22 August 2017.
Klöckner Industrie-Anlagen GmbH v. United Republic of Cameroon ICSID Case No ARB/81/2, Award, 21 October 1983.
Klöckner Industrie-Anlagen GmbH v United Republic of Cameroon ICSID Case No ARB/81/2, Decision on Annulment, 3 May 1985.
LG&E Energy Corp., LG&E Capital Corp. and LG&E International Inc. v. Argentine Republic ICSID Case No ARB/02/1, Decision on Liability, 3 October 2006.
Mamidoil Jetoil Greek Petroleum Products Societe Anonyme S.A. v. Republic of Albania ICSID Case No ARB/11/24, Award, 30 March 2015.
Marco Gavazzi and Stefano Gavazzi v. Romania ICSID Case No ARB/12/25, Decision on Jurisdiction Admissibility and Liability, 21 April 2015.
Marco Gavazzi and Stefano Gavazzi v. Romania ICSID Case No ARB/12/25, Dissenting Opinion by Arbitrator Mauro Rubino-Sammartano I, 21 April 2015.
Marion Unglaube and Reinhard Unglaube v. Costa Rica ICSID Case No ARB/08/1 and ARB/09/20, Award, 16 May 2012.
Maritime International Nominees Establishment v. Republic of Guinea ICSID Case No ARB/84/4, Award, 6 January 1988.
M.C.I. Power Group, L.C. and New Turbine v. Republic of Ecuador ICSID Case No ARB/03/6, Award, 31 July 2007.
M. Meerapfel Sohne AG v. Central African Republic ICSID Case No ARB/07/10, Excerpts of Award, 12 May 2012.
Metal-Tech Ltd. v. Republic of Uzbekistan ICSID Case No ARB/10/3, Award, 4 October 2013.
Perenco Ecuador Limited v. Republic of Ecuador and Empresa Estatal Petróleos del Ecuador ICSID Case No ARB/08/6, Decision on Jurisdiction, 30 June 2011.
Perenco Ecuador Limited v. Republic of Ecuador and Empresa Estatal Petróleos del Ecuador ICSID Case No ARB/08/6, Interim Decision on the Environmental Counterclaim, 11 August 2015.
Perenco Ecuador Limited v. Republic of Ecuador and Empresa Estatal Petróleos del Ecuador ICSID Case No ARB/08/6, Decision on Claimant Application for Dismissal of Respondent Counterclaims, 18 August 2017.
Perenco Ecuador Limited v. Republic of Ecuador and Empresa Estatal Petróleos del Ecuador ICSID Case No ARB/08/6, Award, 27 September 2019.

Quiborax S.A. *and Non Metallic Minerals* S.A. *v. Plurinational State of Bolivia* ICSID Case No ARB/06/2, Award, 16 September 2015.

RSM Production Corporation v. Grenada ICSID Case No ARB/05/14, Award, 13 March 2009.

Saipem S.p.A. v. People's Republic of Bangladesh ICSID Case No ARB/05/07, Decision on Jurisdiction and Recommendation on Provisional Measures, 21 March 2007.

S.A.R.L. *Benvenuti & Bonfant v. People's Republic of the Congo* ICSID Case No ARB/77/2, Award, 8 August 1980.

Salini Costruttori S.P.A. *and Italstrade* S.P.A. *v. Kingdom of Morocco* ICSID Case No ARB/00/4, Decision on Jurisdiction, 16 July 2001.

SGS *Société Générale de Surveillance* S.A. *v. Islamic Republic of Pakistan* ICSID Case No ARB/01/13, Award on Jurisdiction, 6 August 2003.

SGS *Société Générale de Surveillance* S.A. *v. Republic of the Philippines* ICSID Case No ARB/02/6, Decision of the Tribunal on Objections to Jurisdiction, 29 January 2004.

SGS *Société Générale de Surveillance* S.A. *v. Republic of the Philippines* ICSID Case No ARB/02/6, Order of the Tribunal on Further Proceedings, 17 December 2007.

Siemens A.G. *v. Argentine Republic* ICSID Case No ARB/02/8, Decision on Jurisdiction, 3 August 2004.

Southern Pacific Properties (Middle East) Limited v. Arab Republic of Egypt ICSID Case No ARB/84/3, Decision on Jurisdiction, 14 April 1988.

Spyridon Roussalis v. Romania ICSID Case No ARB/06/1, Declaration of W Michael Reisman, 28 November 2011.

Spyridon Roussalis v. Romania ICSID Case No ARB/06/1, Award, 7 December 2011.

Teinver S.A., *Transportes de Cercanías* S.A. *and Autobuses Urbanos del Sur* S.A. *v. Argentine Republic* ICSID Case No ARB/09/1, Decision on Jurisdiction, 21 December 2012.

Tethyan Copper Company Pty Limited v. Islamic Republic of Pakistan ICSID Case No ARB/12/1, Decision on Jurisdiction and Liability, 10 November 2017.

Tokios Tokelės v. Ukraine ICSID Case No ARB/02/18, Decision on Jurisdiction, 29 April 2004.

Tradex Hellas S.A. *v. Republic of Albania* ICSID Case No ARB/94/2, Decision on Jurisdiction, 24 December 1996.

Urbaser S.A. *and Consorcio de Aguas Bilbao Bizkaia, Bilbao Biskaia Ur Partzuergoa v. The Argentine Republic* ICSID Case No ARB/07/26, Decision on Jurisdiction, 19 December 2012.

Urbaser S.A. and Consorcio de Aguas Bilbao Biskaia, Bilbao Biskaia Ur Partzuergoa v. Argentine Republic ICSID Case No ARB/07/26, Award, 8 December 2016.

Venezuela Holdings B.V. et. al. v. Bolivarian Republic of Venezuela ICSID Case No ARB/07/27, Decision on Jurisdiction, 10 June 2010.

Venezuela Holdings B.V. et. al. v Bolivarian Republic of Venzuela ICSID Case No, ARB/07/27, Decision on Annulment, 9 March 2017.

Vestey Group Ltd v. Bolivarian Republic of Venezuela ICSID Case No ARB/06/4, Award, 15 April 2016.

Wena Hotels Ltd v. Arab Republic of Egypt ICSID Case No ARB/98/4, Annulment Proceeding, 5 February 2002.

World Duty Free Co. Ltd v. Republic of Kenya ICSID Case No ARB/00/7, Award, 4 October 2006.

Zhinvali Development Ltd. v. Republic of Georgia ICSID Case No ARB/00/1, Award, 24 January 2003.

ICSID Additional Facility Awards

Anglo American PLC v. Bolivarian Republic of Venezuela ICSID Case No ARB(AF)/14/1, Award, 18 January 2019.

Gold Reserve Inc. v. Bolivarian Republic of Venezuela ICSID Case No ARB(AF)/09/1, Award, 22 September 2014.

Lao Holdings N.V. v. Lao People's Democratic Republic I ICSID Case No ARB(AF)/12/6, Interim Ruling on Issues Arising Under the Deed of Settlement, 19 December 2014.

Lao Holdings N.V. v. Lao People's Democratic Republic I ICSID Case No ARB(AF)/12/6, Decision on the Merits of Claimants Second Material Breach Application, 15 December 2017.

Lao Holdings N.V. v. Lao People's Democratic Republic II ICSID Case No ARB(AF)16/2, Procedural Order No 3, 14 November 2017.

Robert Azinian, Kenneth Davitian & Ellen Baca v. United Mexican States ICSID Case No ARB(AF)/97/2, Award, 1 November 1999.

Rusoro Mining Ltd. v. Bolivarian Republic of Venezuela ICSID Case No ARB(AF)/12/5, Award, 22 August 2016.

Sanum Investments Limited v. Lao People's Democratic Republic II ICSID Case No ADHOC/17/1, Procedural Order No 3, 14 November 2017.

Strabag SE, Raiffeisen Centrobank AG and Syrena Immobilien Holding AG v. Republic of Poland ICSID Case No ADHOC/15/1, Partial Award on Jurisdiction, 4 March 2020.

UNCITRAL Awards

Chevron Corporation (U.S.A.) and Texaco Petroleum Corporation (U.S.A.) v. Republic of Ecuador II PCA Case No 2009–23, First Partial Award on Track I, 17 September 2013.

Chevron Corporation (U.S.A.) and Texaco Petroleum Corporation (U.S.A.) v. Republic of Ecuador II PCA Case No 2009–23, Second Partial Award on Track II, 30 August 2018.

CME Czech Republic B.V. v. Czech Republic UNCITRAL, Partial Award, 13 September 2001.

CME Czech Republic B.V. v. Czech Republic UNCITRAL, Final Award, 14 March 2003.

Copper Mesa Mining Corporation v. Republic of Ecuador PCA Case No 2012–2, Award, 15 March 2016 (redacted).

Hesham Talaat M. Al-Warraq v. Republic of Indonesia UNCITRAL, Final Award, 15 December 2014.

Iberdrola Energia S.A. v. Republic of Guatemala II PCA Case No 2017–41, Final Award, 24 August 2020.

Methanex Corporation v. United States of America UNCITRAL, Final Award, 3 August 2005.

National Grid P.L.C. v. Argentina Republic UNCITRAL, Award, 3 November 2008.

Oxus Gold plc v. Republic of Uzbekistan UNCITRAL, Final Award, 17 December 2015.

Romak S.A. v. Republic of Uzbekistan PCA Case No 2007–07/AA280, Award, 26 November 2009.

Ronald S. Lauder v. Czech Republic UNCITRAL, Final Award, 3 September 2001.

Saluka Investment B.V. v. Czech Republic UNCITRAL, Decision on Jurisdiction over the Czech Republic's Counterclaim, 7 May 2004.

Sergei Paushok, CJSC Golden East Company and CJSC Vostokneftegaz Company v. Government of Mongolia UNCITRAL, Award on Jurisdiction and Liability, 28 April 2011.

South American Silver Limited v. Plurinational State of Bolivia PCA Case No 2013–15, Procedural Order No 2, 1 December 2014.

South American Silver Limited v. Plurinational State of Bolivia PCA Case 2013–15, Award, 22 November 2018.

Ulysseas, Inc. v. Ecuador PCA Case No 2009–19, Final Award, 12 June 2012.

Permanent Court of International Justice Cases

Certain German Interests in Polish Upper Silesia (Merits) PCIJ Rep Series A No 7.

Mavrommatis Palestine Concessions (Merits) PCIJ Rep Series A No 2.

International Court of Justice Cases

Armed Activities on the Territory of the Congo (*Democratic Republic of the Congo v. Uganda*) (Order of 29 November 2001) [2001] ICJ Rep 660.

Case concerning East Timor (*Portugal v. Australia*) (Judgment) [1995] ICJ Rep 89.

Case concerning Oil Platforms (*Islamic Republic of Iran v. United States of America*) (Counterclaim Order of 10 March 1998)[1998] ICJ Rep 190.

Continental Shelf (*Libyan Arab Jamahiriya/Malta*) (Judgment) [1985] ICJ Rep 13.

Jurisdictional Immunities of the State (*Germany v. Italy; Greece intervening*) (Judgment) [2012] ICJ Rep 99.

Legal Consequences for States of the Continued Presence of South Africa in Namibia (*South West Africa*) *notwithstanding Security Council Resolution 276* (*1970*) (Advisory Opinion) [1971] ICJ Rep 16.

South West Africa Second Phase (Judgment) [1966] ICJ Rep 6.

United States Diplomatic and Consular Staff in Tehran (Judgment) [1980] ICJ Rep 3.

Domestic Cases

Milieudefensie et al. v. Royal Dutch Shell plc ECLI:NL:RBDHA:2021:5339 C/09/571932/ HA ZA 19–379.

Nevsun Resources Ltd v Araya [2020] 1 SCR 166.

Occidental v Ecuador [2005] EWCA Civ 1116, [2006] QB 432.

Republic of Ecuador v. Occidental Exploration and Production Company [2005] EWHC 774 (Comm) (HC QBD).

CHAPTER 1

Investment Arbitration and Counterclaims

1.1 Introduction

Investment arbitration focuses almost exclusively on host State conduct when resolving investment disputes. Foreign investors frame investment claims based on how host State conduct potentially breaches a host State's legal obligations. Investment arbitrators evaluate whether a host State has breached its obligations and should be held legally responsible for its acts. Arbitral tribunals calculate a foreign investor's loss by determining how host State conduct has negatively impacted the value of the investment project. Given that the aim of international investment law (IIL) is to regulate host State conduct with respect to foreign investors and their investment projects,[1] it should not be surprising that host State conduct is pivotal to the resolution of investment disputes. However, by unduly concentrating on host State conduct, investment arbitration frequently overlooks the potential impact of foreign investor misconduct on host States.

Foreign investor misconduct is a generic term that captures different types of unacceptable behaviour undertaken by a foreign investor that generate legal consequences.[2] Examples of foreign investor misconduct are wide-ranging, but the term frequently captures conduct like corruption and breaches of international law such as environmental damage or human rights violations.[3] Foreign investor misconduct can negatively impact host States in different ways. Foreign investor misconduct can result in host States being in breach of international obligations. For example, foreign investor misconduct that prevents indigenous communities from accessing traditional lands is contrary to human rights standards that bind host States.[4] Host States may respond to

1 Ibrahim F J Shihata, 'Regulation of Foreign Investment' in AFM Maniruzzaman and others (eds), *International Sustainable Development Law Vol II* (Eolss 2010) 195; James Gathii and Sergio Puig, 'Introduction to the Symposium on Investor Responsibility: The Next Frontier in International Investment Law' (2019) 113 AJIL Unbound 1, 1; Jean Ho, 'The Creation of Elusive Investor Responsibility' (2019) 113 AJIL Unbound 10, 10.

2 Anna Kozyokova, *Foreign Investor Misconduct in International Investment Law* (Springer 2021) 1.

3 ibid.

4 This type of foreign investor misconduct could place the host State in breach of international obligations relating to the right to self-determination (Common Article 1 International

 DOI:10.1163/9789004420953_002

foreign investor misconduct in a way that detrimentally affects the foreign investor, or its investment project, giving rise to an investment dispute. For instance, a host State may terminate a contract following foreign investor misconduct generating an investment claim for unlawful expropriation.[5] Further, host States may need to pay the costs of remedying any wrongful acts caused by foreign investor misconduct.[6] Despite the potential impact of foreign investor misconduct on host States, existing procedures in investment arbitration do not permit host States to easily invoke foreign investor misconduct in investment disputes. As a result, foreign investors can avoid being held accountable for their misconduct in investment arbitration.

Counterclaims have been identified as a potential means by which host States can address foreign investor misconduct in investment arbitration.[7] Counterclaims permit host States to turn an arbitral tribunal's attention away from State conduct and instead focus on the legality of a foreign investor's actions. Nonetheless, there is a significant gap between the legal possibility of using counterclaims for this purpose and the reality of presenting a counterclaim before an arbitral tribunal that can generate foreign investor liability. This

Covenant on Civil and Political Rights (ICCPR) (adopted 16 December 1966, entered into force 23 March 1976) 999 UNTS 171 and International Covenant on Economic, Social and Cultural Rights (ICESCR) (adopted 16 December 1966, entered into force 3 January 1976) 993 UNTS 3; Committee on Economic, Social and Cultural Rights (CESCR), 'General Comment No. 26 (2022) on land and economic, social and cultural rights' (24 January 2023) UN Doc. No. E/C.12/GC/26, [11], [16]), the rights of ethnic, religious or linguistic minorities (ICCPR Article 27) and rights contained in the International Convention on the Elimination of All Forms of Racial Discrimination (adopted 21 December 1965, entered into force 4 January 1969) 660 UNTS 195 (based on Committee on the Elimination of All Forms of Racial Discrimination, General Recommendation 23 on the rights of indigenous peoples, 18 August 1997, [5]).

5 For example, in *South American Silver Limited v. Plurinational State of Bolivia* PCA Case 2013–15, Award, 22 November 2018, the foreign investor was alleged to have violated the indigenous communities' right to self-determination, violated the personal integrity of their women, and endangered their right to a healthy environment in their territories [463]. In response, Bolivia terminated the foreign investor's mining concessions, but it did not provide compensation and was liable for unlawful expropriation [610].

6 For example, a host State may have to pay to remedy environmental damage caused by a foreign investor.

7 See for example, Tomoko Ishikawa, *Corporate Environmental Responsibility in Investor-State Dispute Settlement: The Unexhausted Potential of Current Mechanisms* (Cambridge University Press 2022); Walid Ben Hamida, 'L'arbitrage Etat-investisseur cherche son quilibre perdu: Dans quelle mesure l'Etat peut introduire des demandes reconventionnelles contre l'investisseur priv?' (2005) 7 International Law Forum du droit international 261; Zachary Douglas, 'The enforcement of environmental norms in investment treaty arbitration' in Pierre-Marie Dupuy and Jorge E Viñuales (eds), *Harnessing Foreign Investment to Promote Environmental Protection: Incentives and Safeguards* (Cambridge University Press 2013).

book explains, in practical terms, how host States can integrate foreign investor misconduct into investment disputes by using counterclaim procedures in investment arbitration. The book argues that, by altering State practice and legal argumentation, host States can use counterclaims to hold foreign investors accountable for violations of international law. Host States are then able to decide on a claim-by-claim basis when to employ counterclaims to address foreign investor misconduct. To understand why counterclaims should be used in this way, it is first necessary to evidence how investment arbitration fails to encompass foreign investor misconduct that is contrary to international law.

1.2 Foreign Investors, Investment Arbitration and International Law

Investment arbitration's remit does not currently extend to foreign investor misconduct that breaches international law. This can be attributed to three main factors: (1) international investment agreements (IIAs) privilege foreign investors; (2) international law does not directly regulate foreign investors; and (3) investment arbitration currently lacks procedures that enable host States to effectively draw on foreign investor misconduct in investment disputes. In combination, these factors permit foreign investors to evade liability for breaches of international law in investment arbitration.

The vast majority of IIAs adopt an asymmetrical structure that privileges foreign investors by only imposing obligations on host States.[8] Therefore, investment arbitration does not readily permit host States to hold foreign investors accountable for misconduct because IIAs do not contain a legal foundation for a host State to claim against a foreign investor.[9] The use of asymmetrical obligations in IIAs was traditionally justified on the grounds that the foreign investor was vulnerable[10] to abuses of host State power when operating in the host

8 Gathii and Puig (n 1) 1; Martin Jarrett, *Contributory Fault and Investor Misconduct in Investment Arbitration* (Cambridge University Press 2019) 1–2; Ivar Alvik, 'The Justification of Privilege in International Investment Law: Preferential Treatment of Foreign Investors as a Problem of Legitimacy' (2020) 31 European Journal of International Law 289, 290; see also Jürgen Kurtz, 'On Foreign Investor "Privilege" and the Limits of the Law: A Reply to Ivar Alvik' (2020) 31 European Journal of International Law 313, 313–314.

9 Jarrett (n 8) 1–2; Tomoko Ishikawa, 'Counterclaims and the Rule of Law in Investment Arbitration' (2019) 113 AJIL Unbound 33, 33; Markus Krajewski, 'A Nightmare or a Noble Dream? Establishing Investor Obligations Through Treaty-Making and Treaty-Application' (2020) 5 Business and Human Rights Journal 105, 106; Paul E Trinel, 'Counterclaims and legitimacy in investment treaty arbitration' (2022) 38 Arbitration International 59, 66.

10 For a discussion on foreign investor vulnerability, see Güneş Ünüvar and Aysel Küçüksu, 'From Protection to Governance of Foreign Investment: Vulnerability Theory as a

State.[11] However, a growing body of investment claims demonstrates that host States can also be vulnerable to the acts of foreign investors.[12] For example, in *Metal-Tech* v *Uzbekistan*,[13] the foreign investor made payments to a government official to secure acceptance of the investment.[14] In *Copper Mesa Mining Corporation* v *Ecuador*,[15] the foreign investor, through privately employed security forces, engaged in violent acts against those who opposed the foreign investor's mining project.[16] Finally, in *Burlington* v *Ecuador*[17] and *Perenco* v *Ecuador*,[18] the foreign investors failed to comply with host State environmental laws resulting in environmental damage when operating oil fields.[19] These examples highlight that the privileging of foreign investors in IIAs fails to accurately reflect the balance of power between foreign investors and host States in investment disputes involving foreign investor misconduct.[20] Consequently, by failing to include provisions that restrict foreign investor misconduct,

---

Paradigm Shift in International Investment Law' (*EJIL: Talk!*, 27 December 2019) <https://www.ejiltalk.org/from-protection-to-governance-of-foreign-investment-vulnerability-theory-as-a-paradigm-shift-in-international-investment-law/> accessed 11 May 2021.

11 Gustavo Laborde, 'The Case for Host State Claims in Investment Arbitration' (2010) 1 Journal of International Dispute Settlement 97, 98; Krajewski (n 9) 106; Ishikawa, *Corporate Environmental Responsibility in Investor-State Dispute Settlement: The Unexhausted Potential of Current Mechanisms* (n 7) 8. For a discussion of this point, see Mavluda Sattarova and Oleksandra Vytiaganets, 'Learning from Investment Treaty Law and Arbitration: Developing States and Power Inequalities' in Daniel Behn, Ole K Fauchald and Malcolm Langford (eds), *Legitimacy of Investment Arbitration* (Cambridge University Press 2021).

12 Ishikawa, 'Counterclaims and the Rule of Law in Investment Arbitration' (n 9) 33; Mavluda Sattorova, 'Investor Responsibilities From a Host State Perspective: Qualitative Data and Proposals for Treaty Reform' (2019) 113 AJIL Unbound 22, 22.

13 *Metal-Tech Ltd. v. Republic of Uzbekistan* ICSID Case No ARB/10/3, Award, 4 October 2013.

14 ibid [194]–[227].

15 *Copper Mesa Mining Corporation v. Republic of Ecuador* PCA Case No 2012–2, Award, 15 March 2016 (redacted).

16 See, for example, ibid [4.76]–[4.77], [4.230], [4.245]–[4.246], [4.251]–[4.254] and [4.264]–[4.265].

17 *Burlington Resources Inc. v. Republic of Ecuador* ICSID Case No ARB/08/5, Decision on Counterclaims, 7 February 2017.

18 *Perenco Ecuador Limited v. Republic of Ecuador and Empresa Estatal Petróleos del Ecuador* ICSID Case No ARB/08/6, Award, 27 September 2019.

19 *Burlington Resources Inc. v. Republic of Ecuador* (n 17) section V.B; *Perenco Ecuador Limited v. Republic of Ecuador and Empresa Estatal Petróleos del Ecuador* ICSID Case No ARB/08/6, Interim Decision on the Environmental Counterclaim, 11 August 2015, section III.B; *Perenco Ecuador Limited v. Republic of Ecuador*, Award (n 18) [1023(b)] and Annex A.

20 Laborde (n 11) 98; Ishikawa, 'Counterclaims and the Rule of Law in Investment Arbitration' (n 9) 33; Sattorova (n 12) 26.

IIAs preclude host States from being able to effectively hold foreign investors accountable for their misconduct in investment arbitration.

If host States are to hold foreign investors accountable for their misconduct, host States must source legal obligations that bind foreign investors from beyond IIAs. The legal foundations of foreign investor misconduct can frequently be traced back to principles of international law. For example, corruption is contrary to principles of international public policy,[21] violent acts against protestors breach human rights,[22] and domestic environmental laws frequently implement standards sourced from international environmental law.[23] Despite these connections to international law, host States have difficulty attributing responsibility to foreign investors for breaches of international law because foreign investors do not inherently possess international legal personality.[24] States can confer foreign investors with international legal personality to become actors on the international legal plane.[25] However, most IIAs only confer international legal personality on foreign investors to the extent that enables foreign investors to commence investment claims.[26] Further, international law regimes that govern common forms of foreign investor misconduct, such as international human rights law, international environmental law and international labour law place obligations solely on States.[27] Therefore, as a

21 *World Duty Free Co. Ltd v. Republic of Kenya* ICSID Case No ARB/00/7, Award, 4 October 2006 [157]. This arbitral tribunal finds corruption to be contrary to transnational public policy rather than international law. As to whether corruption amounts to a human rights violation, see Anne Peters, 'Corruption as a Violation of International Human Rights' (2018) 29 European Journal of International Law 1251.

22 For example, the right of peaceful assembly (ICCPR (n 4) Article 21).

23 See Clara Brandi, Dominique Blümer and Jean-Frédéric Morin, 'When Do International Treaties Matter for Domestic Environmental Legislation?' (2019) 19 Global Environmental Politics 14.

24 Patrick Dumberry and Èrik Labelle-Eastaugh, 'Non-state actors in international investment law: The legal personality of corporations and NGOs in the context of investor-state arbitration' in Jean d'Aspremont (ed), *Participants in the International Legal System: Multiple Perspectives on Non-State Actors in International Law* (Routledge 2011) 365.

25 This can be achieved through specific treaty language or by implication through State conduct (R Hansen, 'The International Legal Personality of Multinational Enterprises: Treaty, Custom and the Governance Gap' (2010) 10 Global Jurist 1, 13; Roland Portmann, *Legal Personality in International Law* (Cambridge University Press 2010) 82).

26 Ole Spiermann, 'Individual Rights, State Interests and the Power to Waive ICSID Jurisdiction Under Bilateral Investment Treaties' (2004) 20 Arbitration International 179, 185. See *Republic of Ecuador v. Occidental Exploration and Production Company* [2005] EWHC 774 (Comm) (HC QBD) [61]; *SGS Société Générale de Surveillance S.A. v. Republic of the Philippines* ICSID Case No ARB/02/6, Decision of the Tribunal on Objections to Jurisdiction, 29 January 2004 [154].

27 See Section 5.2.1.

general rule, foreign investors are not directly bound by international law. In the absence of directly binding obligations, States ensure that private actors, like foreign investors, comply with these norms by implementing international legal norms into domestic legal frameworks.[28] Thus, host States can use domestic law and contractual provisions to generate binding legal obligations on foreign investors. In this way, international obligations bind foreign investors indirectly. However, even when international obligations are translated into domestic legal frameworks, it is difficult for host States to challenge foreign investor misconduct in investment arbitration given that investment practice focuses heavily on IIAs.[29] Therefore, the combination of the foreign investors' lack of international legal personality and the privileging of foreign investors in IIAs means that a host State's ability to hold foreign investors accountable for breaches of international law in investment arbitration is restricted.

Nonetheless, host States have attempted to hold foreign investors accountable for their misconduct in investment arbitration. Despite adopting a variety of litigation strategies, their attempts have only met with limited success.[30] Most commonly, host States have relied on foreign investor misconduct in an attempt to demonstrate that investment protection standards have not been breached.[31] This practice can be seen in relation to the fair and equitable treatment standard.[32] This investment protection standard requires, in part, that host States comply with any legitimate expectations that have been relied on by the foreign investor.[33] However, where the foreign investor has sought to rely on legitimate expectations, but has failed to take into account foreseeable host State laws and regulations, a few arbitral tribunals have deemed that this

28 Carlos M Vázquez, 'Direct vs Indirect Obligations of Corporations Under International Law' (2005) 43 Columbia Journal of International Law 927, 930.

29 Jorge E Viñuales, 'Investor Diligence in Investment Arbitration: Sources and Arguments' (2017) 32 ICSID Review – Foreign Investment Law Journal 346, 367.

30 Gathii and Puig (n 1) 1.

31 Karsten Nowrot, *The Other Side of Rights in the Processes of Constitutionalizing International Investment Law: Addressing Investors' Obligations as a New Regulatory Experiment* (Heft 21 Rechtswissenschaftliche Beiträge der Hamburger Sozialökonomie, 2018) 21.

32 For a full discussion of the impact of foreign investor misconduct in relation to the fair and equitable treatment standard, see Peter T Muchlinski, '"Caveat Investor"? The Relevance of the Conduct of the Investor under the Fair and Equitable Treatment Standard' (2006) 55 International and Comparative Law Quarterly 527.

33 Legitimate expectations may be created by the presumed stability of the host State's legal framework, any explicit or implicit representations made by the host State or based on contractual commitments the foreign investor has with the host State (Roland Klager, *'Fair and Equitable Treatment' in International Investment Law* (Cambridge University Press 2011) 164–165).

failure amounts to misconduct and have precluded the foreign investor's fair and equitable treatment claim.[34] Although this approach has proved successful for host States in a small minority of investment disputes,[35] framing foreign investor misconduct in terms of host State obligations can only exonerate host State responsibility. Hence, this strategy does not generate foreign investor accountability for their misconduct that breaches international law.

Foreign investor misconduct has also been addressed using the concept of contributory fault based on Article 39 of the International Law Commission's (ILC) Articles on Responsibility of States for Internationally Wrongful Acts (ARSIWA).[36] This provision requires that when remedying an international wrong, account should be taken of any 'wilfully negligent act or omission' that materially contributes to the injury. Hence, if a host State breaches an investment protection standard, but the foreign investor has contributed to their own loss through wilful negligence or omission, an arbitral tribunal may reduce the compensation payable by the host State to the foreign investor. Contributory fault has been applied inconsistently across a small number of investment awards.[37] Therefore, it does not provide a guaranteed means of holding foreign investors accountable. Nonetheless, in *Copper Mesa Mining* v *Ecuador*, by framing the foreign investor's targeted attacks on protestors as negligence, the arbitral tribunal reduced the compensation payable to the foreign investor by 30 percent.[38] However, a significant limitation to relying on contributory fault

---

34 Yulia Levashova, 'The Accountability and Corporate Social Responsibility of Multinational Corporations for Transgression in Host States through International Investment Law' (2018) 14 Utrecht Law Review 40, 53; Peter T Muchlinski, 'Can International Investment Law Punish Investor's Human Rights Violations? Copper Mesa, Contributory Fault and its Alternatives' (2022) 37 ICSID Review – Foreign Investment Law Journal 359, 362.

35 See, for example, *Marion Unglaube and Reinhard Unglaube v. Costa Rica* ICSID Case No ARB/08/1 and ARB/09/20, Award, 16 May 2012 [258]; *Mamidoil Jetoil Greek Petroleum Products Societe Anonyme S.A. v. Republic of Albania* ICSID Case No ARB/11/24, Award, 30 March 2015 [729]–[735].

36 ILC, Draft Articles on State Responsibility for Internationally Wrongful Acts in 'Report of the International Law Commission on the Work of its 53rd Session' (23 April–1 June and 2 July–10 August 2001) UN Doc. A/56/10. The final version of the Articles are available in James Crawford, *The International Law Commission's Articles on State Responsibility: Introduction, Text and Commentaries* (Cambridge University Press 2002).

37 Jean-Michel Marcoux and Andrea Bjorkland, 'Foreign Investors' Responsibilities and Contributory Fault in Investment Arbitration' (2020) 69 International and Comparative Law Quarterly 877, 880, 881–900; Sattorova (n 12) 24; Martin Jarrett, Sergio Puig and Steven R Ratner, *Investor Accountability: Indirect Actions, Direct Actions by States, and Direct Actions by Individuals* (Academic Forum on ISDS Concept Paper 2021/1, 10 June 2021) 10.

38 *Copper Mesa Mining Corporation v. Republic of Ecuador* (n 15) [7.32].

to address foreign investor misconduct is that it can only reduce the compensation payable by the host State.[39] Thus, the application of contributory fault is contingent on host State liability for a breach of an investment protection standard and cannot independently generate foreign investor accountability for breaches of international law.[40]

Host States have used foreign investor misconduct to deny the foreign investor access to investment arbitration. When an IIA includes an 'in accordance with host State law' clause, consent to investment arbitration is conditional on the foreign investor complying with host State law.[41] Should this type of clause exist in the IIA, and the foreign investor fails to comply with host State law, consent to investment arbitration does not exist.[42] In *Metal-Tech* v *Uzbekistan*, the arbitral tribunal applied this type of clause and concluded that the corruption that secured the investment project was in violation of Uzbek criminal law, which meant that the arbitral tribunal did not have jurisdiction to hear the claim.[43] 'In accordance with host State law' clauses can deny the operation of investment arbitration, however, they are limited to instances of illegality that occur in the pre-investment phase.[44] Thus, by excluding post-establishment breaches of host State law, this litigation strategy only captures a small proportion of foreign investor misconduct.

Finally, host States have challenged foreign investor misconduct by commencing counterclaims against the foreign investor. Counterclaim procedures require host States to generate an independent claim against the foreign investor based on obligations owed by the foreign investor to the host State that have a link to the originating claim.[45] The asymmetrical structure of IIAs

39 For the full legal implications of contributory fault in investment arbitration, see Jarrett (n 8).

40 Ho (n 1) 12–13.

41 Rahim Moloo and Alex Khachaturian, 'The Compliance with the Law Requirement in International Investment Law' (2011) 43 Fordham International Law Journal 1473, 1478; Stephan W Schill, 'Illegal Investments in Investment Treaty Arbitration' (2012) 11 The Law and Practice of International Courts and Tribunals 281, 289; Andrea Carlevaris, 'The Conformity of Investments with the Law of the Host State and the Jurisdiction of International Tribunals' (2008) 9 Journal of World Investment and Trade 35, 49.

42 Moloo and Khachaturian (n 41) 1476; Andrea J Menaker, 'The Determinative Impact of Fraud and Corruption on Investment Arbitrations' (2010) 25 ICSID Review – Foreign Investment Law Journal 67, 69.

43 *Metal-Tech Ltd. v. Republic of Uzbekistan* (n 13) [389].

44 Schill (n 41) 307; *Gustav F W Hamester GmbH & Co KG v. Republic of Ghana* ICSID Case No ARB/07/24, Award, 18 June 2010 [127]–[129]; *Georg Gavrilovic and Gavrilovic d.o.o. v. Republic of Croatia* ICSID Case No ARB/12/39, Award, 25 July 2018 [303].

45 Yavaslau Kryvoi, 'Counterclaims in Investor-State Arbitration' (2012) 21 Minnesota Journal of International Law 216, 220. See Chapter 3.

and the absence of international obligations that bind foreign investors have resulted in limited options for host States to pursue a counterclaim.[46] Further, arbitral tribunals have been reluctant to permit counterclaims based on host State domestic law on the basis that these counterclaims are not sufficiently connected to the investment.[47] However, the relevance of counterclaim procedures has increased significantly after the first successful counterclaims were made by Ecuador in *Burlington* v *Ecuador* and *Perenco* v *Ecuador*, which were based on Ecuador's domestic environmental laws.[48] Despite these recent successes, the vast majority of counterclaims have been rejected, primarily due to a lack of jurisdiction.[49] Consequently, even if a legal foundation for a counterclaim does exist, it remains difficult for host States to meet the procedural requirements to establish a counterclaim. Therefore, the manner in which counterclaims currently operate does not provide a straightforward mechanism for host States to pursue claims of foreign investor misconduct.

In short, the way international law and investment arbitration are structured combine to constrain host States from holding foreign investors accountable for breaches of international law. Host States have found existing litigation strategies in investment arbitration to be ineffective at addressing foreign investor misconduct. Thus, investment arbitration does not currently possess a procedure that permits host States to consistently and comprehensively address foreign investor misconduct that is contrary to international law. As a result, foreign investors are not being held accountable for their misconduct that violates international law in investment arbitration.

1.3 Host State Courts

Many of the challenges faced by host States in regulating foreign investor misconduct in investment arbitration arise because host State courts provide

46 Andrea K Bjorklund, 'The Role of Counterclaims in Rebalancing Investment Law' (2013) 17 Lewis and Clark Law Review 461, 463; Anne Hoffman, 'Counterclaims in Investment Arbitration' (2013) 28 ICSID Review – Foreign Investment Law Journal 438, 447.

47 Kryvoi (n 45) 252. See also *Saluka Investment B.V. v. Czech Republic* UNCITRAL, Decision on Jurisdiction over the Czech Republic's Counterclaim, 7 May 2004 [75].

48 *Burlington Resources Inc. v. Republic of Ecuador* (n 17) section V.B.2; *Perenco Ecuador Limited v. Republic of Ecuador*, Interim Decision on the Environmental Counterclaim (n 19) section III.B.

49 Dafina Atanasova, Carlos Adrían Martínez and Josef Ostřanský, *Counterclaims in Investor-State Dispute Settlement (ISDS) under International Investment Agreements (IIAs)* (Trade and Investment Law Clinic Papers, 2012) 37; Trinel (n 9) 65.

an alternative forum in which host States can hold foreign investors accountable.[50] Consequently, investment arbitration does not need to accommodate foreign investor misconduct. Host State courts can perform this role because foreign investor misconduct occurs within the host State's jurisdiction.[51] However, using host State courts in this manner can result in investment disputes being divided between investment arbitration proceedings to examine host State misconduct and host State court proceedings to consider foreign investor misconduct. The division of an investment dispute in this way can result in disconnected legal proceedings. Nonetheless, parallel investment arbitration and domestic court proceedings are not entirely independent of one another because arbitral tribunals do refer to decisions made by host State courts.[52] These competing considerations mean that, for strategic reasons, resolving foreign investor misconduct claims in domestic courts may not be the best option for host States or foreign investors.

The dual use of investment arbitration and host State courts to resolve investment disputes involving foreign investor misconduct can be problematic for foreign investors and for host States. To engage with separate legal proceedings, foreign investors and host States are likely to have to duplicate resources across two dispute resolution fora.[53] Foreign investors may additionally be reluctant to have host State courts hear misconduct claims for the same reasons that investment claims are usually resolved using investment arbitration[54] – that is, foreign investors may have concerns regarding the existence of judicial bias[55] or

50 Stephan W Schill, 'Access to Justice in Investment Dispute Settlement' (*Kluwer Arbitration Blog*, 2020) <http://arbitrationblog.kluwerarbitration.com/2020/02/10/access-to-justice-in-investment-dispute-settlement/> accessed 12 May 2021. See Laborde (n 11) 98; Ishikawa, 'Counterclaims and the Rule of Law in Investment Arbitration' (n 9) 34; Ishikawa, *Corporate Environmental Responsibility in Investor-State Dispute Settlement: The Unexhausted Potential of Current Mechanisms* (n 7) 60–61.

51 Gabrielle Kaufmann-Kohler and Michele Potestà, 'The Interplay Between Investor-State Arbitration and Domestic Courts in the Existing IIA Framework' in *The European Yearbook of International Economic Law* (Springer International Publishing 2020) 35.

52 Hanno Wehland, 'Domestic Courts and Investment Treaty Tribunals: The Effect of Local Recourse Against Administrative Measures on the Breach of Investment Protection Standards' (2019) 36 Journal of International Arbitration 207, 213.

53 Hege Elisabeth Kjos, 'Counterclaims by Host States in Investment Treaty Arbitration' (2007) 4 Transnational Dispute Management 1, 31.

54 See Christoph Schreuer, 'Do We Need Investment Arbitration?' (2014) 1 Transnational Dispute Management 1.

55 Gus Van Harten, 'Five Justifications for Investment Treaties: A Critical Discussion' (2010) 2 Trade, Law and Development 19, 33; Kaufmann-Kohler and Potestà (n 51) 20; Christoph Schreuer, 'Do We Need Investment Arbitration?' (n 54) 5; Andrea Steingruber,

inefficiency[56] in host State courts.[57] Given these risks, foreign investors are likely to resist host State court proceedings, and in turn, host States will need to strategize how to overcome foreign investor hesitation to appear in host State courts. Hence, attempting to bring a claim in host State courts can take considerable time and increase the costs involved for both parties. Even if a claim is brought, host States will need to be sure that host State courts will act fairly[58] to prevent an investment claim arising based on the court's treatment of the foreign investor.[59] An investment claim for denial of justice based on the host State court proceedings[60] may result in further liability for the host State in investment arbitration. Finally, the host State may also need to enforce a host State court's decision against a foreign investor in another jurisdiction,[61] which can involve further time and costs. Thus, running independent claims in investment arbitration and host State courts is not practicable for either host States or foreign investors.

The issues become more nuanced when the relationship between investment arbitration and domestic legal proceedings are taken into account. Arbitral tribunals may refer to host State court decisions to establish facts. For example, in instances where host State courts have reviewed administrative measures, some arbitral tribunals have relied on the host State courts' findings and have not undertaken an independent review of the host State's conduct.[62]

'Counterclaims: a Critical Analysis of Article 6 of the 2019 The Hague Resolution of the Institut de Droit International on the "Equality of Parties before International Investment Tribunals"' (2020) 35 ICSID Review – Foreign Investment Law Journal 595, 600.

56 Gus Van Harten (n 55) 33; Kaufmann-Kohler and Potestà (n 51) 20; Schreuer, 'Do We Need Investment Arbitration?' (n 54) 7.

57 Ishikawa, 'Counterclaims and the Rule of Law in Investment Arbitration' (n 9) 35; Ishikawa, *Corporate Environmental Responsibility in Investor-State Dispute Settlement: The Unexhausted Potential of Current Mechanisms* (n 7) 25, 62–63.

58 Laborde (n 11) 99.

59 See Mavluda Sattorova, 'Denial of Justice Disguised? Investment Arbitration and the Protection of Foreign Investors from Judicial Misconduct' (2012) 61 International and Comparative Law Quarterly 223.

60 Francesco Francioni, 'Access to Justice, Denial of Justice and International Investment Law' (2009) 20 European Journal of International Law 729, 738.

61 Laborde (n 11) 99; Ishikawa, 'Counterclaims and the Rule of Law in Investment Arbitration' (n 9) 36.

62 See for example, *Robert Azinian, Kenneth Davitian & Ellen Baca v. United Mexican States* ICSID Case No ARB(AF)/97/2, Award, 1 November 1999 [97]–[99]; *Helnan International Hotels A/S v. Arab Republic of Egypt* ICSID Case No ARB/05/19, Award, 7 June 2008 [106]; *Fouad Alghanim & Sons Co. for General Trading & Contracting, W.L.L. and Fouad Mohammed Thunyan Alghanim v. Hashemite Kingdom of Jordan* ICSID Case No ARB/13/38, Award, 14 December 2017 [365]. See also Wehland (n 52) 213–220; Ishikawa, *Corporate*

Thus, there is a risk that if a host State seeks to hold a foreign investor accountable in domestic courts, and the domestic court finds in favour of the host State, the domestic decision will be accepted by the investment tribunal. The host State could use the decision of the host State court to try and minimise its potential liability in an investment claim using one of the limited avenues to establish foreign investor misconduct in investment arbitration.[63] Hence, there is the possibility that host State court proceedings addressing foreign investor misconduct could undermine a foreign investor's investment claim before an arbitral tribunal. Although this risk is comparatively small, it remains a risk that the foreign investor will probably want to avoid.

The apparent benefits to the host State of using host State courts are likely to be outweighed by the host State's potential struggle to obtain a financial remedy against the foreign investor. Whilst compensation is the standard form of remedy in investment arbitration, many domestic courts, such as administrative courts, are unable to award compensation.[64] Even if host State courts do award compensation, it is improbable that compensation will be awarded on the same scale as that found in investment arbitration.[65] As a result, if the host State is found to be liable for breaches of the IIA in investment arbitration, it will not necessarily be able to counter any compensation awarded to the foreign investor with the remedies awarded by some host State courts. Hence, host State courts can generate foreign investor accountability, but may be unable to remedy foreign investor misconduct in the same way as investment arbitration. Therefore, whilst a host State court ruling in favour of the host State could potentially undermine a foreign investor's claim, it may not provide a host State with a full range of legal options.

Host State courts seem to provide an obvious dispute resolution forum in which host States could hold foreign investors accountable for misconduct. However, in practice, there is a high likelihood that host States and foreign investors will duplicate resources across two dispute resolution fora. Foreign investors risk judicial bias, high costs and a judgment that could undermine an investment claim. If host State courts can provide a suitable venue for a foreign

---

Environmental Responsibility in Investor-State Dispute Settlement: The Unexhausted Potential of Current Mechanisms (n 7) 133.

63 A host State could use the litigation strategies outlined in Section 1.2.

64 Kaufmann-Kohler and Potestà (n 51) 26; Armand de Mestral and Lukas Vanhonnaeker, *Reforming Investor-State Arbitration by Recourse to the Domestic Courts of Host States* (Centre for International Governance Innovation, Policy Brief 156, 2019) 5–6.

65 See Martins Paparinskis, 'A Case Against Crippling Compensation in International Law of State Responsibility' (2020) 83 Modern Law Review 1246, 1246–1248.

investor misconduct claim, host States may gain some potential benefit from host State court decisions but may struggle to obtain a financial remedy. Given the complications and inefficiencies for both foreign investors and host States, host State courts do not provide a suitable forum for addressing foreign investor misconduct claims. Therefore, investment arbitration requires an effective mechanism that will permit host States to invoke foreign investor misconduct as part of the investment dispute.

1.4 The Potential Role of Counterclaims in Investment Arbitration

Counterclaim procedures have the potential to operate as an effective mechanism to address foreign investor misconduct in investment arbitration whilst simultaneously avoiding the difficulties of using host State courts to perform this role. The way in which counterclaims currently function has restricted their operation, however, counterclaims possess the necessary attributes to hear claims of foreign investor misconduct. By holding foreign investors accountable for breaches of international law, counterclaims could also help to prevent foreign investor misconduct.

Host States are not always willing to present foreign investor misconduct as a legal argument,[66] and as a result, counterclaims based on foreign investor misconduct remain at the periphery of investment arbitration practice. The failure of host States to present counterclaims can be attributed, in part, to how counterclaims work. Investment arbitration is consent-based,[67] which means that the disputing parties must consent to counterclaims. Thus, if consent to arbitration is not framed in terms that include counterclaims, arbitral tribunals will be precluded from hearing a counterclaim.[68] Counterclaims also need a connection to the originating claim,[69] which means that foreign investor misconduct must comprise a significant aspect of the investment dispute. Not all forms of foreign investor misconduct will meet this criterion, meaning that host States will not seek to rely on counterclaim procedures. Finally, there must be a legal foundation on which to base the counterclaim. As outlined

66 Ho (n 1) 11.

67 Christoph Schreuer, 'Investment Arbitration' in Cesare PR Romano, Karen J Alter and Yuval Shany (eds), *The Oxford Handbook of International Adjudication* (Oxford University Press 2014) 302.

68 Zachary Douglas, *The International Law of Investment Claims* (Cambridge University Press 2009) 257.

69 ibid 260.

in Section 1.2, this can be difficult for a host State to establish. Consequently, the procedural requirements to establish counterclaims have, to date, limited the availability and success rate of counterclaims in investment arbitration. The low success rate may further dissuade host States from presenting foreign investor misconduct in the form of a counterclaim.

Despite these limitations, counterclaims possess the attributes to enable investment arbitration to address foreign investor misconduct. Although counterclaims remain contingent on a foreign investor commencing investment arbitration,[70] counterclaims reverse investment arbitration's asymmetry[71] by ensuring that both host States and foreign investors have the ability to initiate claims.[72] Counterclaims can increase efficiency[73] by resolving all investment related claims in one forum simultaneously,[74] reduce the time and costs associated with parallel dispute resolution proceedings[75] and provide equivalent remedies. Addressing all claims before an arbitral tribunal also reduces the risk of potential bias in host State courts.[76] It will still be difficult to identify obligations that bind foreign investors to form the legal foundation of the counterclaim. However, recent investment arbitration practice suggests that arbitral tribunals may be more amenable to applying a wider range of obligations

70 Anna De Luca, 'UNCITRAL Working Group III: Counterclaims in ISDS – Challenges and Prospects in Light of the UNCITRAL Reform Process' (*Kluwer Arbitration Blog*, 28 March 2020) <http://arbitrationblog.kluwerarbitration.com/2020/03/28/uncitral-working-group-iii-counterclaims-in-isds-challenges-and-prospects-in-light-of-the-uncitral-reform-process/> accessed 13 May 2021.

71 Helene Brubowski, 'Balancing IIA Arbitration Through the Use of Counterclaims' in A De Mestral and C Levesque (eds), *Improving International Investment Agreements* (Taylor and Francis 2013); Ishikawa, 'Counterclaims and the Rule of Law in Investment Arbitration' (n 9) 37; Ishikawa, *Corporate Environmental Responsibility in Investor-State Dispute Settlement: The Unexhausted Potential of Current Mechanisms* (n 7) 65.

72 Ana Vohryzek-Griest, 'State Counterclaims in Investor-State Disputes: A History of 30 Years of Failure' (2009) 15 International Law, Revista Colombian de Derecho Internacional 83, 87–88; Laborde (n 11) 103; Kryvoi (n 45) 220. This was the intention of the drafters of the ICSID Convention. See ICSID, 'Report of the Executive Directors on the Convention on the Settlement of Investment Disputes Between States and Nationals of other States' <https://icsid.worldbank.org/rules-regulations/convention/report/section-one> accessed 22 February 2023.

73 Kryvoi (n 45) 221.

74 ibid; Ishikawa, *Corporate Environmental Responsibility in Investor-State Dispute Settlement: The Unexhausted Potential of Current Mechanisms* (n 7) 64; *Spyridon Roussalis v. Romania* ICSID Case No ARB/06/1, Declaration of W Michael Reisman, 28 November 2011.

75 Kryvoi (n 45) 221.

76 Ishikawa, 'Counterclaims and the Rule of Law in Investment Arbitration' (n 9) 37.

owed by foreign investors to host States within counterclaim procedures.[77] State practice also evidences that some host States may seek to impose international legal obligations directly on foreign investors.[78] These shifts increase the viability of counterclaims going forward. Therefore, counterclaims possess the characteristics that can overcome the existing problems within investment arbitration.

When utilised to their full potential, the widespread use of counterclaims could contribute to the prevention of foreign investor misconduct. Counterclaims permit host States to initiate an independent claim against a foreign investor.[79] Hence, unlike when host States frame foreign investor misconduct claims in terms of investment protection standards or contributory fault, counterclaims permit a host State to hold a foreign investor accountable for their misconduct. Thus, host States can use counterclaims to directly challenge foreign investor misconduct in an investment dispute. If an arbitral tribunal finds a foreign investor liable for a breach of international law, the foreign investor must compensate the host State for any loss suffered.[80] Therefore, foreign investors that breach international law are likely to suffer financial loss[81]

77 For example, *Urbaser S.A. and Consorcio de Aguas Bilbao Biskaia, Bilbao Biskaia Ur Partzuergoa v. Argentine Republic* ICSID Case No ARB/07/26, Award, 8 December 2016. See Anil Yilmaz-Vastardis, 'Is International Investment Law moving the ball forward on IHRL obligations for business enterprises?' (*EJIL: Talk!*, 15 May 2017) <https://www.ejiltalk.org/is-international-investment-law-moving-the-ball-forward-on-ihrl-obligations-for-business-enterprises/> accessed 13 May 2021.

78 See Barnali Choudhury, 'Investor Obligations for Human Rights' (2020) 35 ICSID Review – Foreign Investment Law Journal 82, 88–94; Krajewski (n 9) 114–116.

79 Kryvoi (n 45) 220.

80 Article 34 ARSIWA (n 36) sets out that reparation for breaches of international law can include restitution, compensation and satisfaction, either singly or in combination. Whilst ARSIWA are based on customary international law, and do not bind foreign investors, some rules of state responsibility may still apply to investment arbitration (*Quiborax S.A. and Non Metallic Minerals S.A. v. Plurinational State of Bolivia* ICSID Case No ARB/06/2, Award, 16 September 2015 [555]). Thus, ARSIWA provides guidance regarding the remedies that a host State might be awarded.

81 For example, in *Burlington* v *Ecuador* and *Perenco* v *Ecuador*, Ecuador counterclaimed for nearly double the value of the foreign investors' originating claims to remedy the environmental damage and the damage to infrastructure caused by the foreign investors. Burlington and Perenco both claimed US$1.5 billion for Ecuador's breaches of the IIA (*Burlington Resources Inc. v. Republic of Ecuador* ICSID Case No ARB/08/5, Decision on Reconsideration and Award, 7 February 2017 [37]–[39]; *Perenco Ecuador Limited v. Republic of Ecuador*, Award (n 18) [56]–[62]). However, Ecuador counterclaimed for US$2.8 billion for the costs of remedying the environmental damage and damage to infrastructure caused by Burlington and Perenco (*Burlington Resources Inc. v. Republic*

and reputational damage.[82] If counterclaims are used consistently in investment arbitration, the threat of a possible counterclaim could alter how foreign investors evaluate the risks associated with breaching international law and dissuade them from undertaking activities that amount to foreign investor misconduct.[83]

The scope of counterclaim procedures means that counterclaims are not capable of addressing all facets of foreign investor misconduct. Counterclaims only permit a host State to challenge foreign investor misconduct in investment arbitration.[84] Consequently, local populations that may have been impacted by foreign investor misconduct are reliant on their State to bring a claim.[85] Local populations may not have any influence over the claim and may not receive compensation from their State.[86] Therefore, counterclaims cannot

---

of Ecuador, Decision on Counterclaims (n 17) [53]; *Perenco Ecuador Limited v. Republic of Ecuador*, Interim Decision on the Environmental Counterclaim (n 19) [36]). The compensation awarded to Burlington was valued at US$379.8 million and Ecuador received US$41.7 million for its counterclaim (*Burlington Resources Inc. v. Republic of Ecuador*, Decision on Reconsideration and Award [635]; *Burlington Resources Inc. v. Republic of Ecuador*, Decision on Counterclaims (n 17) [1099]). Perenco was awarded US$449 million and Ecuador $54 million for its counterclaim (*Perenco Ecuador Limited v. Republic of Ecuador*, Award (n 18) [1023]).

82 The extent to which reputational damage impacts foreign investors remains inconclusive. For example, the impact of loss of reputation on a corporation that causes environmental damage often aligns with the economic loss generated by legal liability (see Jonathan M Karpoff, John R Lott Jr. and Eric W Wehrly, 'The Reputational Penalties for Environmental Violations: Empirical Evidence' (2005) 48 The Journal of Law and Economics 653). However, if a corporation causes more than one case of environmental damage, the reputational loss through the media may be more significant because of their prior conduct (HL Zou and others, 'How Do Environmental Violations Harm Corporate Reputation?' (2015) 24 Business Strategy and the Environment 836).

83 Ishikawa, *Corporate Environmental Responsibility in Investor-State Dispute Settlement: The Unexhausted Potential of Current Mechanisms* (n 7) 65.

84 Ishikawa, 'Counterclaims and the Rule of Law in Investment Arbitration' (n 9) 35; Ishikawa, *Corporate Environmental Responsibility in Investor-State Dispute Settlement: The Unexhausted Potential of Current Mechanisms* (n 7) 12; Nicolás M Perrone, 'The "Invisible" Local Communities: Foreign Investor Obligations, Inclusiveness, and the International Investment Regime' (2019) 113 AJIL Unbound 16, 16.

85 Perrone (n 84) 18, 20; Lorenzo Cotula and Nicolás M Perrone, 'Investors' International Law and its Asymmetries: the Case of Local Communities' in Jean Ho and Mavluda Sattarova (eds), *Investors' International Law* (Hart Publishing 2021). See also Tomoko Ishikawa, 'Counterclaims in Investment Arbitration: Is the Host State the Right Claimant?' in Jean Ho and Mavluda Sattarova (eds), *Investors' International Law* (Hart Publishing 2021).

86 Perrone (n 84) 20; Patrick Abel, 'Counterclaims Based on International Human Rights Obligations of Investors in International Investment Arbitration: Fallacies and Potentials of the 2016 ICSID *Urbaser v. Argentina* Award' (2018) 1 Brill Open Law 61, 87.

provide direct access to remedies for local populations affected by foreign investor misconduct. Nonetheless, the potential of counterclaims as a means of challenging foreign investor misconduct should not be dismissed.

At present, host States cannot effectively challenge foreign investor misconduct that breaches international law in investment arbitration. Counterclaims possess the attributes required to overcome the existing challenges of addressing foreign investor misconduct in investment arbitration and their consistent use could dissuade foreign investors from breaching international law. Therefore, counterclaims provide the most viable option to achieve this goal. While not providing direct remedies to local populations, counterclaims form part of a toolbox that can contribute to holding foreign investors to account when they act contrary to norms of international law. However, current practices will need to be adjusted to make counterclaims workable so that they can fulfil this potential.

1.5 Holding Foreign Investors Accountable for Breaches of International Law

This book illustrates that counterclaims can be used to hold foreign investors accountable for misconduct that breaches international law in investment arbitration. Counterclaims permit host States to commence independent legal claims against foreign investors. Thus, by enhancing the effectiveness of counterclaim procedures, host States can hold foreign investors liable for their misconduct. Rather than simply asserting that counterclaims have the ability perform this role, the book comprehensively reviews and analyses arbitral practice to identify shortcomings in how counterclaims are currently employed in investment arbitration. Based on these shortcomings, the book outlines in practical terms how host States can maximise the availability and impact of counterclaim procedures. Thus, the book relies on State practice and litigation strategies as means of steering future arbitral practice to give greater effect to counterclaims procedures. The recommendations made throughout the book are not outside the scope of the arbitration rules, but instead, re-focus current State practice and arbitral jurisprudence to enable greater use of counterclaim procedures. Therefore, whilst the book examines the law of counterclaims in investment arbitration, it additionally guides host States regarding how to best use counterclaims to hold foreign investors accountable for breaches of international law.

The book centres on foreign investor misconduct that can be categorised as a breach of international law. Obligations sourced from international law often lie at the foundation of foreign investor misconduct. Thus, by focusing on international law, it becomes possible to capture prevalent forms of foreign investor misconduct that generate significant problems for host States. Given that international legal principles can be manifested in different ways, international law is defined in broad terms. International law is understood to include international obligations that bind foreign investors directly and obligations that are sourced from international law that bind foreign investors indirectly through their incorporation into domestic law. Domestic law encompasses domestic legislation and private legal obligations that are recognised by domestic legal systems, such as contractual obligations. Framing international law in this way permits host States to construct counterclaims based on international obligations regardless of whether the obligations bind foreign investors directly or indirectly. Increasing the accessibility of counterclaims will enable them to become a mainstream aspect of investment arbitration.

The book addresses counterclaim procedures under the International Centre for the Settlement of Investment Disputes (ICSID) Convention[87] and ICSID Arbitration Rules,[88] the ICSID Additional Facility (AF) Arbitration Rules[89] and the United Nations Commission on International Trade Law (UNCITRAL) Arbitration Rules.[90] These arbitration rules have been selected because they are commonly selected arbitration rules in investment arbitration. It is assumed that counterclaim procedures will continue to exist in investment arbitration in terms that are broadly similar to those found in existing arbitration rules. However, as variations exist between these rules, and arbitration rules may be subject to amendments, focus is placed on both the text of the arbitration rules and the litigation policy that underpins the rule. By giving effect to the dominant litigation policy that applies at each stage of establishing a counterclaim, the recommendations made in the book can withstand minor amendments to the arbitration rules.

Investment arbitration is limited to arbitration initiated by a host State offer to arbitrate sourced from an IIA or the host State's domestic legislation. The book focuses on claims based on investment protection standards (sourced from an IIA or domestic legislation) and contract claims that are brought in

87 Convention on the Settlement of Investment Disputes Between States and Nationals of Other States (adopted 18 March 1965, entered into force 14 October 1966) 575 UNTS 171 (ICSID Convention).

88 ICSID Arbitration Rules (2006) and ICSID Arbitration Rules (2022).

89 ICSID AF Arbitration Rules (2006) and ICSID AF Arbitration Rules (2022).

90 UNCITRAL Arbitration Rules (1976) and UNCITRAL Arbitration Rules (2010).

conjunction with this type of claim. The book excludes contract-based investment arbitration and purely contractual claims[91] because contracts allow claims and counterclaims by both foreign investors and host States based on the terms of the contract (which can potentially include provisions addressing foreign investor obligations). It is assumed that investment arbitration will remain the dominant means of resolving investment disputes. Although reform agendas exist that seek to alter investment arbitration in response to various critiques, these reform agendas do not indicate that investment arbitration will undergo wholesale change.[92] Therefore, the proposals to hold foreign investors accountable for misconduct in violation of international law are presented in conformity with the existing investment arbitration framework.

The book traces the procedural steps that a host State must follow to bring a counterclaim in investment arbitration and highlights what changes are required to enable counterclaims to hold foreign investors accountable for breaches of international law. It also considers what factors might influence whether a host State employs counterclaims in an investment dispute. The book initially examines the jurisdictional requirements to establish a counterclaim and focuses on how host States can use consent to create jurisdiction over counterclaims that avoids the constraints of existing arbitral practice (Chapter 2). The emphasis of the book then turns to the need for a connection between the originating claim and the counterclaim (Chapter 3). It is asserted that host States can encourage arbitral tribunals to capture a wider range of connections by emphasising the good administration of justice instead of focusing on the nature of the legal relationship between the claims. Consideration then turns to the need for the applicable law to encompass the legal obligations that form the basis of the counterclaim (Chapter 4). As the applicable law of the arbitral tribunal is a matter of party consent, it is recommended that host States should specify what law applies to counterclaims and in what circumstances the law should be applied. The book proceeds to examine the sources of law that can form the foundation of the counterclaim, the desirable characteristics of these laws and how host States can maximise the efficacy of laws that could be used

91 Contractual claims in this book refers to claims that do not involve investment protection standards. Claims based on umbrella clauses are not excluded because a breach of contract is framed as a breach of a treaty obligation.

92 For example, UNCITRAL Working Group III has limited the scope of its mandate to address (1) excessive legal costs; (2) duration of proceedings; (3) legal consistency; (4) decisional correctness; (5) arbitral diversity; and (6) arbitral independence and impartiality. See UNCITRAL Working Group III, 'Possible Reform of Investor-State Dispute Settlement (ISDS)' (5 September 2018) UN Doc A/CN.9/WG.III/WP.149.

as the foundation for a counterclaim (Chapter 5). Focus is then placed on how arbitral tribunals interpret legal obligations sourced from beyond IIL at the merits stage of the counterclaim. Although host States can steer arbitral practice with provisions that help arbitral tribunals to interpret law sourced from beyond IIL, arbitral tribunals should ideally refer to experts to minimise the risk of inconsistent decision-making. However, not all arbitral tribunals will be able to appoint experts, so host States will need to balance competing considerations and decide on a claim-by-claim basis whether to use counterclaims to challenge foreign investor misconduct in investment arbitration (Chapter 6). Based on this analysis, the conclusion (Chapter 7) demonstrates how a counterclaim in investment arbitration can be employed by host States to challenge foreign investor misconduct that breaches international law. The conclusion also elaborates on the wider implications of using counterclaims in the proposed manner for international law more generally.

CHAPTER 2

Jurisdiction over Counterclaims

2.1 Introduction

A foreign investor can only be held accountable for breaches of international law using counterclaims in investment arbitration if the arbitral tribunal possesses jurisdiction over counterclaims. If a counterclaim does not fall within the arbitral tribunal's jurisdiction it will be dismissed at the first stage of review.

In investment arbitration, an arbitral tribunal's jurisdiction is derived from the disputing parties' consent[1] and the selected arbitration rules.[2] Therefore, if a host State wishes to rely on counterclaim procedures, it must ensure that party consent encompasses counterclaims and that the jurisdictional requirements in the arbitration rules that govern counterclaims are met.[3] Nonetheless, host States must be strategic when consenting to counterclaims in investment arbitration. If consent to arbitration is framed in expansive terms, it is highly likely to permit counterclaims, but it may also enable foreign investors to commence a wide range of originating claims against the host State. Conversely, if a host State consents to investment arbitration in limited terms, it can reduce the availability of counterclaims. Arbitral tribunals attempt to give effect to the aims of counterclaims where possible, however, the options available to the arbitral tribunal are dictated by party consent. Hence, this chapter examines how host States can use consent, in conjunction with the selected arbitration rules, to generate jurisdiction in investment arbitration that is sufficiently nuanced to bind foreign investors to counterclaims whilst minimising host State exposure to investment claims. The chapter argues that host States can achieve these aims by drafting tailored consent clauses in IIAs and domestic legislation that distinguish between originating claims and counterclaims.

1 Chittharanjan F Amerasinghe, *International Arbitral Jurisdiction* (Brill 2011) 55; Relja Radović, *Beyond Consent: revisiting jurisdiction in investment treaty arbitration* (Brill 2021) 45; Hege Elisabeth Veenstra-Kjos, 'Counter-claims by Host States in Investment Dispute Arbitration "without Privity"' in Philippe Khan and Thomas Wälde (eds), *New Aspects of International Investment Law* (Nijhoff 2007) 599.

2 Andrea Steingruber, *Consent in International Arbitration* (Oxford University Press 2012) 254; Radović (n 1) 45.

3 Dafina Atanasova, Adrián Martínez Benoit and Josef Ostřanský, 'The Legal Framework for Counterclaims in Investment Treaty Arbitration' (2014) 31 Journal of International Arbitration 357, 365.

 | DOI:10.1163/9789004420953_003

Arbitral tribunals can then give effect to the aims of counterclaims without increasing the risk of host State liability.

To develop this argument, this chapter proceeds in three stages. It initially examines the consensual foundations of jurisdiction in investment arbitration to highlight the degree to which host States can influence the terms of party consent to investment arbitration (Section 2.2). The chapter then analyses how consent and jurisdiction have been understood by arbitral tribunals when applying arbitration rules on counterclaims (Section 2.3). This section demonstrates that the way in which consent to counterclaims is currently framed either excludes counterclaims or potentially exposes host States to a wide range of originating claims. It also illustrates that, when given the opportunity, arbitral tribunals seek to facilitate counterclaim procedures. Finally, with reference to recent State practice, the chapter addresses how host States can draft consent to investment arbitration to permit jurisdiction over counterclaims in a way that gives full effect to counterclaims whilst protecting the host State's interests (Section 2.4). To close, the chapter draws some preliminary conclusions (Section 2.5).

2.2 Consent to Investment Arbitration

Investment arbitration is based on party consent.[4] Party consent evidences the disputing parties' agreement to resolve disputes using investment arbitration,[5] but when it is interpreted in conjunction with the selected arbitration rules, it also determines the arbitral tribunal's jurisdiction.[6] Thus, the terms used by the disputing parties when they consent to investment arbitration directly influence whether an arbitral tribunal possesses jurisdiction over counterclaims.[7] Party consent to investment arbitration can be sourced from IIAs or

4 Guiguo Wang, 'Consent in Investor-State Arbitration: A Critical Analysis' (2014) 13 Chinese Journal of International Law 335, 336; Radović (n 1) 45.

5 Clara Reiner and Christoph Schreuer, 'Human Rights and International Investment Arbitration' in Pierre-Marie Dupuy, Francesco Francioni and Ernst-Ulrich Petersmann (eds), *Human Rights in International Investment Law and Arbitration* (Oxford University Press 2009) 83; Ursula Kriebaum, 'Human Rights of the Population of the Host State in International Investment Arbitration' (2009) 10 Journal of World Investment and Trade 653, 660.

6 Zachary Douglas, *The International Law of Investment Claims* (Cambridge University Press 2009) 360–361.

7 Radović (n 1) 53.

domestic legislation.[8] This section argues that, in many instances, host States have sufficient power when drafting these legal instruments to ensure that party consent extends to counterclaims. Therefore, provided that host States exercise this power to influence the terms of party consent, they can maximise the chance that an arbitral tribunal possesses jurisdiction over counterclaims in investment arbitration. To substantiate this argument, IIAs and domestic legislation will be discussed in turn.

Consent to investment arbitration in IIAs is based on public international law.[9] Consequently, IIAs are negotiated by States and the dispute resolution clauses that grant consent to investment arbitration are only binding on the State parties to the IIA.[10] To overcome the lack of direct consent between the host State and the foreign investor, the dispute resolution provision in the IIA is understood to amount to a standing offer to arbitrate.[11] The standing offer is made by the host State to foreign investors that possess the nationality of another contracting State.[12] At the time of consenting, the host State is unaware of what legal claims may arise in the future. When a foreign investor accepts the standing offer (most commonly by commencing investment arbitration proceedings in accordance with the selected arbitration rules) both parties have consented to investment arbitration and the scope of the investment claim becomes clear.[13] Consequently, party consent to investment

8 Michele Potestà, 'The Interpretation of Consent to ICSID Arbitration Contained in Domestic Investment Laws' (2011) 27 Arbitration International 149, 152; *Venezuela Holdings B.V. et. al. v. Bolivarian Republic of Venezuela* ICSID Case No ARB/07/27, Decision on Jurisdiction, 10 June 2010 [64]; *CEMEX Caracas Investments B.V. and CEMEX Caracas II Investments B.V. v. Bolivarian Republic of Venezuela* ICSID Case No ARB/08/15, Decision on Jurisdiction, 30 December 2010 [58].

9 Radović (n 1) 63.

10 Steingruber (n 2) 229.

11 James Crawford, 'Treaty and Contract in Investment Arbitration' (2008) 24 Arbitration International 351, 360; Paul Michael Blyschak, 'State Consent, Investor Interests and the Future of Investment Arbitration: Reanalyzing the Jurisdiction of Investor-State Tribunals in Hard Cases' (2009) 9 Asper Review of International Business and Trade Law 99, 133; Gustavo Laborde, 'The Case for Host State Claims in Investment Arbitration' (2010) 1 Journal of International Dispute Settlement 97, 112; Yavaslau Kryvoi, 'Counterclaims in Investor-State Arbitration' (2012) 21 Minnesota Journal of International Law 216, 226.

12 Steingruber (n 2) 201.

13 Stefan Dudas, 'Treaty Counterclaims under the ICSID Convention' in Crina Baltag (ed), *ICSID Convention after 50 Years: Unsetttled Issues* (Kluwer Law International 2017) 395; Wang (n 4) 336; Konstanze Von Papp, 'Biting the Bullet or Redefining Consent in Investor-State Arbitration: Pre-Arbitration Requirements After *BG Group v Argentina*' (2015) 16 Journal of World Investment and Trade 695, 699; Atanasova, Benoit and Ostřanský (n 3) 366; Hanno Wehland, 'Jurisdiction and Admissibility in Proceedings under the ICSID

arbitration under an IIA is initiated by the terms of the host State's standing offer,[14] but requires two separate acts of consent.[15]

IIAs confer host States with control over the terms of their consent to arbitration because a host State can set out the parameters of their consent independently of the foreign investor. Nonetheless, this does not provide a host State with complete control over the terms of their consent to arbitration because it must negotiate the terms of the IIA with other States. IIA negotiations are influenced by the respective bargaining power of each State[16] and often reflect the preferences of the more powerful State's domestic actors.[17] Consequently, State parties that import capital may agree to consent to counterclaims to protect their interests as a potential host State. However, some capital exporting States may be more resistant to consenting to counterclaims because they are less likely to be subject to investment claims and want to protect their nationals that invest in foreign jurisdictions. Hence, the terms of the dispute resolution clauses are likely to vary depending on which States are involved in the negotiations. Yet, the strength of one State's bargaining power can be mitigated by other States' negotiating expertise.[18] Thus, whilst many States will not be able to dictate the terms of consent to arbitration in an IIA, if the negotiating States can be convinced of the benefits of counterclaims, it should still be possible for most States to consent to arbitration in a way that includes counterclaims.

The foreign investor must accept the host State's standing offer to perfect the consent to investment arbitration. A question arises as to whether a foreign investor can exclude consent to counterclaims when accepting the standing offer. Whether this is possible depends on how consent is understood to function. One understanding identifies the scope of consent based on the common elements that are shared between the host State's standing offer and the

---

Convention and the Additional Facility Rules' in Crina Baltag (ed), *ICSID Convention After 50 Years: Unsetttled Issues* (Kluwer Law International 2017) 239; Steingruber (n 2) 206.

14 Dudas (n 13) 395; Abhimanyu George Jain, 'Consent to Counterclaims in Investor-State Arbitration: a post-Roussalis analysis' (2013) 16 International Arbitration Law Review 135, 140.

15 Dudas (n 13) 395; Amerasinghe (n 1) 49–50. For a general discussion, see Jan Paulsson, 'Arbitration Without Privity' (1995) 10 ICSID Review – Foreign Investment Law Journal 232.

16 Todd Allee and Clint Peinhardt, 'Evaluating Three Explanations for the Design of Bilateral Investment Treaties' (2014) 66 World Politics 47, 62–63.

17 ibid 63–65.

18 See Tarald Laudal Berge and Øyvind Stiansen, 'Negotiating BITS with Models: The Power of Expertise' (10th Annual Conference on the Political Economy of International Organizations, University of Bern, Switzerland, January 12–14, 2017).

foreign investor's acceptance.[19] Adopting this viewpoint, the foreign investor's acceptance of the standing offer will be limited to the scope of its originating claim, and would, in the absence of further consent,[20] exclude consent to counterclaims.[21] An alternative viewpoint asserts that party consent is only aligned when the foreign investor accepts the standing offer in its entirety, which occurs when the foreign investor commences a claim.[22] In accordance with this approach, the foreign investor cannot limit or expand the terms of the host State's standing offer. The extent to which the host State can control the terms of consent to arbitration will depend on which standpoint is adopted. The arbitral tribunal in *Urbaser* v *Argentina*[23] deemed that the foreign investor's acceptance must mirror the terms of the host State's standing offer. In this investment dispute, the foreign investor argued that its consent was limited to claims made against the host State, thereby ruling out any potential losses

---

19 Ibrahim FJ Shihata and Antonio R Parra, 'The Experience of the International Centre for Settlement of Investment Dispute' (1999) 14 ICSID Review – Foreign Investment Law Journal 299, 320. See Hamid Walid Ben Hamida, 'L'arbitrage Etat-investisseur cherche son quilibre perdu: Dans quelle mesure l'Etat peut introduire des demandes reconventionnelles contre l'investisseur priv?' (2005) 7 International Law Forum du droit international 261, 269.

20 See *Burlington Resources Inc. v. Republic of Ecuador* ICSID Case No ARB/08/5, Decision on Counterclaims, 7 February 2017 [60]–[62] for an example of consent to counterclaims after the initiation of investment arbitration.

21 See for example, Christoph Schreuer, *The ICSID Convention: A Commentary* (Cambridge University Press 2001) 746 who states that '[i]f the investor accepts the offer to arbitrate [contained in a BIT] only in respect of its specific claim, consent will be restricted by the terms of the acceptance. If the investor accepts the offer of jurisdiction by instituting proceedings, consent only exists to the extent necessary to deal with the investor's request. But if a counterclaim of the State is closely connected to the investor's complaint, it is arguable that it will be covered by the mutual consent of the parties'. For discussions of this point, see Steingruber (n 2) 304–305; Zachary Douglas, 'The enforcement of environmental norms in investment treaty arbitration' in Pierre-Marie Dupuy and Jorge E Viñuales (eds), *Harnessing Foreign Investment to Promote Environmental Protection: Incentives and Safeguards* (Cambridge University Press 2013) 469; Tomoko Ishikawa, *Corporate Environmental Responsibility in Investor-State Dispute Settlement: The Unexhausted Potential of Current Mechanisms* (Cambridge University Press 2022) 91–92.

22 Pierre Lalive and Laura Halonen, 'On the Availability of Counterclaims in Investment Treaty Arbitration' (2011) II Czech Yearbook of International Law 141, 150; Douglas, *The International Law of Investment Claims* (n 6) 258. This position has been adopted by UNCITRAL Working Group III in Draft provision 11(2) on counterclaims (UNCITRAL Working Group III, 'Possible reform of investor-State dispute settlement (ISDS): Draft provisions on procedural and cross-cutting issues' (26 July 2023) UN Doc No. A/CN.9/WG.III/WP.231, 6).

23 *Urbaser S.A. and Consorcio de Aguas Bilbao Biskaia, Bilbao Biskaia Ur Partzuergoa v. Argentine Republic* ICSID Case No ARB/07/26, Award, 8 December 2016.

sustained by the Argentine Republic.[24] The arbitral tribunal noted that the foreign investor's acceptance of the standing offer did not specifically exclude counterclaims and its silence on the issue meant that the availability of counterclaims was not addressed explicitly or implicitly.[25] In any event, the arbitral tribunal considered that it was not possible for the foreign investor to accept a right for both parties to bring claims based on the dispute resolution clause and then deny this right by restricting the terms of their acceptance because neither ICSID or UNCITRAL arbitration permit a unilateral delimitation of a tribunal's competence.[26] Thus, a foreign investor's acceptance of the standing offer to arbitrate in more limited terms would not result in an agreement between the parties.[27] The approach taken in *Urbaser* v *Argentina* aligns with the majority of arbitral practice, which focuses on the terms of the standing offer to establish jurisdiction in investment arbitration. Thus, based on this award, the scope of a host State's offer to arbitrate takes precedence over the foreign investor's acceptance, granting the host State more control over the terms of party consent to arbitration.

In short, subject to negotiations with other States, host States can formulate consent to arbitration in IIAs independently of the foreign investor, which must be accepted by the foreign investor in the same terms. Therefore, host States, to a relatively large degree, can dictate the terms of their consent to arbitration in an IIA, which permits them to include counterclaims within the terms of their consent.

Although used less frequently,[28] consent to investment arbitration can also be granted through domestic legislation. Domestic legislation permits host States to unilaterally formulate the terms of their consent to arbitration in national law.[29] The host State will need to comply with its constitutional law to create the domestic legislation. Domestic legislation that contains a unilateral offer to arbitrate creates a similar legal framework to that found in an IIA.[30] The

24 ibid [1145].

25 ibid [1146].

26 ibid [1147]. See ICSID Convention Article 25(1).

27 *Urbaser S.A. and Consorcio de Aguas Bilbao Biskaia, Bilbao Biskaia Ur Partzuergoa v. Argentine Republic* (n 23) [1147].

28 See Jarrod Hepburn, 'Domestic Investment Statutes in International Law' (2018) 112 American Journal of International Law 658, 659.

29 ibid.

30 The language used in domestic legislation will not necessarily be drafted in these terms. If it is not, a unilateral offer to arbitrate may not exist. For example, in the *Venezuela Holdings B.V. et. al. v. Bolivarian Republic of Venezuela* (n 8) and *CEMEX Caracas Investments B.V. and CEMEX Caracas II Investments B.V. v. Bolivarian Republic of Venezuela* (n 8) awards, the language in Article 22 of Venezuela's Foreign Investment Law contained a proviso

arbitral tribunal in *SPP* v *Egypt*[31] deemed that the unilateral offer to arbitrate set out in the Egyptian Foreign Investment Law[32] was sufficient to amount to host State consent to arbitration without the need for further action from the host State.[33] As a result, arbitration provisions in domestic legislation are considered to be standing offers to arbitrate when drafted in similar terms.[34] The standing offer is made by the host State in advance of investment disputes and the foreign investor consents to arbitration by initiating an investment claim in accordance with the terms of the offer.[35] However, unlike IIAs which limit the standing offer to nationals of other contracting States, an offer set out in domestic legislation extends to all foreign investors.[36] Thus, domestic legislation allows host States to formulate open offers to arbitrate investment disputes. Therefore, when making a unilateral offer, host States have control over the terms of consent to arbitration in domestic legislation in a manner that permits them to include consent to counterclaims.

Host States frequently have sufficient power over the terms of consent to arbitration to ensure that consent encompasses counterclaims. IIAs and domestic legislation that contain a unilateral offer generate standing offers to arbitrate. Therefore, host States can consent to arbitration in advance of an investment dispute on their preferred terms. Whilst negotiating strategies may impact provisions in IIAs, and domestic legislation is subject to national law-making processes, host States possess the power to ensure that consent to arbitration encompasses counterclaims and can exercise this power to formulate consent in these terms. Notwithstanding that host States have control over consent to

---

that was interpreted to mean that the treaty or agreement needed to provide for the mandatory submission of disputes to international arbitration. As to the different types of language that can be used see Makane Moïse Mbengue, 'Consent to Arbitration Through National Investment Legislation' (*Investment Treaty News*, 19 July, 2012) <https://www.iisd.org/itn/en/2012/07/19/consent-to-arbitration-through-national-investment-legislation/> accessed 12 July 2020.

31 *Southern Pacific Properties (Middle East) Limited v. Arab Republic of Egypt* ICSID Case No ARB/84/3, Decision on Jurisdiction, 14 April 1988.

32 Egypt Law No. 43 of 1974 concerning the Investment of Arab and Foreign Funds and the Free Zone.

33 *Southern Pacific Properties (Middle East) Limited v. Arab Republic of Egypt* (n 31) [82].

34 Steingruber (n 2) 199.

35 ibid, 200; see for example, *Tradex Hellas S.A. v. Republic of Albania* ICSID Case No ARB/94/2, Decision on Jurisdiction, 24 December 1996, [D.6.4]. Investment arbitration can be commenced in any other way permitted by the domestic legislation, see Lucy Reed, Jan Paulsson and Nigel Blackaby (eds), *Guide to ICSID Arbitration* (2nd edn, Kluwer Law International 2011) 56.

36 Steingruber (n 2) 199.

arbitration, consent only provides one source of an arbitral tribunal's jurisdiction. It is how consent interacts with arbitration rules that ultimately dictates the extent of an arbitral tribunal's jurisdiction over counterclaims.

2.3 Jurisdiction over Counterclaims

Whether an arbitral tribunal has jurisdiction to hear a counterclaim depends on the availability of counterclaim procedures under the applicable arbitration rules. However, the applicable arbitration rules provide the outer-limits of the arbitral tribunal's jurisdiction over counterclaims.[37] The disputing parties can choose to further delimit the arbitral tribunal's jurisdiction by consenting to arbitration in narrower terms.[38] Hence, if party consent is framed in more restrictive terms, a counterclaim may be within the general jurisdiction of the arbitral tribunal but not within the arbitral tribunal's competence.[39] Thus, to determine whether jurisdiction over a counterclaim exists, an arbitral tribunal must identify whether counterclaims are permitted based on the arbitration rules and determine whether the disputing parties' consent extends to counterclaims in the specific dispute before them.[40]

The way in which an arbitral tribunal identifies whether party consent extends to counterclaims depends on the form of legal instrument that sets out the party consent. Consent to arbitration in an IIA requires an arbitral tribunal to interpret the host State's standing offer and the foreign investor's acceptance of the offer. The host State's offer is made in a treaty, and consequently, will be interpreted in accordance with the rules of treaty interpretation[41] set out in Articles 31–33 of the Vienna Convention on the Law of Treaties (VCLT).[42]

37 Wehland (n 13) 230.

38 ibid; Douglas, *The International Law of Investment Claims* (n 6) 234–235; Charles Oman, *Policy Competition for Foreign Direct Investment* (OECD 2000) para 139.

39 Wehland (n 13) 230; Ina C. Popova and Fiona Poon, 'From Perpetual Respondent to Aspiring Counterclaimant? State Counterclaims in the New Wave of Investment Treaties' (2015) 2 BCDR International Arbitration Review 223, 227; Viejo Heiskanen, 'Ménage à trois? Jurisdiction, Admissibility and Competence in Investment Treaty Arbitration' (2014) 29 ICSID Review – Foreign Investment Law Journal 231, 235–236; Gerold Zeiler, 'Jurisdiction, Competence and Admissibility of Claims in ICSID Arbitral Proceedings' in Christina Binder and others (eds), *International Investment Law for the 21st Century: Essays in Honour of Christoph Schreuer* (Oxford University Press 2009) 81.

40 Wang (n 4) 338.

41 Steingruber (n 2) 231; Radović (n 1) 67.

42 Vienna Convention on the Law of Treaties (adopted 23 May 1969, entered into force 27 January 1980) 1155 UNTS 331. These rules exist in the same form in customary international

The foreign investor's acceptance of the standing offer is not considered to be a treaty, but instead, a contract governed by international law.[43] The English Court of Appeal in *Occidental Exploration & Production Company* v *Republic of Ecuador*[44] considered that applying international law to the foreign investor's acceptance of the standing offer better served the purpose of investor protection.[45] The Court of Appeal's position can be justified based on the foreign investor's consent to arbitration being in response to the host State's standing offer set out in an IIA.[46] Thus, the standing offer and its acceptance are both likely to be interpreted with reference to international law.

Standing offers to arbitrate made in domestic legislation have been interpreted in an inconsistent manner.[47] Arbitral tribunals have focused on applying national law (including principles of statutory interpretation), rules of treaty interpretation and international law governing unilateral declarations made by States, but have placed emphasis on different elements.[48] For example, the majority in *SPP* v *Egypt*[49] considered that the standing offer should be interpreted with reference to 'general principles of statutory interpretation taking into consideration, where appropriate, relevant rules of treaty interpretation and principles of international law applicable to unilateral declarations'.[50] The

law. See Romesh Weeramantry, 'Treaty Interpretation, the ICSID Convention and Investment Treaties' in Crina Baltag (ed), *ICSID Convention after 50 Years: Unsettled Issues* (Kluwer Law International 2017); c.f. Yulia Andreeva, 'Interpreting Consent to Arbitration as a Unilateral Act of State: A Case Against Conventions' (2011) 27 Arbitration International 129.

43 *Republic of Ecuador v. Occidental Exploration and Production Company* [2005] EWHC 774 (Comm) (HC QBD) [2005] [32]–[33]. See Charles Brower and Shashank P Kumar, 'Investomercial Arbitration: Whence Cometh It? What Is It? Whither Goeth It?' (2015) 30 ICSID Review – Foreign Investment Law Journal 35, 44.

44 *Republic of Ecuador v. Occidental Exploration and Production Company* (n 43).

45 *Occidental v Ecuador* [2005] EWCA Civ 1116, [2006] QB 432 [33].

46 Douglas, *The International Law of Investment Claims* (n 6) 76.

47 Romesh Weeramantry, *Treaty Interpretation in Investment Arbitration* (Oxford University Press 2012) 167. The variation in wording may contribute to the diverse interpretations. See Potestà (n 8) 154–160.

48 For example, in *Tradex Hellas S.A. v. Republic of Albania*, the tribunal did not apply a particular approach, but evaluated the wording of the offer. As the law included the clearly worded phrase 'the Republic of Albania hereby consents' (Article 8(2) Albania's Foreign Investment Law 1993), the failure to espouse the approach taken is arguably less problematic. See Andrés A Mezgravis, 'The Standard of Interpretation Applicable to Consent and its Revocation in Investment Arbitration' (2011) 8 Transnational Dispute Management 1 and Potestà (n 8) 160–162 on competing considerations.

49 *Southern Pacific Properties (Middle East) Limited v. Arab Republic of Egypt* (n 31).

50 ibid [61]. However, the dissenting arbitrator preferred to interpret the standing offer based solely on principles of national law. See also *Zhinvali Development Ltd. v. Republic*

arbitral tribunals in *Mobil* v *Venezuela*[51] and CEMEX v *Venezuela*[52] both interpreted standing offers set out in Venezuela's domestic legislation to be unilateral acts of the State that should be governed by international law together with the State's domestic law.[53] However, these tribunals specifically denied the applicability of the ILC's Guiding Principles on Unilateral Declarations of States (2006).[54] In part, arbitral tribunals' use of varied interpretative methods results from the lack of academic understanding regarding how to legally frame consent to arbitration sourced from domestic legislation.[55] Nonetheless, the diverse approaches make it more challenging to identify whether a host State has definitively included counterclaims in their consent to arbitration.

The assorted approaches to interpreting party consent make it necessary to refer to a wide selection of arbitral practice to understand how arbitral tribunals establish jurisdiction over counterclaims. Based on arbitral practice, this section argues that party consent is currently drafted in expansive or restrictive terms that do not enable arbitral tribunals to give effect to counterclaims in investment arbitration. Party consent in expansive terms may create jurisdiction over counterclaims, but simultaneously creates jurisdiction over originating claims. Party consent in restrictive terms can deny jurisdiction over counterclaims before a dispute arises. Neither approach enables arbitral tribunals to implement the policies that support the use of counterclaims in investment arbitration. Yet, arbitral tribunals employ these policies when the terms of party consent are ambiguous. Thus, the prevailing formulations of party consent inhibit counterclaims in investment arbitration. To illustrate these practices, this section considers how party consent has been interpreted in conjunction with the ICSID Convention and the ICSID Arbitration Rules, the ICSID AF Arbitration Rules and UNCITRAL Arbitration Rules before discussing the implications of this arbitral practice for host States.

---

of Georgia ICSID Case No ARB/00/1, Award, 24 January 2003 that emphasised that the standing offer should be interpreted using national law, but subject to principles of international law ([339]ff); c.f. *Ceskoslovenska obchodní banka, a.s. v. Slovak Republic* ICSID Case No ARB/97/4, Decision of the Tribunal on Objections to Jurisdiction, 24 May 1999, in which the tribunal based its decision on international law without any reservation.

51 *Venezuela Holdings B.V. et. al. v. Bolivarian Republic of Venezuela* (n 8).

52 *CEMEX Caracas Investments B.V. and CEMEX Caracas II Investments B.V. v. Bolivarian Republic of Venezuela* (n 8).

53 *Venezuela Holdings B.V. et. al. v. Bolivarian Republic of Venezuela* (n 8) [96], and *CEMEX Caracas Investments B.V. and CEMEX Caracas II Investments B.V. v. Bolivarian Republic of Venezuela* (n 8) [46].

54 *Venezuela Holdings B.V. et. al. v. Bolivarian Republic of Venezuela* (n 8) [90] and *CEMEX Caracas Investments B.V. and CEMEX Caracas II Investments B.V. v. Bolivarian Republic of Venezuela* (n 8) [83].

55 Hepburn (n 28) 659.

2.3.1 *ICSID Convention and ICSID Arbitration Rules*

An arbitral tribunal's ability to determine a counterclaim in ICSID arbitration is governed by Article 46 ICSID Convention (which is mirrored in Rule 40(1) ICSID Arbitration Rules (2006) and Rule 48 ICSID Arbitration Rules (2022)). These provisions provide that, unless the parties otherwise agree, counterclaims must fall 'within the consent of the parties' and otherwise be 'within the jurisdiction of the Centre'.[56] Therefore, an arbitral tribunal must determine whether the counterclaim meets the requirements set out in Article 25 ICSID Convention which delimits the jurisdiction of ICSID. If these elements are met, the counterclaim must additionally fall within the scope of party consent to arbitration. These conditions will be examined in turn.

The jurisdictional limits of ICSID reflect its origins as a dedicated forum for the resolution of investment disputes.[57] Article 25(1) ICSID Convention limits the personal jurisdiction of ICSID to State parties to the ICSID Convention and foreign investors that have the nationality of a different contracting State.[58] Hence, the host State must ensure that it is seeking to enforce obligations that are owed to the State, rather than to a different legal entity.[59] The counterclaim must additionally seek to enforce obligations owed to the host State by the foreign investor (and not third parties).[60] Therefore, to fall within ICSID's personal jurisdiction, counterclaims must be confined to obligations that bind the disputing parties.[61]

56 ICSID Convention Article 46 states in full 'Except as the parties otherwise agree, the Tribunal shall, if requested by a party, determine any incidental or additional claims or counter-claims arising directly out of the subject-matter of the dispute provided that they are within the scope of the consent of the parties and are otherwise within the jurisdiction of the Centre'.

57 ICSID, 'Report of the Executive Directors on the Convention on the Settlement of Investment Disputes Between States and Nationals of other States' <https://icsid.worldbank.org/rules-regulations/convention/report/section-one> accessed 22 February 2023 [11].

58 The foreign investor must possess this nationality at the time of consent to arbitration and when the request to proceed to arbitration is registered (ICSID Convention Article 25(2)(a)).

59 See *Alex Genin, Eastern Credit Limited, INC. and A.S. Baltoil v. Republic of Estonia* ICSID Case No ARB/99/2, Award, 25 June 2001 [378] and fn 101.

60 *Hesham Talaat M. Al-Warraq v. Republic of Indonesia* UNCITRAL, Final Award, 15 December 2014 [669]. Although an UNCITRAL award, the principle is transferable.

61 See Brower and Kumar (n 43) 50–51 and Berk Demirkol, 'Non-treaty Claims in Investment Treaty Arbitration' (2018) 31 Leiden Journal of International Law 59, at 64–65 on how this affects contractual claims.

The subject matter jurisdiction of ICSID is determined by the phrase 'any legal dispute arising out of an investment'.[62] This phrase requires that several preconditions are met. The first element is that the dispute must be 'legal', that is, it must concern the scope of a legal right or obligation, or a remedy in relation to a legal right or obligation.[63] In *Teinver* v *Argentina*,[64] the tribunal rejected the Respondent's counterclaim because it merely identified the relationship between the counterclaim and the investment and failed to identify any legal right or obligation in its pleadings.[65] Thus, to establish that a counterclaim is within ICSID's subject matter jurisdiction, the legal basis of the counterclaim must be made explicit.

The need for the counterclaim to arise 'directly out of an investment' requires that the dispute displays a sufficient nexus with the investment.[66] This criterion must be distinguished from the need for the counterclaim to 'arise directly out of the subject matter of the dispute', which is a separate element of Article 46 ICSID Convention (see Section 3.3.1).[67] A dispute that arises directly out of an investment can be contrasted to disputes over rights and obligations of general application. In the resubmitted case of *Amco* v

62 ICSID Convention Article 25(1).

63 ICSID (n 57) 44. See *Fedax N.V. v. The Republic of Venezuela* ICSID Case No ARB/96/3, Decision of the Tribunal on Objections to Jurisdiction, 11 July 1997 [15]; *Tokios Tokelės v. Ukraine* ICSID Case No ARB/02/18, Decision on Jurisdiction, 29 April 2004 [106]; *AES Corporation v. Argentine Republic* ICSID Case No ARB/02/17, Decision on Jurisdiction, 26 April 2005 [43]–[44]; *M.C.I. Power Group, L.C. and New Turbine v. Republic of Ecuador* ICSID Case No ARB/03/6, Award, 31 July 2007 [63]; *Abaclat and Others (formerly Giovanna a Beccara and Others) v. Argentine Republic* ICSID Case No ARB/07/5, Decision on Jurisdiction and Admissibility, 4 August 2011 [255]; Aron Broches, *Selected Essays: World Bank, ICSID and Other Subjects of Public and Private International Law* (Martinus Nijhoff 1995) 168; Yavaslau Kryvoi, *International Centre for Settlement of Investment Disputes* (Kluwer Law International 2010) 55.

64 *Teinver S.A., Transportes de Cercanías S.A. and Autobuses Urbanos del Sur S.A. v. Argentine Republic* ICSID Case No ARB/09/1, Decision on Jurisdiction, 21 December 2012.

65 ibid [1066].

66 This requirement does not refer to the direct nature of the investment but rather that the dispute stems directly from an investment. See *Fedax N.V. v. The Republic of Venezuela* ICSID Case No ARB/96/3, Decision of the Tribunal on Objections to Jurisdiction, 11 July 1997 [25]–[29]; *Ceskoslovenska obchodní banka, a.s. v. Slovak Republic* (n 50) [71]–[74]; *Siemens A.G. v. Argentine Republic* ICSID Case No ARB/02/8, Decision on Jurisdiction, 3 August 2004 [150]; Omar E Garcia-Bolivar, 'Foreign Investment Disputes under ICSID: A Review of its Decisions on Jurisdiction' (2004) 5 Journal of World Investment and Trade 187, 190; Kryvoi, *International Centre for Settlement of Investment Disputes* (n 63) 56. This is in contrast to general commercial disputes which fall outside of ICSID's jurisdiction.

67 See Steingruber (n 2) 304.

Indonesia,[68] Indonesia's counterclaim for repayment of taxes based on alleged tax fraud was beyond ICSID's subject matter jurisdiction because this particular case of tax fraud did not arise directly out of the investment.[69] A similar decision was reached in *Meerapfel Sohne* v *Central African Republic*,[70] where a counterclaim based on non-payment of tax and tax fraud was dismissed due to the claims being subject to domestic jurisdiction (and by implication, being of general application).[71] Consequently, claims that are peripheral, or that indirectly relate to an investment, will be considered to fall outside of ICSID's jurisdiction.[72] Notwithstanding, if general rights or obligations specifically impact an investment, this criterion is fulfilled.[73] Thus, the arbitral tribunal in *Urbaser* v *Argentina*[74] did not consider that international human rights law was inherently beyond ICSID's jurisdiction because the subject matter did not automatically exclude the existence of a dispute arising out of an investment.[75] Hence, to fall within ICSID's subject matter jurisdiction, a host State counterclaim must evidence a direct relationship between the dispute and an investment.

Finally, ICSID's subject matter jurisdiction requires the existence of an investment. The ICSID Convention does not provide a definition of 'investment', instead leaving it to the parties to determine what amounts to an investment as an element of party consent to arbitration.[76] Consequently, the

---

68 *Amco Asia Corporation and others v. Republic of Indonesia* ICSID Case No ARB/81/1, Decision on Jurisdiction in Resubmitted Proceeding, 10 May 1988.

69 ibid [126]; c.f. *S.A.R.L. Benvenuti & Bonfant v. People's Republic of the Congo* ICSID Case No ARB/77/2, Award, 8 August 1980 [4.104].

70 *M. Meerapfel Sohne AG v. Central African Republic* ICSID Case No ARB/07/10, Excerpts of Award, 12 May 2012.

71 ibid [447].

72 Garcia-Bolivar (n 66) 190; Ugljesa Grusic, 'The Evolving Jurisdiction of the International Centre for Settlement of Investment Disputes' (2009) 10 Journal of World Investment and Trade 69, 82.

73 *Amco Asia Corporation and others v. Republic of Indonesia* (n 68) states at [125]: [I]t is correct to distinguish between rights and obligations that are applicable to legal or natural persons who are within the reach of a host State's jurisdiction, as a matter of general law; and rights and obligations that are applicable to an investor as a consequence of an investment agreement entered into with that host state. Legal disputes relating to the latter will fall under Article 25(1) of the Convention. Legal disputes concerning the former in principle fall to be decided by the appropriate procedures in the relevant jurisdiction unless the general law generates an investment dispute under the Convention.

74 *Urbaser S.A. and Consorcio de Aguas Bilbao Biskaia, Bilbao Biskaia Ur Partzuergoa v. Argentine Republic* (n 23).

75 ibid [1154].

76 ICSID (n 57) 44. See Broches (n 63) 168; Grusic (n 72) 82; Kryvoi, *International Centre for Settlement of Investment Disputes* (n 63) 57.

arbitral tribunal must determine whether the specific dispute is covered by the disputing parties' definition of investment sourced from the legal instrument that generates consent. Some arbitral tribunals have sought to identify objective characteristics of an investment in addition to those formulated by the disputing parties.[77] In these instances, what amounts to an investment remains subject to the terms of party consent but will also need to meet objective criteria relating to the foreign investor's contribution to the investment, the duration of the investment, the existence of risk and the investment's contribution to the economic development of the host State.[78] If a counterclaim relates to a dispute that is not captured by the State's definition of an investment (and if applicable, the objective criteria of an investment) ICSID will not possess subject matter jurisdiction.

In short, a counterclaim will need to fall within ICSID's jurisdiction. Thus, the counterclaim must be based on obligations owed by the foreign investor to the host State. Further, the subject matter of the counterclaim must address a legal issue that can be directly related to an investment. An investment is defined by the disputing parties but may also be subject to additional criteria. In addition to being within the personal and subject matter jurisdiction, the counterclaim must also comply with any applicable time limitations.[79] If these conditions are met, the counterclaim falls within the scope of ICSID's jurisdiction, and the first element of Article 46 ICSID Convention is fulfilled. To comply with the second element, an arbitral tribunal must determine whether the counterclaim is within the terms of party consent.

Prior to examining arbitral practice based on the terms of party consent, a preliminary issue arises as to whether party consent to counterclaims can be inferred from the selection of ICSID arbitration because the arbitration rules permit counterclaim procedures. This issue arose in *Roussalis* v *Romania*.[80] The dispute resolution clause governing the dispute, Article 9 of the Romania-Greece Bilateral Investment Treaty (BIT), limited party consent to disputes based on host State obligations under the BIT.[81] Relying on the general rule

---

77 See Radović (n 1) 133–135.

78 These are the criteria from the so-called *Salini* test, resulting from the award in *Salini Costruttori S.P.A. and Italstrade S.P.A. v. Kingdom of Morocco* ICSID Case No ARB/00/4, Decision on Jurisdiction, 16 July 2001. See Radović (n 1) 135.

79 ICSID Arbitration Rules (2006) Rule 40(2) and Rule 40(3); ICSID Arbitration Rules (2022) Rule 48(2).

80 *Spyridon Roussalis v. Romania* ICSID Case No ARB/06/1, Award, 7 December 2011.

81 Article 9 of the Romania-Greece BIT (adopted 23 May 1997, entered into force 11 June 1998) states '[d]isputes between an investor of a Contracting Party and the other Contracting Party concerning an obligation of the latter under this Agreement, in relation to an investment of the former'.

of treaty interpretation set out in Article 31 VCLT, the majority of the arbitral tribunal held the dispute resolution clause 'undoubtedly limited jurisdiction' to claims initiated by foreign investors based on host State obligations[82] and rejected the counterclaim on this basis.[83] However, in his declaration,[84] Reisman presented an opposing view. Reisman's understanding of consent under ICSID was that 'when the State Parties to a BIT contingently consent, *inter alia*, to ICSID jurisdiction, the consent component of Article 46 of the Washington Convention is *ipso facto* imported into any ICSID arbitration which an investor then elects to pursue'.[85] Reisman contended that if the majority view was taken, there would be the need for the host State to pursue its claims in a domestic forum, which the investor had elected to avoid by selecting ICSID arbitration and pursuing a counterclaim.[86] Thus, the majority's decision would give rise to duplication, inefficiency and additional costs,[87] which would be 'an ironic, if not absurd, outcome, at odds ... with the objectives of international investment law'.[88] Reisman's reasoning was subsequently employed in *Goetz* v *Burundi*.[89] The terms of the applicable dispute resolution clause, set out in Article 8 of the Belgium-Luxembourg-Burundi BIT,[90] did not evidence party consent to counterclaims, but unlike Article 9 of the Romania-Greece BIT, this provision did not exclude their operation. Rather than interpreting Article 8 of the Belgium-Luxembourg-Burundi BIT to identify the scope of party consent, the arbitral tribunal focused on the foreign investor's initiation of ICSID arbitration.[91] Citing Reisman's reasoning, the arbitral tribunal held that the foreign investor's acceptance of the host state's standing offer of ICSID arbitration was sufficient to permit counterclaims in the absence of any express exclusion.[92]

82 *Spyridon Roussalis v. Romania* (n 80) [869].
83 ibid [871]–[872].
84 *Spyridon Roussalis v. Romania* ICSID Case No ARB/06/1, Declaration of W Michael Reisman, 28 November 2011.
85 ibid.
86 ibid.
87 ibid.
88 ibid.
89 *Antoine Goetz and others v. Republic of Burundi* [*II*] ICSID Case No ARB/01/2, Award, 21 June 2012.
90 Article 8 of the Belgium-Luxembourg-Burundi BIT (adopted 13 April 1989, entered into force 12 September 1993) conferred the tribunal with jurisdiction over 'any legal dispute between a Contracting Party and an investor of the other Contracting Party concerning an investment of the latter'.
91 *Antoine Goetz and others v. Republic of Burundi* [*II*] (n 89) [278].
92 ibid [281]. The need for judicial economy was also taken into account in the dissent in *Marco Gavazzi and Stefano Gavazzi v. Romania* ICSID Case No ARB/12/25, Dissenting Opinion by Arbitrator Mauro Rubino-Sammartano I, 21 April 2015 [42].

Thus, party consent has been understood to extend to counterclaims when a foreign investor initiates ICSID arbitration when their use is not otherwise denied or not expressly contemplated by the disputing parties.

Reisman's position illustrates how investment arbitrators may seek to give effect to counterclaims in investment arbitration. Reisman identified an opportunity to generate jurisdiction over counterclaims by implicitly finding party consent to counterclaims based on the policies that underpin Article 46 ICSID Convention. He justified his interpretation based on the need to minimise the duplication of claims across dispute resolution fora because host States have no option but to commence independent legal proceedings when party consent in restrictive terms excludes counterclaims. Nonetheless, by prioritising the availability of counterclaims within the ICSID arbitration rules, Reisman's position challenges party consent's central role in establishing investment arbitration.[93] Hence, Reisman's use of this opportunity to give effect to counterclaims has been widely criticised and remains controversial.[94] Whilst Reisman's approach was adopted in *Goetz* v *Burundi*, relying on his reasoning remains a high-risk strategy for host States seeking to establish jurisdiction over counterclaims. Not all arbitral tribunals will be amenable to Reisman's perspective. In fact, despite the application of the ICSID Arbitration Rules (2006), one arbitral tribunal pre-emptively excluded the operation of counterclaims based on the lack of references to counterclaims in an IIA.[95] Further, an arbitral tribunal could be understood to be exceeding its powers if it overlooks

93 Andrea Steingruber, 'Counterclaims: a Critical Analysis of Article 6 of the 2019 The Hague Resolution of the Institut de Droit International on the "Equality of Parties before International Investment Tribunals"' (2020) 35 ICSID Review – Foreign Investment Law Journal 595, 607; Dudas (n 13) 392; Ishikawa (n 21) 93.

94 See for example, Atanasova, Benoit and Ostřanský (n 3) 358.

95 In *Marco Gavazzi and Stefano Gavazzi v. Romania* ICSID Case No ARB/12/25, Decision on Jurisdiction Admissibility and Liability, 21 April 2015, the majority of the arbitral tribunal did not find consent to counterclaims on the basis that there was no express reference to counterclaims in the Italy-Romania BIT (adopted 29 May 1991, entered into force 1 April 1993), contrary to the presumption in Article 46 ICSID Convention that counterclaims can be filed. The arbitral tribunal relied on Article 8(2) Italy-Romania BIT, which refers to the foreign investors' right to claim against the host State, to override a broad definition of disputes in Article 8(1) Italy-Romania BIT. The majority's approach was rejected in the dissent (*Marco Gavazzi and Stefano Gavazzi v. Romania*, Dissenting Opinion by Arbitrator Mauro Rubino-Sammartano I, (n 92) [42]). See Tomoko Ishikawa, '*Marco Gavazzi and Stefano Gavazzi v Romania*: A New Approach to Determining Jurisdiction over Counterclaims in ICSID Arbitration?' (2017) 32 ICSID Review – Foreign Investment Law Journal 721.

the terms in which party consent is granted.[96] If this view is taken, the award could be annulled on this basis.[97] Reisman's stance illustrates that some investment arbitrators seek to give effect to counterclaims where possible, even if this particular approach remains problematic. Nonetheless, party consent to counterclaims that is inferred from the choice of the ICSID Arbitration Rules remains at the periphery of arbitral practice. Consequently, it is necessary to examine party consent to arbitration that is based on agreement.

Party consent to ICSID arbitration must be evidenced in writing.[98] Therefore, whether party consent to counterclaims exists will depend on the exact wording of the party consent. Nonetheless, in general terms, the wider the terms of party consent, the more likely it is that an ICSID arbitral tribunal will extend its jurisdiction to encompass counterclaims. Party consent that includes 'all disputes' or 'any legal dispute' concerning an investment has been interpreted to permit either the foreign investor or the host State to bring a claim, thereby encompassing counterclaims.[99] Thus, when party consent does not draw a distinction with regards to which party may bring a claim, foreign investors cannot prevent counterclaims from being made by merely initiating investment arbitration.[100] This style of interpretation is evident in *Inmaris* v *Ukraine*.[101] The arbitral tribunal accepted that Article 11 of the Germany-Ukraine BIT, which conferred the tribunal with jurisdiction 'with regard to investments between either Contracting Party and a national or company of the other Contracting Party', was drafted in broad enough terms to capture counterclaims.[102] This type of clause has been interpreted to include counterclaims based on treaty provisions, contractual obligations and domestic law. In *Tethyan Copper Company* v *Pakistan*,[103] the arbitral tribunal considered that the language 'dispute …

96 An arbitral tribunal's powers are sourced from party consent. Therefore, if an arbitral tribunal acts without party consent, it arguably is exceeding its powers.

97 ICSID Convention Article 52(1)(b). Anne K Hoffman, 'Chapter 36: Counterclaims' in Meg Kinnear and others (eds), *Building International Investment Law: The First 50 Years of ICSID* (Kluwer Law International 2015) 508–509; Dudas (n 13) 393–394.

98 ICSID Convention Article 25. The use of a standing offer is sufficient to meet the writing requirement.

99 Douglas, *The International Law of Investment Claims* (n 6) 257; Dudas (n 13) 396. See for example, *Metal-Tech Ltd. v. Republic of Uzbekistan* ICSID Case No ARB/10/3, Award, 4 October 2013 [410].

100 *Urbaser S.A. and Consorcio de Aguas Bilbao Biskaia, Bilbao Biskaia Ur Partzuergoa v. Argentine Republic* (n 23) [1143]–[1144].

101 *Inmaris Perestroika Sailing Maritime Services GmbH and others v. Ukraine* ICSID Case No ARB/08/8, Excerpts of Award, 1 March 2012.

102 ibid [432].

103 *Tethyan Copper Company Pty Limited v. Islamic Republic of Pakistan* ICSID Case No ARB/12/1, Decision on Jurisdiction and Liability, 10 November 2017.

relating to an investment' covered disputes over the IIA, the investment contract and the regulatory framework governing the investment. This position was justified on the basis that the terms of the party consent did not evidence an intention to limit consent to originating claims and that the drafters of the ICSID Convention sought to permit claims by both disputing parties.[104] The arbitral tribunal's interpretation of party consent in *Tethyan Copper Company* v *Pakistan* is particularly inclusive given that arbitral tribunals rarely accept domestic law as the foundation of a counterclaim irrespective of whether domestic law is linked to international law (see Chapter 3).[105] Nevertheless, party consent that is drafted in wide terms has been interpreted by arbitral tribunals in a way that usually permits counterclaims.

Conversely, narrow dispute resolution clauses that limit party consent to obligations in an IIA, or specific categories of claims, will preclude certain counterclaims. Party consent that is limited to claims under IIAs are highly likely to prevent all counterclaims because IIAs rarely confer host States with rights.[106] Examples of this type of provision are found in Article 26 of the Energy Charter Treaty, Articles 1116 and 1117 of North American Free Trade Agreement (NAFTA) and in some BITs.[107] When dispute resolution clauses limit the application of investment arbitration to specific types of claims, counterclaims that do not fall within the scope of party consent will be excluded. For example, provisions that limit claims to matters of the quantum of compensation following an

104 ibid, [1419]–[1420] and [1425].

105 Other arbitral tribunals have required subsequent party consent before permitting counterclaims based on domestic law (*Burlington Resources Inc. v. Republic of Ecuador* (n 20)). See Steingruber, 'Counterclaims: a Critical Analysis of Article 6 of the 2019 The Hague Resolution of the Institut de Droit International on the "Equality of Parties before International Investment Tribunals"' (n 93) 643–644.

106 Douglas, *The International Law of Investment Claims* (n 6) 235. Attempts to overcome this limitation based on the inclusion of an umbrella clause in the IIA, which enables a tribunal to consider contractual breaches on the international plane, cannot be used to bring obligations that bind the foreign investor within the jurisdiction of the tribunal. However, it will depend on the wording of the umbrella clause. See *Spyridon Roussalis v. Romania* (n 80) [871]–[876].

107 For example, Energy Charter Treaty (adopted 17 December 1994, entered into force 16 April 1998) 2080 UNTS 95, Article 26(6) states '[a] tribunal established under paragraph (4) shall decide the issues in dispute in accordance with this Treaty and applicable rules and principles of international law'. See Douglas, *The International Law of Investment Claims* (n 6) 257; Lalive and Halonen (n 22) 147. In *Vestey* v *Venezuela*, consent to arbitration in Article 8 of the United Kingdom-Venezuela, Bolivarian Republic BIT (adopted 15 March 1995, entered into force 1 August 1996) was limited to disputes concerning host State obligations in the BIT, thereby excluding counterclaims (*Vestey Group Ltd v. Bolivarian Republic of Venezuela* ICSID Case No ARB/06/4, Award, 15 April 2016 [333]).

expropriation will not encompass counterclaims.[108] However, not all dispute resolution clauses that limit claims are this narrow. Should a contract contain an alternative dispute resolution clause, counterclaims based on the contract are unlikely to fall within the arbitral tribunal's jurisdiction. For example, the arbitral tribunal in *Elsamex* v *Honduras*[109] rejected those aspects of Honduras' counterclaim that relied on Honduran civil legislation as these claims were the subject of alternative dispute resolution provisions in the contract.[110] However, counterclaims relating to the contract that were within the terms of party consent were permitted.[111] Hence, any limitations placed in the terms of consent, such as limiting consent to obligations sourced from IIAs, or to specific categories of claims, have the potential to exclude counterclaims from the jurisdiction of the arbitral tribunal.

Whilst party consent is generally framed in either broad or narrow terms, some arbitral tribunals have had to reconcile party consent that is internally inconsistent. The decisions made by the arbitral tribunals in these instances are based on the specific terms of the party consent and the surrounding factual circumstances. In *Hamester v Ghana*,[112] Article 12(1) of the Federal Republic of Germany-Ghana BIT enabled the arbitral tribunal to consider disputes concerning host State obligations in the BIT. The tribunal noted the 'restricted scope' of the consent given, but also took into account that Articles 12(3) and (4) of the BIT recognised 'that the State party may be "aggrieved" and "shall have the right to refer the dispute to" arbitration'.[113] Although this language hints at consent to counterclaims, the arbitral tribunal did not need to consider the precise scope of consent because the counterclaim had not been fully developed.[114] In *Gavazzi* v *Romania*,[115] Article 8(1) of the Italy-Romania BIT permitted 'any dispute' to be heard by investment arbitration but Article 8(2) only granted the foreign investor the right to claim against the host State. Article 8(3) allowed a host State to elaborate a defence against a claim. The

108 For example, the China-Hungary BIT (adopted 29 May 1991, entered into force 1 April 1993) sets out consent in Article 10(1) in the following terms: 'Any dispute between either Contracting State and the investor of the other Contracting State concerning the amount of compensation for expropriation may be submitted to an arbitral tribunal'.

109 *Elsamex, S.A. v. Republic of Honduras* ICSID Case No ARB/09/4, Award, 16 November 2012.

110 ibid [303].

111 ibid [304].

112 *Gustav F W Hamester GmbH & Co KG v. Republic of Ghana* ICSID Case No ARB/07/24, Award, 18 June 2010.

113 ibid [354].

114 Lalive and Halonen (n 22) 149.

115 *Marco Gavazzi and Stefano Gavazzi v. Romania* (n 95).

tribunal distinguished between the legal effects of a defence and a counterclaim,[116] and held that there was no jurisdiction over counterclaims.[117] The arbitral tribunal's decision was informed by the existence of the same claim being commenced by the host State in domestic proceedings[118] and that the claim was based on Romanian law, which did not form part of the arbitral tribunal's applicable law.[119] In both of these disputes, the arbitral tribunals were required to discern whether counterclaims were permissible, however they were unable to give effect to counterclaims due to the surrounding circumstances.

The foreign investor and the host State may reach an agreement that counterclaims shall be heard after an investment dispute has already arisen. Subsequent consent to counterclaims is an independent form of consent that is separate to that found in a host State's standing offer.[120] In *Burlington* v *Ecuador*,[121] the parties agreed part way through the proceedings that investment arbitration was the most appropriate forum for the counterclaim to 'ensure maximum judicial economy and consistency'.[122] The agreement clearly amounted to party consent.[123] An arbitral tribunal's ruling regarding a counterclaim also amounts to agreement. In *Perenco* v *Ecuador*,[124] the tribunal's prior ruling on the counterclaim implied that it had jurisdiction over the counterclaim and found the counterclaim to be admissible.[125] As there was a prior decision on this point, it was *res judicata*, and could not be revisited.[126] Consequently, the foreign investor was deemed to have agreed to the counterclaim at the time the arbitral tribunal made its decision.[127] Hence, party consent can be express or implied when a dispute already exists.

---

116 ibid [152].

117 ibid [154].

118 ibid.

119 ibid [156]. See Chapter 4 on applicable law.

120 Steingruber, 'Counterclaims: a Critical Analysis of Article 6 of the 2019 The Hague Resolution of the Institut de Droit International on the "Equality of Parties before International Investment Tribunals"' (n 93) 601. As to the potential implications of this, see Andrea K Bjorklund, 'The Role of Counterclaims in Rebalancing Investment Law' (2013) 17 Lewis and Clark Law Review 461, 474–475.

121 *Burlington Resources Inc. v. Republic of Ecuador* (n 20).

122 ibid [60].

123 ibid [62].

124 *Perenco Ecuador Limited v. Republic of Ecuador and Empresa Estatal Petróleos del Ecuador* ICSID Case No ARB/08/6, Decision on Claimant Application for Dismissal of Respondent Counterclaims, 18 August 2017.

125 ibid [43], [44] and [51].

126 ibid [41].

127 *Perenco Ecuador Limited v. Republic of Ecuador* ICSID Case No ARB/08/6, Interim Decision on the Environmental Counterclaim, 11 August 2015 [81].

The terms of party consent will vary between legal instruments. Nonetheless, ICSID arbitral practice highlights certain trends with regards to how party consent is interpreted. Party consent framed in broad terms gives rise to a higher chance of an arbitral tribunal finding consent to counterclaims. Conversely, party consent will not permit counterclaims when consent is limited to claims made by the foreign investor, or when counterclaims fall within a category of claims outside the scope of consent. In those instances where party consent is ambiguous, arbitral tribunals will seek to give effect to counterclaims where this is feasible. In the examples above where party consent was granted in inconsistent terms, the surrounding circumstances precluded consent to counterclaims. However, consent to counterclaims has been inferred by virtue of the existence of Article 46 ICSID Convention – although there is limited arbitral practice that has employed this approach. It may also be possible for the disputing parties to agree to counterclaims after an investment dispute has arisen, either explicitly or implicitly.

In conclusion, the terms in which party consent is granted is determinative of the extent of an ICSID arbitral tribunal's jurisdiction. Provided that the requirements of Article 25 ICSID Convention are met, arbitral practice highlights that when consent to arbitration is framed in broad terms the arbitral tribunal is likely to find jurisdiction over counterclaims. Other instances where jurisdiction over counterclaims has been established, for example, based on implicit party consent to counterclaims, remain at the periphery of arbitral practice. Therefore, ICSID arbitral practice evidences that for an arbitral tribunal to possess jurisdiction over counterclaims, consent to arbitration should be framed in wide terms.

2.3.2 *ICSID Additional Facility Arbitration Rules*

ICSID's AF permits the use of arbitration when either the host State or the foreign investor's home State are party to the ICSID Convention.[128] Given that one State is not party to the ICSID Convention it does not apply,[129] and as a result, the AF cannot require that the dispute falls within ICSID's jurisdiction. Therefore, to establish a counterclaim, Article 47(1) ICSID AF Arbitration Rules (2006) and Rule 58(1) ICSID AF Arbitration Rules (2022) provide that two conditions must be met: (1) the parties must not oppose the operation of counterclaims; and (2) the counterclaim must be within the scope of the arbitration agreement. Consequently, the arbitral tribunal must interpret the terms

128 ICSID AF Rules (2006) Article 2(a); ICSID AF Rules (2022) Article 2(1).

129 ICSID AF Rules (2006) Article 3; ICSID AF Rules (2022) Article 3.

of party consent to determine whether a counterclaim is within the arbitral tribunal's jurisdiction.

Arbitral practice relating to counterclaims in ICSID AF arbitration is limited. Nonetheless, arbitral practice establishes that counterclaims will not be within an arbitral tribunal's jurisdiction when the parties limit their consent to claims relating to host State breaches of an IIA.[130] Given the limited arbitral practice, it remains unclear how broadly party consent must be framed to encompass counterclaims. It is likely that party consent that does not exclude any form of dispute will meet this threshold, but in the absence of definitive arbitral practice, is it not clear whether any other formulation of party consent will give rise to jurisdiction over counterclaims in ICSID AF arbitration.

2.3.3 *UNCITRAL Arbitration Rules*

The UNCITRAL Arbitration Rules permit jurisdiction over counterclaims. However, there are two different versions of the rules and the provisions in each version are worded differently. Which provision applies will depend on which set of rules are selected by the disputing parties.[131] In its earlier formulation, Article 19(3) UNCITRAL Arbitration Rules (1976) limited the operation of counterclaims to claims 'arising out of the same contract', reflecting that these rules were drafted for use in international commercial arbitration. This proved problematic in the context of treaty-based investment arbitration where a contract did not regularly form the foundation of the dispute.[132] Even if an IIA was viewed as a contract, an IIA does not traditionally contain obligations for foreign investors, which precludes counterclaim procedures.[133] Article 21(3) UNCITRAL Arbitration Rules (2010) permits the respondent to commence a counterclaim 'provided that the arbitral tribunal has jurisdiction over it'. Consequently, in accordance with this provision, the terms of party consent will determine whether counterclaims are permitted.

---

130 *Anglo American PLC v. Bolivarian Republic of Venezuela* ICSID Case No ARB(AF)/14/1, Award, 18 January 2019 [528]; *Rusoro Mining Ltd. v. Bolivarian Republic of Venezuela* ICSID Case No ARB(AF)/12/5, Award, 22 August 2016 [627]–[628].

131 However, the UNCITRAL Arbitration Rules (2010) cannot be applied retrospectively (see Jan Paulsson and Georgios Petrochilos, *UNCITRAL Arbitration* (Kluwer Law International 2018) 1).

132 See Atanasova, Benoit and Ostřanský (n 3) 364; Michael Waibel and Jake Rylatt, *Counterclaims in International Law* (Legal Studies Research Paper Series, University of Cambridge, Faculty of Law, Paper No 66/2014, 2014) 13.

133 Waibel and Rylatt (n 132) 13.

Party consent that is constructed in wide terms is more likely to permit counterclaims.[134] The arbitral tribunal in *Saluka v Czech Republic*[135] took an expansive view of party consent even though it was bound by the UNCITRAL Arbitration Rules (1976). In this dispute, the arbitral tribunal considered party consent based on Article 8 of the Netherlands-Czech Republic BIT which conferred jurisdiction over 'any legal dispute' between the host State and a foreign investor regarding its investment. Despite the limitations of Article 19(3) UNCITRAL Arbitration Rules (1976), the arbitral tribunal proceeded to establish how counterclaims were customarily achieved by reference to both the UNCITRAL and ICSID Arbitration Rules (in addition to other international dispute resolution fora such as the US-Iran Claims Tribunal).[136] In taking this approach, the arbitral tribunal arguably exceeded its powers. Nonetheless, in deciding that the arbitral tribunal's jurisdiction extended to host State counterclaims, it reasoned that 'the language of Article 8, in referring to "All disputes," is wide enough to include disputes giving rise to counterclaims'.[137] The arbitral tribunal in *Paushok* v *Mongolia*[138] endorsed the approach taken in *Saluka* when interpreting a similar dispute resolution clause.[139] The phrase 'all disputes' has the potential to encompass both treaty and contract claims. Consequently, when party consent is framed in broad terms, it will capture a variety of counterclaims.

Conversely, dispute resolution clauses in narrow terms will exclude some counterclaims.[140] When party consent excludes specific types of claims, a counterclaim founded on that type of claim will not be permitted. In the *Chevron and Texaco* v *Ecuador* award,[141] an environmental cross-claim could not be brought by the host State[142] based on the terms of a settlement agreement

134 Douglas, *The International Law of Investment Claims* (n 6) 257, 258; Lalive and Halonen (n 22) 146.

135 *Saluka Investment B.V. v. Czech Republic* UNCITRAL, Decision on Jurisdiction over the Czech Republic's Counterclaim, 7 May 2004.

136 ibid [61]. This is despite the more limited jurisdiction of the US-Iran Claims Tribunal, which limits counterclaims to those that arise from the 'same contract, transaction or occurrence'.

137 ibid [39].

138 *Sergei Paushok, CJSC Golden East Company and CJSC Vostokneftegaz Company v. Government of Mongolia* UNCITRAL, Award on Jurisdiction and Liability, 28 April 2011.

139 ibid [689].

140 See, for example, *Karkey Karadeniz Elektrik Uretim A.S. v. Islamic Republic of Pakistan* ICSID Case No ARB/13/1, Award, 22 August 2017, [1007]; *Iberdrola Energia S.A. v. Republic of Guatemala II* PCA Case No 2017–41, Final Award, 24 August 2020 [386]–[391].

141 *Chevron Corporation (U.S.A.) and Texaco Petroleum Corporation (U.S.A.) v. Republic of Ecuador II* PCA Case No 2009–23, Second Partial Award on Track II, 30 August 2018.

142 ibid [7.42].

which released the foreign investor from liability for environmental damage resulting from oil concessions.[143] Consequently, the tribunal found that it had no jurisdiction over the counterclaim.[144] When party consent excludes the host State from bringing a claim, counterclaims will also be excluded. In *Oxus* v *Uzbekistan*,[145] party consent was limited to claims brought by foreign investors against the host State.[146] Hence, the arbitral tribunal found that counterclaims were not permitted.[147] Significantly, the arbitral tribunal distinguished the terms of this provision from the type used in *Saluka* and *Paushok*,[148] and consequently failed to find a basis on which the contractual breach that formed the basis of the counterclaim could be addressed by the arbitral tribunal.[149] In reaching this conclusion, the arbitral tribunal rejected the application of an umbrella clause to the counterclaim because the umbrella clause expressly applied only to host State obligations and it considered that the contractual dispute resolution clause removed the arbitral tribunal's jurisdiction over this aspect of the dispute.[150] The arbitral tribunal confirmed that the effect of Article 21(3) UNCITRAL Arbitration Rules (2010) is that 'counter-claims are admissible and can be submitted to the extent that they *already* fall under the scope of jurisdiction of the Arbitral Tribunal'.[151] Hence, Article 21(3) UNCITRAL Arbitration Rules (2010) requires an arbitral tribunal to focus exclusively on the terms of party consent when determining the arbitral tribunal's jurisdiction over counterclaims. Therefore, any limitations to party consent that impact the ability of the host State to bring a counterclaim will preclude the arbitral tribunal from establishing jurisdiction over counterclaims.

In instances where the dispute resolution clause is not explicit, or ambiguous, the tribunal may need to infer the limits of its jurisdiction from the surrounding circumstances. The arbitral tribunal in *Al-Warraq* v *Indonesia*[152] had to interpret an ambiguous IIA to determine if it had jurisdiction over counterclaims. The arbitral tribunal primarily interpreted Article 17 Organization

143 ibid.
144 ibid [7.44].
145 *Oxus Gold plc v. Republic of Uzbekistan* UNCITRAL, Final Award, 17 December 2015.
146 ibid [948].
147 ibid [959].
148 ibid [950].
149 ibid [958].
150 ibid.
151 ibid [944].
152 *Hesham Talaat M. Al-Warraq v. Republic of Indonesia* (n 60).

of the Islamic Conference (OIC) Investment Agreement[153] to determine if its jurisdiction extended to counterclaims. The tribunal took into account that Article 17 OIC Investment Agreement permits counterclaims as it uses the term 'disputes' ambiguously, makes reference to 'each party' resorting to arbitration (Article 17(2)(a)), and obliges States to implement decisions against foreign investors (Article 17(2)(d)), which presupposes that a State party has a right to bring a counterclaim.[154] It also considered Article 9 OIC Investment Agreement, which imposes an obligation on the foreign investor to comply with host State law, thereby raising this obligation to an international level and generating the potential for a counterclaim.[155] Finally, reference to the choice of the UNCITRAL Arbitration Rules and a letter of agreement that referred to counterclaims provided additional support for this conclusion.[156] Based on this analysis, the arbitral tribunal found it had jurisdiction over the counterclaims.[157] Party consent that is ambiguous makes it difficult for an arbitral tribunal to discern the limits of its jurisdiction. In *Aven* v *Costa Rica*,[158] the tribunal was required to interpret Article 10 DR-CAFTA[159] to determine if a counterclaim based on environmental damage caused by the foreign investor was within its jurisdiction. Although Article 10.16 states that any claim must be based on the host State having breached an obligation under Section A DR-CAFTA, Article 10.11 in Section A permits host States to adopt, maintain or enforce measures to ensure that investment projects are undertaken in an environmentally sensitive manner. The tribunal recognised that these environmental measures were capable of binding a foreign investor and a violation of which would amount to a breach of domestic and international law.[160] On this basis, the tribunal held that a foreign investor is also capable of breaching an obligation sourced in section

153 Agreement on Promotion, Protection and Guarantee of Investments amongst the Member States of the Organization of the Islamic Conference (adopted 5 June 1981, entered into force February 1998).

154 *Hesham Talaat M. Al-Warraq v. Republic of Indonesia* (n 60) [661].

155 ibid [663].

156 ibid [664].

157 ibid [666]. On the interpretation of the OIC Investment Agreement, see Hossein Abedian and Reza Eftekhar, 'Consent to Investor-State Arbitration in the Second Largest International Investment Protection Agreement: The Correct Interpretive Approach to Article 17 of the OIC Investment Agreement' (2018) 35 Journal of International Arbitration 59.

158 *David R. Aven and others v. Republic of Costa Rica* ICSID Case No UNCT/15/3, Final Award, 18 September 2018.

159 Free Trade Agreement between Central America, the Dominican Republic and the United States of America (DR-CAFTA) (adopted 5 August 2004, entered into force 1 January 2009).

160 *David R. Aven and others v. Republic of Costa Rica* (n 158) [734].

A DR-CAFTA,[161] especially given that the subject matter of the counterclaim related to environmental law.[162] Further, Article 10.15 DR-CAFTA refers in general to "an investment dispute", and when taken together with Article 10.16 DR-CAFTA, there is no implication that consent is limited to disputes in which a foreign investor initiates a claim because the respondent could be the foreign investor.[163] On this basis, the tribunal possessed prima facie jurisdiction over the counterclaim.[164]

In these awards, the arbitral tribunals are given the opportunity to give effect to counterclaims and rely on similar factors to infer jurisdiction. First, both tribunals find that the applicable IIA creates an obligation for the foreign investor that exists in international law. This creates a direct link between the counterclaim and the instrument that generates consent to arbitration. Second, when consent to counterclaims is not explicit, but equally not limited or excluded, consent is inferred. Consequently, in these circumstances, arbitral tribunals are willing to imply that party consent includes counterclaims.

The *Aven* v *Costa Rica* award additionally supports its conclusion with reference to judicial economy by citing Reisman's dissenting opinion in *Roussalis* v *Romania*.[165] Nonetheless, the use of judicial economy in this award differs to its use in Reisman's dissent in *Roussalis* v *Romania* and the majority in *Goetz* v *Burundi* given that, in those awards, the terms of party consent were not individually scrutinised. In *Aven* v *Costa Rica*, judicial economy supplemented the analysis of party consent. Applying judicial economy as a supplementary justification makes the stance taken in *Aven* v *Costa Rica* less controversial, especially because the amendments to the UNCITRAL Arbitration Rules that gave rise to the more flexible terms found in Article 21(3) UNCITRAL Arbitration Rules (2010) were intended to recognise a wider range of potential counterclaims.[166]

Thus, when arbitral tribunals infer whether consent to counterclaims exists, they attempt to give effect to the policies that underpin counterclaim procedures. This arbitral practice indicates that host States may be able to remain silent on counterclaims in their party consent and still enable counterclaims to

161 ibid [735]. Articles 10.9.3, 10.11 and 17 of DR-CAFTA can make foreign investors liable for breaches of international law in this field [737].

162 ibid [738]–[739].

163 ibid [740].

164 ibid [742].

165 ibid [741].

166 David D Caron and Lee Caplan, *The UNCITRAL Arbitration Rules: A Commentary* (Oxford University Press 2013) 427.

fall within the arbitral tribunal's jurisdiction. Nonetheless, this approach does not guarantee that jurisdiction over counterclaims will be established in every instance. Therefore, party consent that is explicit is more likely to ensure that jurisdiction over counterclaims is established.

Under both versions of the UNCITRAL Arbitration Rules, party consent forms the foundation of the arbitral tribunal's jurisdiction. Party consent in broad terms is most likely to include counterclaims. However, where consent to counterclaims is not expressly dealt with, arbitral tribunals have attempted to support the operation of counterclaims by referring to factors such as the existence of binding obligations on foreign investors in the IIA, silence as to the use of counterclaims and judicial economy. Despite this approach, arbitral practice based on the UNCITRAL Arbitration Rules indicates that host States should explicitly include counterclaims in the terms of their consent to arbitration.

2.3.4 *Analysis of Arbitral Practice*

Arbitral practice addressing jurisdiction over counterclaims conducted under the ICSID Convention and ICSID Arbitration Rules, the ICSID AF Arbitration Rules and the UNCITRAL Arbitration Rules evidences three general trends.

First, arbitral tribunals are most likely to establish jurisdiction over counterclaims when party consent is framed in wide terms that allow either disputing party to bring a claim or permit all types of claims.[167] Consenting to investment arbitration in wide terms confers the arbitral tribunal with a broad jurisdictional scope. Party consent drafted in these terms is potentially problematic for host States because party consent establishes jurisdiction over both originating claims and counterclaims. Thus, if a host State consents to arbitration in wide terms, this potentially permits a foreign investor to commence a wide range of originating claims, conceivably increasing the host State's liability for breaches of IIL. Counterclaims are intended to provide balance to investment arbitration proceedings.[168] Arbitral practice that establishes jurisdiction over counterclaims whilst simultaneously enhancing the host State's risk of being exposed to originating claims undermines this purpose of counterclaims. However, when consent to arbitration is clearly established in these terms, an arbitral tribunal must interpret these terms rather than questioning the reasoning of the disputing parties. Consequently, when party consent is framed in

167 See Douglas, *The International Law of Investment Claims* (n 6) 257; Demirkol (n 61) 63.
168 Kryvoi, 'Counterclaims in Investor-State Arbitration' (n 11) 218.

wide terms, arbitral tribunals cannot give effect to the policies that underpin counterclaims.

A second theme is that party consent in more restrictive terms often results in counterclaims being excluded from the arbitral tribunal's jurisdiction. This is frequently because the counterclaim is based on an obligation that is not captured within the terms of party consent, or because consent is limited to claims initiated by the foreign investor. Consent in narrow terms may be used to try and minimise the scope of an arbitral tribunal's jurisdiction over originating claims. Alternatively, counterclaims may be excluded because consent to arbitration is given in advance of an investment dispute arising. Consequently, at the time of consenting, host States do not know what types of disputes may arise, the nature of the claims that may be raised against them, and whether a counterclaim will be required. Nevertheless, when party consent clearly denies the operation of counterclaims, arbitral tribunals have no discretion to permit counterclaims unless the disputing parties subsequently consent to them. Therefore, arbitral tribunals cannot give effect to counterclaims when party consent in a standing offer is framed in narrow terms that exclude the counterclaim.

The final trend is that, when the disputing parties do not rely on the more common wide and narrow categorisations of party consent, arbitral tribunals will attempt to give effect to counterclaim procedures where possible. Consent to counterclaims may be implied based on the disputing parties' choice of arbitration rules or because of ambiguity regarding the scope of party consent. When determining whether consent to counterclaims is present, arbitral tribunals frequently refer to policy considerations that underpin the function of counterclaims in investment arbitration to support their position. By focussing on the policies that underlie counterclaims, these arbitral tribunals can give greater effect to how counterclaims were intended to operate. However, these opportunities have been limited due to party consent frequently being framed in broad or narrow terms, meaning that the reasoning employed by these arbitral tribunals remains at the periphery of arbitral practice. Therefore, the policy considerations that seek to give effect to counterclaims cannot be effectively employed by arbitral tribunals.

In summary, arbitral tribunals are willing to give effect to counterclaims where possible, but party consent that is framed in broad or narrow terms dictates how arbitral tribunals are able to give effect to counterclaims. Therefore, the way in which party consent is usually granted does not enable host States to take full advantage of counterclaim procedures. Consequently, it is necessary to find a different way for host States to consent to counterclaims.

2.4 Recalibrating Consent to Counterclaims

Host States have the ability, in many instances, to control the terms in which they consent to investment arbitration.[169] Therefore, host States can reframe how they consent to counterclaims by amending the terms of their consent in IIAs and domestic legislation. In so doing, host States can direct how arbitral tribunals interpret party consent, which enables them to alter existing arbitral practice.[170] This section argues that host States can realign the terms of their consent to investment arbitration by drafting tailored consent clauses in legal instruments that generate party consent. By granting consent to investment arbitration in more nuanced terms, host States can be more specific regarding how they wish counterclaims to operate and can confer arbitral tribunals with the ability to give full effect to the policies that underlie counterclaim procedures in investment arbitration. If tailored consent clauses distinguish between jurisdiction over originating claims and counterclaims, they could also reduce a host State's potential liability.

At present, the dominant practice is to draft party consent in either broad or narrow terms. In contrast to this approach, recent State practice in IIAs formulates consent to investment arbitration in more nuanced terms. Not all of these provisions are in force or permit recourse to investment arbitration. However, the manner in which they are drafted is instructive. The consent clauses in these IIAs display two attributes that could be employed by host States to give greater effect to counterclaims. First, party consent to counterclaims is set out independently from consent to originating claims. For example, Article 28.9 of the Common Market for Eastern and Southern Africa (COMESA) Agreement states:

> A Member State against whom a claim is brought by a COMESA investor under this Article may assert as a defence, counterclaim, right of set off or other similar claim, that the COMESA investor bringing the claim has not fulfilled its obligations.[171]

169 See Section 2.2 above.

170 See Jeremy Sharpe, 'From Delegation to Prescription: Interpretative Authority in International Investment Agreements' in Charles Brower and others (eds), *By Peaceful Means: International Adjudication and Arbitration* (Oxford University Press 2024).

171 Investment Agreement for the COMESA Common Investment Area (adopted 23 May 2007, not yet in force). This provision is not binding because the COMESA Agreement is not yet in force. Nonetheless, this provision provides a model of how host States can directly establish party consent over counterclaims.

By formulating party consent that distinguishes between originating claims and counterclaims, host States can expressly consent to counterclaims in investment arbitration without simultaneously expanding an arbitral tribunal's jurisdiction over originating claims.

Second, party consent can be drafted to specifically capture what is encompassed by counterclaim procedures. For example, the ability of host States to tailor the scope of consent provisions based on the nature of the obligation is evident in Article 43 of the Pan-African Investment Code (PAIC).[172] Article 43(1) provides that when a Member State alleges that an investor or its investment has failed to comply with the 'Code, or other relevant rules and principles of domestic and international law', this is to be taken into account by the decision-making body[173] to determine what effect it has on the claim or any damages that may be awarded. Article 43(2) permits a Member State to counterclaim against an investor for an alleged breach of the PAIC. Hence, the PAIC specifies what sources of law that a decision-making body can take into account when addressing allegations of foreign investor misconduct, and explicitly sets out which can form the basis of a counterclaim. As will be demonstrated in Chapter 4, linking jurisdictional clauses with applicable law clauses may not be the best practice. Nonetheless, this type of clause evidences that party consent can be drafted in a way that captures specific elements of counterclaims, rather than using generic phrases that additionally capture a wide range of originating claims.

Tailored consent provisions overcome the difficulties associated with party consent being drafted in broad or narrow terms. Party consent in more nuanced terms clearly delimits the scope of an arbitral tribunal's jurisdiction and creates specificity regarding the availability of counterclaims. Consent in these terms can steer arbitral tribunals more effectively and give greater effect to counterclaims by permitting arbitral tribunals to apply the policies that underpin counterclaim procedures. By distinguishing between consent to originating claims and counterclaims, host States can avoid unnecessarily expanding an arbitral tribunal's jurisdiction over originating claims, thereby limiting their potential liability.

Whilst these types of provisions provide opportunities for host States to alter arbitral practice regarding counterclaims, the manner in which host States formulate these provisions will be central to how effectively they

---

172 African Union Commission, Draft Pan-African Investment Code, December 2016.

173 This provision is not aimed at investment arbitration because the PAIC does not permit investment arbitration as a means of resolving investment disputes. Nonetheless, the language used could be applied to consent to investment arbitration.

achieve this goal. Arbitral tribunals apply the rules of treaty interpretation to determine the limits of the host State's standing offer, which determines the scope of their jurisdiction. Arbitral tribunals frequently fail to apply the rules of treaty interpretation in the manner intended.[174] Consequently, host States should be prepared for variations in how the IIA will be interpreted and should try to make consent over counterclaims as clear as possible. In particular, host States will need to ensure that party consent is formulated as a unilateral offer to arbitrate. This will require language that reflects that the provision in the IIA amounts to host State consent and that investment arbitration is mandatory. If this form of language is not used, it may be necessary for the disputing parties to consent to investment arbitration at a future date rather than relying on a standing offer. Should an investment dispute arise in the absence of consent, host States are unlikely to be able to control the terms of party consent in the way they can when formulating a standing offer. Thus, it is important that party consent that seeks to precisely delimit an arbitral tribunal's jurisdiction is drafted as a unilateral offer. When formulated in this way, this style of provision has the potential to enable host States to minimise the risks that arise in current arbitral practice and change future arbitral practice.

Despite the benefits, only a small number of IIAs frame consent to counterclaims in nuanced terms.[175] This may, in part, be attributed to the limited need for new IIAs given that many host States are bound by pre-existing treaties that will continue to apply for many years. However, the limited use of these provisions could also be indicative that States are reluctant to agree to party consent

174 Christoph Schreuer, 'Diversity and Harmonisation of Treaty Interpretation in Investment Arbitration' in Malgosia Fitzmaurice, Olufemi Elias and Panos Merkouris (eds), *Treaty Interpretation and the Vienna Convention on the Law of Treaties: 30 Years On* (Brill 2010) 129; Michael Waibel, 'International Investment Law and Treaty Interpretation' in Rainer Hofmann and Christian Tams (eds), *International Investment Law and General International Law – From Clinical Isolation to Systemic Integration?* (Nomos 2011) 29.

175 These include the Southern African Development Community (SADC) Model Bilateral Investment Treaty Template, Article 19.2, Article 29; Economic Community of West African States (ECOWAS) Supplementary Act A/SA.3/12/08 Adopting Community Rules on Investment and the Modalities for their Implementation with ECOWAS, Article 18(5) (although investment arbitration is not an option); Belgium-Luxembourg Economic Union Model BIT 2019, Article 19 D(2); Slovakia Model BIT 2019, Article 17(2); Iran-Slovakia BIT (adopted 19 January 2016, entered into force 30 August 2017) Article 14(3); United Arab Emirates-Slovakia BIT (adopted 22 September 2016, entered into force 5 Febuary 2018) Article 17(3); Argentina- United Arab Emirates BIT (adopted 16 April 2018, not yet in force) Article 28(4). No express references to counterclaims were found in the United Nations Conference on Trade and Development database of domestic legislation giving consent to investment arbitration.

in these terms. The majority of treaty practice that has adopted these terms are in regional IIAs or between States with similar investment profiles (i.e. capital importing States). Thus, the power dynamics that underpin IIA negotiations may mean that consent in these terms is not possible in every instance. However, host States that possess negotiating expertise have the potential to counter power differentials by convincing States of the benefits of this style of provision. As very few States only export capital, many States should have an interest in drafting consent in similar terms to those found in these IIAs and could be convinced to adopt similar provisions when revisiting the terms of their IIAs.

In contrast, domestic legislation is not subject to these power limitations. Hence, host States can adopt this model of consent in foreign investment legislation subject to their national law-making processes. Similarly to IIAs, host States will need to ensure that the terms of the domestic legislation clearly amount to a unilateral offer. Whether this is achieved is a matter of interpretation of the wording used in the legislation.[176] At present, there is no clear interpretative method that is widely used by arbitral tribunals to interpret domestic legislation. Therefore, the language used must clearly amount to a unilateral offer to arbitrate.[177] Provisions in domestic legislation may not amount to a standing offer if they indicate that the host State maintains discretion regarding whether to proceed to arbitration.[178] Therefore, host States seeking to make a unilateral offer using domestic legislation should use precise language to ensure that consent to investment arbitration is explicit.

In summary, host States have the power to introduce consent clauses into IIAs and domestic legislation in more nuanced terms than the prevalent forms of consent clauses. Provided that host States frame party consent as a unilateral offer to arbitrate, they can control the terms of party consent and ensure that consent to counterclaims is granted independently from party consent to originating claims and that the legal foundations of the counterclaim are made clear. Consequently, host States do not need to increase their exposure to investment claims and can limit their potential liability. Should host States adopt nuanced provisions as a standard approach when they consent to investment arbitration, arbitral tribunals are more likely to establish

176 There is considerable diversity in how consent to investment arbitration has been drafted in domestic legislation. See Potestà (n 8) 154–160.

177 As to the difficulties associated with interpreting domestic law when establishing consent to arbitration, see, for example Solveiga Palevičienė, 'Consent to Arbitration and the Legacy of the *SPP v. Egypt* Case' (2014) 7 Baltic Journal of Law & Politics 149; Potestà (n 8).

178 Potestà (n 8) 157.

jurisdiction counterclaims in investment arbitration enabling counterclaims to play a larger role in investment arbitration.

2.5 Preliminary Conclusions

Counterclaims must fall within the jurisdiction of the arbitral tribunal if they are to provide a foundation to hold foreign investors accountable under international law. To comply with the jurisdictional requirements of an arbitral tribunal they must align with any requirements set out in the applicable arbitration rules and fall within the scope of party consent. IIAs and domestic legislation provide host States with the ability to dictate terms of party consent because unilateral offers to consent create a standing offer that foreign investors must accept in the same terms. Host States can, in many instances, consent to arbitration using language that evidences that counterclaims fall within the scope of party consent. When party consent is interpreted in conjunction with the ICSID Convention and the ICSID Arbitration Rules, the ICSID AF Arbitration Rules, or the UNCITRAL Arbitration Rules, the jurisdictional scope of the arbitral tribunal is determined. To ensure that this includes counterclaims, party consent drafted in broad terms has been most conducive to establish jurisdiction. However, party consent drafted in broad terms increases the overall jurisdiction of the arbitral tribunal, which potentially allows foreign investors to use investment arbitration to resolve a wide range of investment disputes. Party consent drafted in narrow terms will exclude some, if not all, counterclaims. Arbitral tribunals try to give effect to counterclaims where possible, but broad or narrow formulations of consent dictate the extent of an arbitral tribunal's powers. To address this problem, recent State practice in IIAs evidences a more sophisticated approach to party consent. Provisions in these IIAs specify what types of claims a host State can commence. Therefore, recent formulations of party consent clearly permit counterclaims without the need to resort to generically worded party consent that has the potential to increase the scope of originating claims or exclude counterclaims. Although this is yet to be transferred to domestic legislation, in principle, there is nothing to prevent a similar approach from being adopted. Consequently, host States can consent to counterclaims in investment arbitration in a manner that ensures that counterclaims are within the arbitral tribunal's jurisdiction, but minimises the risks associated with how party consent is currently generated.

CHAPTER 3

The Nexus between Claims and Counterclaims

3.1 Introduction

For an arbitral tribunal to hear a counterclaim there must be a sufficient connection between the originating claim and the counterclaim. If a connection between the claims is not apparent, an arbitral tribunal will not proceed any further with the counterclaim.[1]

A connection between originating claims and counterclaims is required in investment arbitration so that arbitral tribunals can better administer justice[2] by simultaneously addressing related claims in the same forum.[3] Consequently, a host State must demonstrate that a counterclaim is linked to the originating claim. However, the connection between an originating claim and a counterclaim that seeks to hold a foreign investor accountable for violations of international law may not be obvious. Claims in investment arbitration are predominantly based on investment protection standards contained in IIAs. Conversely, counterclaims based on international law can draw from a wide range of obligations that will not necessarily be sourced from the same legal instrument or even the same legal order as the originating claim.[4] Thus, originating claims and counterclaims based on international law may initially appear to be unrelated. This chapter examines how arbitral tribunals

1 The legal implications of failing to establish the connection between the claim and the counterclaim remain unclear. The need for a sufficient connection between the claim and the counterclaim has been described by investment tribunals variably as a matter of jurisdiction, admissibility or both (see for example, *Alex Genin, Eastern Credit Limited, INC. and A.S. Baltoil v. Republic of Estonia* ICSID Case No ARB/99/2, Award, 25 June 2001 [376]–[378]; *Metal-Tech Ltd. v. Republic of Uzbekistan* ICSID Case No ARB/10/3, Award, 4 October 2013 [407]). For the purposes of this book, whether a nexus exists between a claim and a counterclaim is considered to be a question of admissibility rather than a jurisdictional requirement. This approach is adopted because a counterclaim can fall within the jurisdiction of an investment tribunal (see Chapter 2) but still fail to possess a sufficient connection to the originating claim.

2 Hege Elisabeth Kjos, *Applicable Law in Investor-State Arbitration: The Interplay between National and International Law* (Oxford University Press 2013) 128, 147; Walid Ben Hamida, 'L'arbitrage Etat-investisseur cherche son quilibre perdu: Dans quelle mesure l'Etat peut introduire des demandes reconventionnelles contre l'investisseur priv?' (2005) 7 International Law Forum du droit international 261, 270–1.

3 Kjos (n 2) 128.

4 ibid 149.

 | DOI:10.1163/9789004420953_004

understand the relationship between claims and counterclaims to determine how counterclaims based on international law can be viewed as possessing the requisite nexus. It argues that arbitral tribunals tend to identify a nexus when claims are based on reciprocal legal obligations. However, host States can encourage arbitral tribunals to find a wider range of connections using (1) express provisions in IIAs and foreign investment legislation; and (2) by presenting legal argumentation that is based on the good administration of justice. If host States can demonstrate that a connection between a claim and a counterclaim does not always need a reciprocal legal foundation, arbitral tribunals are more likely to find the required nexus to establish a counterclaim based on international law.

The chapter advances this argument in three phases. It first illustrates how arbitral tribunals use a connection between originating claims and counterclaims to give effect to the good administration of justice (Section 3.2). The chapter then proceeds to examine how arbitral tribunals have understood what amounts to a connection between an originating claim and a counterclaim (Section 3.3). This section highlights that arbitral tribunals primarily recognise connections between the disputing parties' claims when they are based on reciprocal legal obligations because arbitral tribunals commonly define disputes in terms of competing legal claims. However, this type of legal connection does not necessarily capture the full extent to which originating claims and counterclaims interact in investment arbitration. Consequently, arbitral tribunals do not give full effect to the good administration of justice and restrict the operation of counterclaims based on international law. Finally, the chapter sets out how host States can encourage arbitral tribunals to permit counterclaims based on international law by (1) using express provisions in IIAs and foreign investment legislation to define disputes in broader terms; and (2) by presenting legal argumentation based on the good administration of justice (Section 3.4). The chapter culminates by setting out preliminary conclusions (Section 3.5).

3.2 The Good Administration of Justice and Counterclaims

Investment arbitration classically addresses whether a host State has breached investment protection standards.[5] Investment protection standards create

5 Arnaud de Nanteuil, 'Counterclaims in Investment Arbitration: Old Questions, New Answers' (2018) 17 Law and Practice of International Courts and Tribunals 374, 376.

asymmetrical obligations, so host States are required to respond to foreign investor claims.[6] When host States commence counterclaims, the roles of the disputing parties are reversed and foreign investors must respond to the counterclaim. As a result, the addition of a counterclaim changes the dynamics of investment arbitration by creating reciprocity between the disputing parties.

Whilst host States have the procedural right to commence counterclaims, the introduction of the host State's counterclaim has the potential to complicate the dispute, cause delays, increase costs and prejudice the foreign investor's interests.[7] Therefore, arbitral tribunals must consider the extent to which the counterclaim impacts the integrity of the legal proceedings and affects the interests of the disputing parties.[8] The good administration of justice requires that disputes are resolved in an efficient, effective and equitable manner to ensure a just result.[9] To achieve these aims, the substantive content of the good administration of justice encompasses considerations such as the time and cost implications of introducing new claims, the equality of the disputing parties and judicial economy.[10] The vague content of the good administration of justice[11] means that decision-makers apply it in a flexible[12] and context specific manner.[13] Decision-makers possess an inherent power to apply the good administration of justice,[14] but aspects of the good administration of justice may also be mirrored by procedural rules.[15] Hence, irrespective of whether the procedural rules refer to the good administration of justice, decision-makers

6 ibid.

7 Andrea K Bjorklund, 'The Role of Counterclaims in Rebalancing Investment Law' (2013) 17 Lewis and Clark Law Review 461, 477.

8 See Julien Cazala, 'Good Administration of Justice' in *Max Planck Encyclopedia of International Procedural Law* (2019) para 18, para 28; Hege Elisabeth Veenstra-Kjos, 'Counterclaims by Host States in Investment Treaty Arbitration' (2007) 4 Transnational Dispute Management 1, 29.

9 Chester Brown, 'Inherent Powers in International Adjudication' in Cesare PR Romano, Karen Alter and Yuval Shany (eds), *The Oxford Handbook of International Adjudication* (Oxford University Press 2013) 843; Cazala (n 8) para 2; Fulvio Maria Palombino, 'Judicial Economy and Limitation of the Scope of the Decision in International Adjudication' (2010) 23 Leiden Journal of International Law 909, 912.

10 For a discussion of these concepts, see Cazala (n 8).

11 ibid para 8.

12 ibid; Kjos (n 2) 148.

13 Veenstra-Kjos (n 8) 31, Cazala (n 8) para 9, para 33.

14 Brown (n 9) 843; Cazala (n 8) para 6; Palombino (n 9) 910; Zachary Douglas, 'The enforcement of environmental norms in investment treaty arbitration' in Pierre-Marie Dupuy and Jorge E Viñuales (eds), *Harnessing Foreign Investment to Promote Environmental Protection: Incentives and Safeguards* (Cambridge University Press 2013) 430.

15 See Veenstra-Kjos (n 8) 30; Brown (n 9) 843; Palombino (n 9) 910–912.

are tasked with evaluating whether the dispute resolution process can accommodate the introduction of a new claim.

Arbitral tribunals use the nexus between a claim and a counterclaim to give effect to the good administration of justice by evaluating the impact of a counterclaim on the investment arbitration proceedings. To illustrate, when a counterclaim is closely connected to the originating claim, the arbitral tribunal can address the evidence and legal arguments that arise in the counterclaim in conjunction with the originating claim.[16] Hence, the burden on the foreign investor is minimal.[17] Further, counterclaims that are related to the claim can prevent the proliferation of legal proceedings across different dispute resolution fora, which saves time and costs[18] and minimises the risk of inconsistent decisions.[19] Thus, the good administration of justice will favour hearing a closely connected counterclaim because it can be dealt with efficiently, it is not detrimental to the integrity of the proceedings and the benefits outweigh any burden on the foreign investor. Conversely, the introduction of an unrelated counterclaim can make proceedings less efficient. It might raise new jurisdictional questions,[20] introduce claims that the arbitral tribunal is not well-equipped to address[21] and add time and costs to the investment arbitration proceedings. These factors undermine the efficiency of the legal proceedings and prejudice the foreign investor's interests.[22] In this case, the good administration of justice is impaired.

In short, the good administration of justice is a vague concept that is applied flexibly to ensure that disputes are resolved in an efficient and equitable manner. Arbitral tribunals use the requirement of a nexus between a claim and a counterclaim in investment arbitration to identify whether hearing a counterclaim is judicious and give effect to the good administration of justice by excluding unrelated counterclaims.[23]

---

16 Alison Dundes Renteln, 'Encountering Counterclaims' (1987) 15 Denver Journal of International Law and Policy 379, 380; Bjorklund (n 7) 475.

17 Veenstra-Kjos (n 8) 5.

18 ibid; Renteln (n 16) 380.

19 Veenstra-Kjos (n 8) 5; Renteln (n 16) 380.

20 See José Antonio Rivas, 'ICSID Treaty Counterclaims: Case Law and Treaty Evolution' in Jean E Kalicki and Anna Joubin-Bret (eds), *Reshaping the Investor-State Dispute Settlement System: Journeys for the 21st Century* (Brill 2015) 781 regarding concerns that counterclaims should not extend an ICSID arbitral tribunal's jurisdiction.

21 This was a concern of the drafters of the ICSID Convention. See Yavaslau Kryvoi, 'Counterclaims in Investor-State Arbitration' (2012) 21 Minnesota Journal of International Law 216, 223.

22 Bjorklund (n 7) 477.

23 This has been described as a filtering process. See Veenstra-Kjos (n 8) 30.

3.3 The Nexus between Claims and Counterclaims in Investment Arbitration

When deciding whether a nexus exists, an arbitral tribunal must appraise the relationship between the claim and the counterclaim and decide if the claims form part of the same dispute. To determine if a sufficient connection between an originating claim and a counterclaim exists, an arbitral tribunal will (1) characterise the originating claim; (2) determine the scope of the dispute based on its characterisation;[24] (3) characterise the counterclaim; and (4) decide whether the counterclaim displays a nexus to the dispute. Consequently, whether a connection exists between the claims is contingent on how an arbitral tribunal defines a dispute.

Arbitral practice that discusses what constitutes a dispute frequently draws from the International Court of Justice's (ICJ) jurisprudence.[25] Therefore, arbitral tribunals often classify a dispute as a conflict that takes the form of competing causes of action,[26] opposing legal views[27] or disagreements over the rights and obligations of the parties.[28] A central component of these definitions is discord regarding the parties' legal positions. Nevertheless, some arbitral practice reflects a less stringent approach regarding what comprises a dispute. These arbitral tribunals have variously recognised that whether a

24 This assessment requires an arbitral tribunal to use the originating claim as a reference point. It is only by referring to the originating claim that the arbitral tribunal can evaluate considerations related to the good administration of justice such as the impact of jurisdictional limitations, the extent to which evidence is shared between the claims, the availability of alternative dispute resolution fora and the cost and time implications of hearing the counterclaim.

25 See for example, *Case concerning East Timor (Portugal v. Australia)* (Judgment) [1995] ICJ Rep 89, 99. See also *Mavrommatis Palestine Concessions* (Merits) PCIJ Rep Series A No 2, which defines a dispute as 'a disagreement on a point of law or fact, a conflict of legal views or of interests between two persons' (11).

26 *Amco Asia Corporation and others v. Republic of Indonesia* ICSID Case No ARB/81/1, Decision on Jurisdiction in Resubmitted Proceeding, 10 May 1988 [135].

27 *Emilio Agustín Maffezini v. Kingdom of Spain* ICSID Case No ARB/97/7, Decision on Jurisdiction, 25 January 2000 [98]; *Helnan International Hotels A/S v. Arab Republic of Egypt* ICSID Case No ARB 05/19, Decision on Jurisdiction, 17 October 2006 [52].

28 *Industria Nacional de Alimentos, S.A. and Indalsa Perú, S.A. (formerly Empresas Lucchetti, S.A. and Lucchetti Perú, S.A.) v. Republic of Peru* ICSID Case No ARB/03/4, Award, 7 February 2005 [48]; *SGS Société Générale de Surveillance S.A. v. Republic of the Philippines* ICSID Case No ARB/02/6, Order of the Tribunal on Further Proceedings, 17 December 2007 [19]; *Teinver S.A., Transportes de Cercanías S.A. and Autobuses Urbanos del Sur S.A. v. Argentine Republic* ICSID Case No ARB/09/1, Decision on Jurisdiction, 21 December 2012 [110].

dispute exists is context dependent[29] and that single disputes may be comprised of claims from different sources that arise at different times.[30] When a dispute is framed in these terms, arbitral tribunals can consider the surrounding circumstances in addition to the existence of opposing legal claims. How expansively or flexibly an arbitral tribunal defines a dispute may influence whether it finds a connection between a claim and a counterclaim. Given this, it becomes necessary to examine how arbitral tribunals have understood what amounts to a connection between an originating claim and a counterclaim with reference to these definitions.

Arbitral tribunals identify whether a connection exists on a case-by-case basis and each dispute will display different variables that may influence the arbitral tribunal's decision. Consequently, it is not possible to definitively determine what amounts to a sufficient connection between an originating claim and a counterclaim. However, by identifying trends in arbitral practice, it is feasible to isolate the factors that arbitral tribunals consider when deciding whether an appropriate nexus exists. This section argues that arbitral tribunals predominantly look for reciprocal legal obligations when identifying a nexus because they frequently define disputes in terms of conflicting legal obligations. This approach fails to capture the full extent to which originating claims and counterclaims interact in investment arbitration, does not give full effect to the good administration of justice and limits the operation of counterclaims based on international law. To support this argument, this section reviews arbitral practice based on the ICSID Convention and the ICSID Arbitration Rules, the ICSID AF Arbitration Rules and the UNCITRAL Arbitration Rules in turn, before considering the extent to which arbitral practice gives effect to the good administration of justice.

3.3.1 *ICSID Convention and ICSID Arbitration Rules*

The need for a connection between claims and counterclaims in ICSID arbitration is addressed by Article 46 ICSID Convention, which requires that a counterclaim must arise 'directly out of the subject-matter of the dispute'. The wording of this provision is replicated in Rule 40(1) ICSID Arbitration Rules (2006) and Rule 48(1) ICSID Arbitration Rules (2022). The language used in these provisions is similar to Article 25(1) ICSID Convention that delimits ICSID's jurisdictional scope to disputes that 'arise directly out of an investment'

---

29 *Industria Nacional de Alimentos, S.A. and Indalsa Perú, S.A. v. Republic of Peru* ICSID Case No ARB/03/4, Decision on Annulment, 5 September 2007 [91].

30 *CMS Gas Transmission Company v. Republic of Argentina* ICSID Case No ARB/01/8, Decision of the Tribunal on Objections to Jurisdiction, 17 July 2003 [109].

(see Section 2.3.1). Yet, despite the similarity in wording, these provisions serve different purposes because they regulate discrete connections. Article 25(1) ICSID Convention addresses what claims may be commenced before an ICSID investment tribunal[31] based on the existence of a connection between the claim and an investment. In contrast, Article 46 ICSID Convention applies when an investment dispute has already been initiated,[32] and dictates that arbitral tribunals look for a connection between the claim and the counterclaim using the object of the dispute[33] as the reference point. Thus, Article 25(1) ICSID Convention and Article 46 ICSID Convention perform distinct roles.

When ascertaining whether a connection exists based on Article 46 ICSID Convention, ICSID arbitral tribunals have most frequently sought to find legal connections between claims and counterclaims. An example of a legal connection can be illustrated by a contract claim. For example, if one contracting party commences a claim for non-payment, the other contracting party can respond by initiating a counterclaim for failure to perform. The claim and counterclaim are legally connected because both claims are based on legal obligations that are sourced from the same contract. Contractual claims are not the focus of this book, however, the first ICSID award that considered Article 46 ICSID Convention was a contractual dispute. In *Klöckner* v *Cameroon*,[34] the legal relationship between the disputing parties was established by a series of contracts, which the arbitral tribunal described as creating unified and 'interdependent' contractual relationships.[35] Even though the counterclaim was founded on a different contract to the claim, the interrelated nature of the obligations meant that the counterclaim was deemed to share the same legal foundation as the

---

31 Andrea Steingruber, 'Counterclaims: a Critical Analysis of Article 6 of the 2019 The Hague Resolution of the Institut de Droit International on the "Equality of Parties before International Investment Tribunals"' (2020) 35 ICSID Review – Foreign Investment Law Journal 595, 624.

32 ibid.

33 *Enron Creditors Recovery Corporation (formerly Enron Corporation) and Ponderosa Assets, L.P. v. Argentine Republic* ICSID Case No ARB/01/3, Decision on Jurisdiction, 14 January 2004 [283]. This distinction was made clear in *Antoine Goetz and others v. Republic of Burundi [II]* ICSID Case No ARB/01/2, Award, 21 June 2012 [283] ('Le Tribunal observe à cet égard qu'il convient de distinguer l'exigence ainsi posée par l'article 46 de la Convention en ce qui concerne la recevabilité des demandes reconventionnelles de celle posée par le paragraphe premier de l'article 25 de la même Convention en ce qui concerne la compétence du Centre. L'article 25 exige une relation directe avec un investissement, l'article 46 un rapport direct avec l'objet du différend').

34 *Klöckner Industrie-Anlagen GmbH v. United Republic of Cameroon* ICSID Case No ARB/81/2, Award, 21 October 1983 [137].

35 ibid.

claim and gave rise to a close connection. Therefore, a contract (or a series of interrelated contracts) establishes a close connection between claims and counterclaims because it creates a common legal foundation. Although formulated in a contractual context, the approach adopted by the arbitral tribunal in *Klöckner* v *Cameroon* has influenced subsequent arbitral practice. For example, in *Grenada Private Power Limited and WRB Enterprises, Inc.* v *Grenada,*[36] the arbitral tribunal merged the requirement for a connection with the need for the causes of action to constitute 'an indivisible whole'.[37] Consequently, the arbitral tribunal required the same legal source to form the foundation of a dispute in a way that makes it 'impractical to unbundle the claims'.[38] The arbitral tribunal undertook this analysis with reference to Article 25(1) ICSID Convention rather than Article 46 ICSID Convention.[39] Nonetheless, it can be seen that the reasoning in *Klöckner* has been influential in ICSID arbitral practice even if this approach was not employed in relation to the correct provision.

A shared legal connection can exclude other types of connections that may exist between a claim and a counterclaim. In *Elsamex* v *Honduras*,[40] Honduras raised a counterclaim based on the contractor performing the contract to a poor standard and failing to remedy defects in a timely manner.[41] The host State founded its counterclaim on breach of contract and by relying on analogies with its Civil Code and negligence.[42] The sole arbitrator found that the counterclaims based on breach of contract were admissible[43] but rejected the counterclaims that drew analogies with the Civil Code and negligence.[44] The non-contractual counterclaims were rejected because the contractual clauses directly applied and the arbitrator's jurisdiction only extended to disputes over the contract or any ancillary contracts.[45] Hence, the contract established both the jurisdictional and substantive limits of any counterclaim.

These awards highlight that legal connections can be established for the purposes of Article 46 ICSID Convention when the legal obligations that underpin the claim and the counterclaim are derived from the same source.

---

36 *Grenada Private Power Limited and WRB Enterprises, Inc. v. Grenada* ICSID Case No ARB/17/13, Award, 19 March 2020.

37 ibid [359].

38 ibid.

39 ibid [357]–[358].

40 *Elsamex, S.A. v. Republic of Honduras* ICSID Case No ARB/09/4, Award, 16 November 2012.

41 ibid [295].

42 ibid [296]–[298].

43 ibid [305].

44 ibid [303].

45 ibid [303]–[304].

In investment disputes, contracts are the main instruments that can establish a reciprocal legal relationship. IIAs generally create asymmetrical obligations between the foreign investor and the host State so they cannot provide the foundation for both claims and counterclaims. Thus, arbitral tribunals have primarily identified a close connection when a claim and a counterclaim are based on contractual obligations.

The focus on contractual connections in arbitral practice has meant that arbitral tribunals rarely identify a legal connection when counterclaims are based on the host State's domestic legislation. When counterclaims are founded on domestic legislation, the scope of the arbitral tribunal's jurisdiction may influence the outcome. As set out in Section 2.3.1, in *Amco* v *Indonesia*[46] the arbitral tribunal rejected Indonesia's counterclaim for repayment of taxes based on alleged tax fraud because it did not have jurisdiction over disputes that related to rights and obligations of general application.[47] The obligations were of general application because the source of the obligations that founded Indonesia's counterclaim was domestic tax law.[48] Although the discussion in *Amco* v *Indonesia* related to Article 25(1) ICSID Convention, which employs different language, a similar understanding has been translated to determinations regarding whether a counterclaim provides for the good administration of justice under Article 46 ICSID Convention. In *Meerapfel Sohne* v *Central African Republic*,[49] the tribunal found that a sufficient connection between the claim and the counterclaim was present.[50] Yet, the arbitral tribunal concluded that it did not have jurisdiction over the counterclaims that related to non-payment of taxes and alleged tax fraud as these should be addressed as matters within national jurisdiction.[51] Therefore, it is not possible to entirely disaggregate questions related to jurisdiction and the need for a nexus when counterclaims are based on domestic legislation.

Even if a counterclaim based on domestic legislation is within the arbitral tribunal's jurisdiction, the arbitral tribunal may still wish to identify a contractual connection. In *RSM* v *Grenada*,[52] the foreign investor's criminal acts were not deemed to be sufficiently linked to the investment dispute, despite being

46 *Amco Asia Corporation and others v. Republic of Indonesia* (n 26).

47 ibid [125].

48 ibid [126].

49 *M. Meerapfel Sohne AG v. Central African Republic* ICSID Case No ARB/07/10, Excerpts of Award, 12 May 2012.

50 ibid [446].

51 ibid [447].

52 *RSM Production Corporation v. Grenada* ICSID Case No ARB/05/14, Award, 13 March 2009.

factually related.[53] This was because the obligation not to undertake the criminal acts was not incorporated into the contract and could not be founded on contractual or tortious grounds.[54] Thus, the arbitral tribunal required the legal connection to be established based on a legal right that was directly related to the performance of the contract. Consequently, arbitral tribunals have consistently been reluctant to engage with counterclaims when domestic legislation is their only legal foundation (whether the counterclaim is based on international law or not).

ICSID arbitral tribunals have concentrated on finding legal connections between claims and counterclaims. As a result, counterclaims that are based on a factual link between the claim and the counterclaim have not formed a central part of ICSID arbitral practice. However, in *Urbaser* v *Argentina*,[55] the arbitral tribunal recognised that a factual link could connect a claim and a counterclaim. The arbitral tribunal observed a factual link between the investment claim and a human rights counterclaim on the basis that 'the principal claim and the claim opposed to it are based on the same investment, or the alleged lack of sufficient investment, in relation to the same Concession'.[56] This factual link was sufficient to establish a connection[57] because the arbitral tribunal found that a human rights counterclaim does not prima facie imply that the dispute does not directly relate to an investment[58] and separate legal proceedings would risk divergent decisions in relation to the same investment.[59] The arbitral tribunal's reliance on a factual connection was the best way to give effect to the good administration of justice given the interrelated nature of the claims. Although the arbitral tribunal was willing to proceed on the basis of the factual connection, the arbitral tribunal additionally identified that a legal connection was established to the extent that the counterclaim did not solely rely on domestic legislation.[60] Whilst reaffirming the position in relation to legal connections, this award is more significant for finding that a factual connection between a claim and a counterclaim has the potential to generate a sufficiently close connection for the purposes of Article 46 ICSID Convention.

53 ibid [469]–[473].

54 ibid.

55 *Urbaser S.A. and Consorcio de Aguas Bilbao Biskaia, Bilbao Biskaia Ur Partzuergoa v. Argentine Republic* ICSID Case No ARB/07/26, Award, 8 December 2016.

56 ibid [1151].

57 ibid.

58 ibid [1154].

59 ibid [1151].

60 ibid.

Not all ICSID arbitral tribunals have fully elaborated their reasoning when addressing Article 46 ICSID Convention. Hence, in these instances it is difficult to discern the precise foundation on which the connection was established. In some awards, the scope of the dispute has determined whether counterclaims are sufficiently connected to the originating claim. For example, in *Benvenuti & Bonfant* v *Congo*,[61] the tribunal relied on the counterclaim being related 'directly to the object of the dispute'.[62] Similarly, in *Inmaris* v *Ukraine*,[63] there was no direct discussion of the connection requirement, but the tribunal stated that the counterclaim 'is a component of the larger dispute that Claimants have consented to submit to this arbitration'.[64] In *Burlington* v *Ecuador*,[65] the arbitral tribunal held that the counterclaims complied with the nexus requirement on the basis that the subject matter was Burlington's investments.[66] Based on this general link, and in contrast to other ICSID arbitral practice, the arbitral tribunal permitted the use of Ecuador's domestic legislation on environmental protection to establish a counterclaim. Arbitral tribunals have established connections based on the foreign investor's claims. In *Goetz* v *Burundi*,[67] the host State halted the activities of the foreign investor, including a bank, which led to an investment claim. The requisite connection was found because the counterclaim related to the damage that flowed from the foreign investor's alleged failure to comply with the conditions of a free-zone certificate.[68] In *Tethyan Copper Company* v *Pakistan*,[69] the arbitral tribunal emphasised that there is 'no general rule' against a host State counterclaim being based on legal obligations sourced from beyond the IIA.[70] Instead, the arbitral tribunal considered that 'there indeed can be such a close or intimate connection if the analysis of the investor's Treaty claims necessarily includes the examination of the contractual and regulatory instruments on which the

61 *S.A.R.L. Benvenuti & Bonfant v. People's Republic of the Congo* ICSID Case No ARB/77/2, Award, 8 August 1980.

62 ibid [4.104].

63 *Inmaris Perestroika Sailing Maritime Services GmbH and others v. Ukraine* ICSID Case No ARB/08/8, Excerpts of Award, 1 March 2012.

64 ibid [432].

65 *Burlington Resources Inc. v. Republic of Ecuador* ICSID Case No ARB/08/5, Decision on Counterclaims, 7 February 2017.

66 ibid [62].

67 *Antoine Goetz and others v. Republic of Burundi* [*II*] (n 29).

68 ibid [285].

69 *Tethyan Copper Company Pty Limited v. Islamic Republic of Pakistan* ICSID Case No ARB/12/1, Decision on Jurisdiction and Liability, 10 November 2017.

70 ibid [1414].

counterclaims are based'.[71] These awards indicate that counterclaims that align with specific aspects of the claim or are directly linked to the operation of the investment can possess the necessary connection. However, they also evidence that whether a connection exists depends on how factors that are specific to the dispute combine with how the arbitral tribunal understands the content of the good administration of justice.

In summary, to comply with Article 46 ICSID Convention a nexus must exist between a claim and a counterclaim. Although not all arbitral tribunals have applied the connection requirement correctly, ICSID arbitral practice prioritises legal connections based on contractual obligations. ICSID arbitral practice is reluctant to establish a nexus based on domestic legislation but can identify legal links between the claim and the counterclaim based on the legal issues in dispute.[72] Factual links between a claim and a counterclaim are not frequently addressed but can also generate a close connection. Nonetheless, not all awards conform with these generalisations, indicating that ICSID arbitral tribunals take a flexible approach when considering whether a nexus exists between claims and counterclaims.

3.3.2 *ICSID Additional Facility Arbitration Rules*

The ICSID AF Arbitration Rules do not explicitly require a connection between claims and counterclaims. Article 47(1) ICSID AF Arbitration Rules (2006) and Rule 58(1) ICSID AF Arbitration rules (2022) only require ancillary claims (which includes counterclaims) to fall within the scope of the parties' arbitration agreement. Consequently, counterclaims will be permitted if they fall within the arbitral tribunal's jurisdiction (see Section 2.3.2). Nevertheless, arbitral tribunals may exercise their inherent powers to give effect to the good administration of justice when ancillary claims are raised.[73] Thus, in *ADF* v *USA*,[74] the arbitral tribunal relied on Article 48(1) ICSID AF Arbitration Rules

---

71 ibid.

72 Counterclaims have also been considered to have a sufficient connection when a host State seeks to recover the costs of defending actions in other legal proceedings when a foreign investor does not comply with a provision that exclusively permits ICSID arbitration as a forum for resolving disputes. In *Maritime International Nominees Establishment v. Republic of Guinea* ICSID Case No ARB/84/4, Award, 6 January 1988, the arbitral tribunal gives effect to the good administration of justice in costs claims by providing a remedy when a forum selection clause has not been complied with by a disputing party ([73]–[79]).

73 As to this prospect, see de Nanteuil (n 5) 396.

74 *ADF Group Inc. v. United States of America* ICSID Case No ARB(AF)/00/1, Award, 9 January 2003.

(1978) to draw an analogy with ICSID arbitration and impose a connection test in relation to the ancillary claim.[75] The arbitral tribunal did not find a connection because the foreign investor's ancillary claim did not relate to the same investment project.[76] The *ADF* v *USA* award was subsequently mentioned in *Lao Holdings/Sanum* v *Lao*.[77] This arbitral tribunal noted that the express requirements of Article 47(1) ICSID AF Arbitration Rules (2006) were met because the additional claims were within the scope of the arbitral tribunal's jurisdiction.[78] Nonetheless, the arbitral tribunal discussed whether it was also necessary to identify a nexus between the claim and the ancillary claim.[79] The arbitral tribunal did not need to reach a conclusion as to whether a nexus was required because a clear connection between the claims was established based on the terms of the Netherlands-Laos BIT and the subject matter of the dispute.[80] Thus, ICSID AF arbitral practice has not specifically addressed whether a connection between a claim and a counterclaim must exist. However, in the context of other ancillary claims, arbitral tribunals have taken opposing positions regarding whether there is a need for a nexus. As arbitral tribunals rely on their inherent powers to give effect to the good administration of justice in ICSID AF arbitration, arbitral practice is likely to vary on a case-by-case basis.

3.3.3 *UNCITRAL Arbitration Rules*

The UNCITRAL Arbitration Rules require different types of connections between an originating claim and a counterclaim depending on which version of the UNCITRAL Arbitration Rules apply. Article 19(3) UNCITRAL Arbitration Rules (1976) requires a contractual connection between the claims, which reflects that this version of the rules was intended for use in commercial arbitration. The rule was amended to reflect that a wider range of counterclaims are applicable in investment arbitration.[81] Hence, Article 21(3) UNCITRAL

75 ibid [144].

76 ibid.

77 *Lao Holdings N.V. v. Lao People's Democratic Republic II* ICSID Case No ARB(AF)16/2, Procedural Order No 3, 14 November 2017; *Sanum Investments Limited v. Lao People's Democratic Republic II* ICSID Case No ADHOC/17/1, Procedural Order No 3, 14 November 2017.

78 *Lao Holdings N.V. v. Lao People's Democratic Republic II* (n 77) [7]; *Sanum Investments Limited v. Lao People's Democratic Republic II* (n 77) [7].

79 *Lao Holdings N.V. v. Lao People's Democratic Republic II* (n 77) [8]; *Sanum Investments Limited v. Lao People's Democratic Republic II* (n 77) [8].

80 *Lao Holdings N.V. v. Lao People's Democratic Republic II* (n 77) [9]–[14]; *Sanum Investments Limited v. Lao People's Democratic Republic II* (n 77) [9]–[14].

81 Jan Paulsson and Georgios Petrochilos, *UNCITRAL Arbitration* (Kluwer Law International 2018) 172; Steingruber (n 31) 628.

Arbitration Rules (2010) only requires an arbitral tribunal to have jurisdiction over a counterclaim. Based on this provision, there is no requirement for a connection between the claims and arbitral tribunals must exercise their inherent powers to give effect to the good administration of justice.[82] Consequently, UNCITRAL arbitral practice gives effect to the good administration of justice in two different ways.

The need for a contractual connection based on Article 19(3) UNCITRAL Arbitration Rules (1976) has resulted in arbitral practice that takes a restrictive approach to counterclaims. The limits of this provision were first considered in *Saluka v Czech Republic*.[83] The arbitral tribunal reviewed the UNCITRAL Arbitration Rules, the ICSID Arbitration Rules and the provisions establishing the US-Iran Claims Tribunal to identify what 'customarily' amounts to a connection between claims and counterclaims.[84] Thus, the arbitral tribunal considered sources that did not directly apply to the dispute and were drafted in different terms. Nonetheless, based on the ICSID award *Klöckner v Cameroon*,[85] and with reference to jurisprudence from the US-Iran Claims tribunal,[86] the arbitral tribunal determined that counterclaims must arise from the same legal source as the originating claim.[87] In investment arbitration, this type of connection usually only exists in contractual relationships. Therefore, the arbitral

82 Although there is not a specific provision regarding how an arbitral tribunal should give effect to the good administration specifically in relation to counterclaims, the good administration of justice is reflected in the terms of Article 17(1) UNCITRAL Arbitration Rules (2010) which states 'Subject to these Rules, the arbitral tribunal may conduct the arbitration in such manner as it considers appropriate, provided that the parties are treated with equality and that at an appropriate stage of the proceedings each party is given a reasonable opportunity of presenting its case. The arbitral tribunal, in exercising its discretion, shall conduct the proceedings so as to avoid unnecessary delay and expense and to provide a fair and efficient process for resolving the parties' dispute'. This provision mirrors an arbitral tribunal's inherent powers.

83 *Saluka Investment B.V. v. Czech Republic* UNCITRAL, Decision on Jurisdiction over the Czech Republic's Counterclaim, 7 May 2004.

84 ibid [61].

85 *Klöckner Industrie-Anlagen GmbH v. United Republic of Cameroon* (n 34). See Section 3.3.1 for a discussion of this award.

86 *Saluka Investment B.V. v. Czech Republic* (n 83) [68]–[74]. Jurisdiction over counterclaims in the US-Iran Claims Tribunal is limited to 'any counterclaim that arises out of the same contract, transaction or occurrence that constitutes the same subject matter of [the] national's claims' (Iran-United States Claims Tribunal Claims Settlement Declaration (19 January 1981) 20 ILM 223 Article II(1)).

87 *Saluka Investment B.V. v. Czech Republic* (n 83) [79]. See Pierre Lalive and Laura Halonen, 'On the Availability of Counterclaims in Investment Treaty Arbitration' (2011) II Czech Yearbook of International Law 141, 154.

tribunal gave direct effect to the language found in Article 19(3) UNCITRAL Arbitration Rules by adopting a narrow understanding[88] of what amounts to a connection between the claims.

By implication, Article 19(3) UNCITRAL Arbitration Rules excludes counterclaims based on domestic legislation. The arbitral tribunal in *Saluka v Czech Republic*[89] explicitly rejected counterclaims that were founded on 'general obligations' sourced from the domestic legislation of the host State[90] based on the *Amco v Indonesia*[91] award.[92] A similar approach was taken in *Paushok v Mongolia*,[93] which addressed multiple counterclaims based on Mongolia's domestic law. The arbitral tribunal found that the counterclaims based on Mongolian tax law fell within the exclusive jurisdiction of Mongolia, and on this basis, did not constitute 'an indivisible part' of the claim or create 'a reasonable nexus'.[94] The arbitral tribunal was particularly concerned about generating extra-territorial jurisdiction for Mongolia's public law and tax laws, which would be contrary to the principle of non-extraterritorial enforceability of public law.[95] As a result, the tribunal considered that tax laws should be subject to national jurisdiction.[96] Other counterclaims based on domestic law were rejected because the obligations were not owed by the foreign investor.[97]

88 Kjos (n 2) 152; Thomas Kendra, 'State Counterclaims in Investment Arbitration – A New Lease of Life?' (2013) 29 Arbitration International 575, 582; Tomoko Ishikawa, *Corporate Environmental Responsibility in Investor-State Dispute Settlement: The Unexhausted Potential of Current Mechanisms* (Cambridge Unversity Press 2022) 105.

89 *Saluka Investment B.V. v. Czech Republic* (n 83).

90 ibid [75].

91 *Amco Asia Corporation and others v. Republic of Indonesia* (n 26).

92 The arbitral tribunal rejected Indonesia's counterclaim for repayment of taxes based on alleged tax fraud because it did not have jurisdiction over disputes that related to rights and obligations of general application (ibid [125]). See Section 2.3.1.

93 *Sergei Paushok, CJSC Golden East Company and CJSC Vostokneftegaz Company v. Government of Mongolia* UNCITRAL, Award on Jurisdiction and Liability, 28 April 2011.

94 ibid [694].

95 ibid [695]. Regarding the merits of this position, see Shao Xuan Shao, 'Environmental and Human Rights Counterclaims in International Investment Arbitration: at the Crossroads of Domestic and International Law' (2021) 24 Journal of International Economic Law 157, 170; Ishikawa (n 88) 125–126.

96 *Sergei Paushok, CJSC Golden East Company and CJSC Vostokneftegaz Company v. Government of Mongolia* (n 93) [695]. The tribunal also found that close connections were not present in relation to counterclaims for unpaid court costs incurred when the Bank of Nova Scotia defended a claim raised by the foreign investor in the English Courts that gave rise to Mongolia's liability ([697]).

97 ibid [696].

It is probable that these types of concerns will be applied to counterclaims based on domestic legislation regardless of whether they give effect to international law or not. Hence, for a variety of reasons, counterclaims based on domestic legislation are highly unlikely to fall within the scope of Article 19(3) UNCITRAL Arbitration Rules.

In contrast, Article 21(3) UNCITRAL Arbitration Rules (2010) dispenses with the need for a connection to exist between claims and counterclaims. Therefore, arbitral tribunals must rely on their inherent powers to give effect to the good administration of justice. Despite the change in language and legal source, UNCITRAL arbitral practice has not changed significantly. Thus, arbitral practice focuses on the need for a legal connection between claims and counterclaims based on a shared legal foundation. The need for a legal connection is illustrated by *Oxus* v *Uzbekistan*,[98] where the host State presented multiple counterclaims. Although the arbitral tribunal was bound by the UNCITRAL Arbitration Rules (2010), the host State's submissions cited awards made under the ICSID Arbitration Rules.[99] Consequently, the arbitral tribunal applied the most beneficial position from the *Saluka* v *Czech Republic* award to the host State.[100] The arbitral tribunal rejected all the counterclaims. One counterclaim was rejected because its foundation was the general law of the host state.[101] A forum selection and choice of law clause precluded the tribunal from proceeding to hear another counterclaim where a close connection did exist.[102] Finally, the arbitral tribunal did not proceed to hear a counterclaim based on an umbrella clause in the BIT. An umbrella clause is an international obligation that requires a host State to comply with contractual terms.[103] The arbitral tribunal decided that an umbrella clause could not be used in reverse to frame a foreign investor's breaches of domestic law as international obligations because the umbrella clause only referred to host State obligations.[104] Therefore, there was no shared foundation that could establish a legal connection between the originating claims and those counterclaims that fell within the arbitral tribunal's jurisdiction. Nevertheless, a legal connection can be established when reciprocal obligations are present in an IIA. The

98 *Oxus Gold plc v. Republic of Uzbekistan* UNCITRAL, Final Award, 17 December 2015.

99 ibid [951].

100 ibid [952].

101 ibid [955]–[956].

102 ibid [957]–[958] (citing *Saluka Investment B.V. v. Czech Republic* (n 83)).

103 Katia Yannaca-Small, 'The Umbrella Clause: Is the Umbrella Closing?' in Katia Yannaca-Small (ed), *Arbitration under International Investment Agreements: A Guide to the Key Issues* (2nd edn, Oxford University Press 2018) 402–403.

104 *Oxus Gold plc v. Republic of Uzbekistan* (n 98) [958].

arbitral tribunal in *Al-Warraq* v *Indonesia*[105] recognised that a treaty obligation to respect host State law 'confirms the absence of restrictions on the nature of the counterclaim, and specifically the absence of an express restriction on counterclaims arising from the investment'.[106] Despite the professed absence of any limitations, the arbitral tribunal additionally identified that the counterclaim related to both to the investment and the foreign investor's claims, thereby establishing a connection.[107] Thus, although Article 21(3) UNCITRAL Arbitration Rules (2010) does not require a nexus, when exercising their inherent power to give effect to the good administration of justice, UNCITRAL arbitral tribunals seek out a legal connection.

In summary, arbitral practice gives effect to the language of Article 19(3) UNCITRAL Arbitration Rules (1976) by requiring a contractual connection between originating claims and counterclaims. In the absence of a need for any connection in Article 21(3) UNCITRAL Arbitration Rules (2010), UNCITRAL arbitral tribunals continue to require a legal connection to give effect to the good administration of justice. As a result, UNCITRAL arbitral practice recognises counterclaims that are based on reciprocal legal obligations sourced from contracts or IIAs but rejects counterclaims based on domestic legislation.

3.3.4 *Analysis of Arbitral Practice*

Investment arbitration practice governing the need for a nexus between claims and counterclaims varies depending on which arbitration rules apply to the dispute. It remains unclear whether a connection is required under the ICSID AF Arbitration Rules. However, ICSID AF arbitral practice is likely to develop on a case-by-case basis until a consistent pattern emerges. Conversely, arbitral practice conducted under the ICSID Convention and ICSID Arbitration Rules and the UNCITRAL Arbitration Rules reveals a strong trend. When governed by these arbitration rules, arbitral tribunals primarily seek to identify a legal connection between originating claims and counterclaims.[108] The way these arbitral tribunals find legal connections between claims and counterclaims has the potential to preclude counterclaims based on international law in investment arbitration.

105 *Hesham Talaat M. Al-Warraq v. Republic of Indonesia* UNCITRAL, Final Award, 15 December 2014.

106 ibid [667].

107 ibid [668].

108 Anne Hoffman, 'Counterclaims in Investment Arbitration' (2013) 28 ICSID Review – Foreign Investment Law Journal 438, 451.

The existence of a connection between a claim and a counterclaim is linked to how expansively an arbitral tribunal defines the scope of a dispute. Arbitral practice routinely finds a nexus when the claim and the counterclaim are presented as opposing legal claims. The focus on a legal connection between the claims suggests that arbitral tribunals define a dispute based on the ICJ's jurisprudence that focuses on a legal disagreement between the disputing parties. However, arbitral practice has further restricted what amounts to a dispute by requiring the competing legal obligations to be derived from the same legal source. Thus, to be able to support a counterclaim, the legal source must generate reciprocal legal obligations. In an investment dispute, reciprocity is usually only created by contracts. Therefore, to establish a legal connection, the foreign investor must have commenced a contract claim. The need for a contractual claim as the foundation of the dispute can be attributed to the context in which the nexus between claims and counterclaims was first discussed in ICSID arbitration and UNCITRAL arbitration. The first ICSID award to apply Article 46 ICSID Convention was a contractual claim and the arbitral tribunal's focus on the relationship between the contractual claims has informed subsequent ICSID arbitral practice. Similarly, Article 19(3) UNCITRAL Arbitration Rules (1976) requires a contractual connection because these arbitration rules were drafted for the purposes of commercial arbitration. Although the need for a contractual connection has been removed from Article 21(3) UNCITRAL Arbitration Rules, arbitral practice continues to reflect the original formulation of the rule. Nevertheless, by continuing to apply considerations that are pertinent to contractual claims, arbitral tribunals have adopted a very narrow definition of a dispute.

When arbitral tribunals adopt a restricted definition of a dispute, they do not necessarily capture the full extent to which originating claims and counterclaims interact in investment arbitration. For instance, by requiring reciprocal obligations that arise from the same legal source, arbitral practice prevents counterclaims that respond to claims based on IIAs and foreign investment legislation. Investment protection standards set out in an IIA or foreign investment legislation do not generate reciprocal obligations because they only bind host States.[109] Thus, unless the IIA or foreign investment legislation contains additional obligations that bind foreign investors,[110] counterclaims will almost always be based on different legal instruments.[111] Arbitral practice that requires a reciprocal legal obligation renders counterclaims in investment arbitration

109 de Nanteuil (n 5) 376.

110 ibid. A small minority of IIAs contain foreign investor obligations (see Section 5.2.1).

111 Kjos (n 2) 149.

almost redundant.[112] However, not all arbitral practice has taken such a limited view of what amounts to dispute. Hence, by referring to arbitral practice that has not solely focused on legal connections, it is possible to examine other types of connections that could create a nexus between a claim and a counterclaim. Consequently, it is necessary to consider the arbitral practice in relation to factual connections, domestic legislation, and general connections between claims and counterclaims in more detail.

Factual connections between claims and counterclaims have not formed an integral part of arbitral practice. Nonetheless, broadening the definition of a dispute to encompass both legal and factual connections potentially captures a wider range of counterclaims. The arbitral tribunal in *Urbaser* v *Argentina*[113] framed the investment dispute expansively. By focusing on how the claims and counterclaims centred on the investment, the arbitral tribunal widened the scope of the dispute to encompass a counterclaim based on human rights. The arbitral tribunal justified its position with reference to the good administration of justice by highlighting that hearing the claim and counterclaim together would reduce the risk of inconsistent decisions. Therefore, if a factual connection can be established, all claims that arise from the factual matrix can be evaluated to determine whether a sufficient connection exists,[114] and all closely connected claims can be resolved together. The use of a factual connection in ICSID arbitration should not be problematic. Article 46 ICSID Convention was modelled on Article 80(1) ICJ Rules of Court,[115] which permits counterclaims that are 'directly connected with the subject-matter of the claim of the other party'.[116] When drawing from the ICJ Rules of Court, the drafters of

112 See Ishikawa (n 88) 106.

113 *Urbaser S.A. and Consorcio de Aguas Bilbao Biskaia, Bilbao Biskaia Ur Partzuergoa v. Argentine Republic* (n 55).

114 Kjos (n 2) 148.

115 Kendra (n 88) 577.

116 This is the 1978 version of the International Court of Justice, Rules of Court (1978) (adopted 14 April 1978, entered into force 1 July 1978). A counterclaim may be presented provided that it 'is directly connected with the subject-matter of the claim of the other party and that it comes within the jurisdiction of the Court'. The Rules were amended in 2001 and Article 80(1) now reads 'The Court may entertain a counter-claim only if it comes within the jurisdiction of the Court and is directly connected with the subject-matter of the claim of the other party'. When applying this rule, the ICJ looks for both factual and legal connections to the originating claim (See for example, *Case concerning Oil Platforms (Islamic Republic of Iran v. United States of America)* (Counterclaim Order of 10 March 1998)[1998] ICJ Rep 190 [138]; *Armed Activities on the Territory of the Congo (Democratic Republic of the Congo v. Uganda)* (Order of 29 November 2001) [2001] ICJ Rep 660 [36]).

the ICSID Convention favored the position that a factual connection would be sufficient.[117] Therefore, the foundations exist for finding connections based on the factual matrix of the dispute. Despite this potential, arbitral practice has largely failed to consider whether factual connections can be used to demonstrate a nexus between originating claims and counterclaims.

Arbitral tribunals have habitually rejected counterclaims sourced from domestic legislation based on the reasoning set out in *Amco* v *Indonesia*. More specifically, arbitral tribunals have relied on the proposition that generally applicable domestic legislation does not generate an investment dispute for the purposes of Article 25(1) ICSID Convention to extrapolate that a counterclaim based on domestic legislation cannot share a connection with an originating claim. The foundation for this position is unclear. The *Amco* v *Indonesia* award does not support a general proposition that arbitral tribunals do not have jurisdiction over counterclaims in investment arbitration if they are based on domestic legislation. Rather, *Amco* v *Indonesia* permits jurisdiction to be established when breaches of domestic legislation generate an investment dispute.[118] Employing this logic, it should be possible for counterclaims based on domestic legislation to have a sufficiently close connection to the originating claim if the application of the legislation specifically relates to the investment. By requiring that the domestic legislation applies directly to the investment, arbitral tribunals could still uphold the position that disputes involving generally applicable domestic legislation, such as tax law, should be heard in a domestic dispute resolution forum. The award in *Burlington* v *Ecuador* illustrates that subject matter governed by domestic legislation can display a clear connection to an investment dispute. In *Burlington* v *Ecuador*, the arbitral tribunal had jurisdiction to hear the counterclaim based on the foreign investor's consent. The arbitral tribunal permitted a counterclaim based on Ecuador's domestic environmental legislation on the basis that environmental damage formed part of a larger dispute over an investment in oil mining operations.[119] Hence, by focusing on whether the domestic legislation is relevant to the investment dispute, arbitral tribunals can justify a connection

117 This decision was made when it was anticipated that most ICSID arbitration would be contract-based claims rather than treaty-based claims. In this context the drafter stated 'the factual connection between the original claim and the ancillary claim is so close as to require the adjudication of the latter in order to achieve the final settlement of the dispute, the object being to dispose all grounds of dispute arising out of the same subject matter' (Note B(a) to ICSID Arbitration Rule 40, 1 ICSID Reports 100).

118 *Amco Asia Corporation and others v. Republic of Indonesia* (n 26) [125].

119 See Shao (n 95) 172.

between claims and counterclaims. Consequently, by partially transposing the jurisdictional limitations found in *Amco* v *Indonesia* to the nexus requirement, arbitral practice discounts connections between claims and counterclaims based on domestic legislation.

By focusing on legal connections, arbitral practice omits general connections between claims and counterclaims. ICSID arbitral practice demonstrates that there can be flexibility in how arbitral tribunals identify connections by adopting a generic understanding of what comprises a dispute. ICSID arbitral tribunals exercise their judgment to balance competing factors when deciding whether a connection exists. UNCITRAL arbitral tribunals cannot take this approach when applying Article 19(3) UNCITRAL Arbitration Rules (1976) given that a contractual connection must be found. However, this textual restriction has been overcome in Article 21(3) UNCITRAL Arbitration Rules. Thus, by continuing to require a legal connection, UNCITRAL arbitral practice fails to use a wider notion of what amounts to a dispute, which makes it difficult for a host State to counterclaim against an investment claim.[120] As a result, UNCITRAL arbitral practice disregards relevant factors that could give rise to a connection between a claim and a counterclaim.

Arbitral practice illustrates that connections that are based on factual links, domestic legislation and general relationships between claims and counterclaims are regularly overlooked by arbitral tribunals when they seek to identify a nexus between claims and counterclaims. By excluding a range of potentially legitimate connections between claims and counterclaims, arbitral practice fails to give full effect to the good administration of justice. The purpose of the good administration of justice is to ensure that disputes are resolved in an efficient, effective and equitable way to achieve just outcomes. Counterclaims that are based on domestic legislation, are factually connected to the originating claim, or that display factors that justify them being heard together with the originating claim may contribute to these aims. Depending on the degree of closeness exhibited, counterclaims with these types of connections may not be prejudicial to a foreign investor and could prevent the duplication of resources, minimise the risk of inconsistent decision-making and reduce the time and costs involved in resolving a dispute. The need for a nexus between claims and counterclaims is intended to allow arbitral tribunals to evaluate whether counterclaims negatively impact the integrity of investment arbitration. Arbitral tribunals cannot make this evaluation if arbitral practice

120 See Melissa Ordonez, 'States' Counterclaims: how hard is it to counterattack in international investment arbitration?' (2019) 22 International Arbitration Law Review 27, 33.

regularly fails to recognise some types of connections that can potentially give effect to the good administration of justice. Consequently, arbitral practice only recognises a modified version of the good administration of justice.

By applying an abridged version of the good administration of justice, arbitral tribunals restrict the operation of counterclaims based on international law. Counterclaims based on international law will not usually meet the criteria for a reciprocal legal connection because different legal orders will typically govern the claim and the counterclaim.[121] Hence, counterclaims based on international law will need to be founded on one of the limited numbers of IIAs that contain foreign investor obligations or be based on contractual obligations. Counterclaims that rely on principles of international law that have been incorporated into domestic legislation will be excluded because arbitral tribunals do not recognise connections based on domestic legislation, even if the domestic legislation specifically applies to an investment. Finally, it is unclear if a counterclaim that is founded on the factual matrix of an investment dispute could generate a connection because factual connections have not become part of mainstream investment arbitration jurisprudence. Thus, counterclaims based on international law will be very difficult to establish. The limitations evident in arbitral practice appear to be arbitrary given that those arbitral tribunals that have engaged with counterclaims based on these sources of law have identified a connection between originating claims and counterclaims, enabling them to give effect to the good administration of justice. The source of the constraint in arbitral practice appears to be linked to arbitral tribunals adopting definitions of disputes that focus on opposing legal claims that are prevalent in the ICJ's jurisprudence. Nonetheless, alternative definitions of disputes in arbitral practice focus on examining the wider context to determine the scope of a dispute[122] or emphasise that disputes can include claims that arise at different times and from different legal instruments.[123] Should arbitral tribunals adopt these definitions of a dispute, they can take a more flexible and expansive approach to identifying a nexus between a claim and a counterclaim. This would enable arbitral tribunals to give full effect to the good administration of justice and permit counterclaims based on international law in investment arbitration.

121 Veenstra-Kjos (n 8) 33.

122 *Industria Nacional de Alimentos, S.A. and Indalsa Perú, S.A. v. Republic of Peru* (n 29) [91].

123 *CMS Gas Transmission Company v. Republic of Argentina* (n 30) [109].

3.4 Establishing the Nexus between a Claim and Counterclaim

Host States need to refocus how arbitral tribunals understand the nexus between claims and counterclaims in investment arbitration so that arbitral tribunals permit counterclaims based on international law. In effect, host States must influence how arbitral tribunals give effect to the good administration of justice. Given that arbitral tribunals possess inherent powers to give effect to the good administration of justice, and may also be guided by arbitration rules, host States cannot proscribe how arbitral tribunals should exercise their judgment. However, host States can attempt to counteract the trends that are evident in arbitral practice that are likely to prevent arbitral tribunals from accepting counterclaims based on international law. This section argues that host States can encourage arbitral tribunals to adopt a broader understanding of what amounts to a dispute by specifying what amounts to a connection between an originating claim and a counterclaim in IIAs and foreign investment legislation. Further, host States can present legal argumentation that emphasises how the counterclaim based on international law gives effect to the policies that underpin the good administration of justice. Both approaches can potentially contribute to arbitral tribunals identifying a nexus between claims and counterclaims based on international law.

Whether a connection is found between an originating claim and a counterclaim is contingent on how an arbitral tribunal defines a dispute. The broader the definition of a dispute, the more likely that an arbitral tribunal will identify a sufficiently close connection. When arbitral tribunals rely on definitions of a dispute that focus on opposing legal claims, arbitral practice restricts counterclaims to those that are based on reciprocal legal obligations or share the same legal source. Counterclaims based on international law do not frequently display these attributes. Therefore, arbitral tribunals need to adopt a wide definition of a dispute to find a connection between originating claims and this category of counterclaims. To encourage arbitral tribunals to extend the definition of a dispute beyond a legal disagreement, host States have included provisions in IIAs and foreign investment legislation that specify that host States may make a counterclaim 'in connection with the factual and legal basis of the claim'.[124] Provisions in these terms effectively require an arbitral tribunal to adopt an expanded definition of a dispute. To comply with this provision,

124 See for example, Comprehensive and Progressive Agreement for Trans-Pacific Partnership 2018 (adopted 8 March 2018, entered into force 30 December 2018) Article 9.19(2); China-Mauritius Free Trade Agreement (FTA) 2019 (adopted 17 October 2019, not yet in force) Article 8.24(4).

an arbitral tribunal must consider both the legal foundation of the claims and the factual matrix of the investment dispute when identifying whether a connection exists between the claims. The inclusion of the factual matrix in the definition of a dispute increases the chances that an arbitral tribunal will identify a connection between originating claims and counterclaims that are not based on reciprocal legal obligations or do not share the same legal source. Consequently, this style of provision may increase the chances that a nexus will arise between originating claims and counterclaims based on international law.

Although a wider definition of a dispute in this type of provision overcomes the reluctance of arbitral tribunals to engage with factual connections, it does not resolve all the challenges associated with legal connections identified in arbitral practice. For example, the reference to legal connections does not prevent an arbitral tribunal from maintaining the same understanding of a legal connection that is already evident in arbitral practice. Hence, arbitral tribunals could continue to focus on contractual claims and overlook counterclaims based on domestic legislation (it if directly applies to an investment) unless a clear factual link exists. As a result, counterclaims based on international law may still be excluded if arbitral tribunals continue to apply the existing criteria that governs whether a legal connection exists or not.

Nonetheless, it remains possible for host States to circumvent existing arbitral practice by using more comprehensive clauses in IIAs and foreign investment legislation to specify when a nexus exists. For example, UNCITRAL Working Group III has prepared a draft provision addressing the availability of counterclaims as part of its review of procedural issues in investment arbitration.[125] Draft Provision 11(1) provides that a host State can make a counterclaim that (1) arises directly out of the subject matter of the claim; (2) is in connection with the factual and legal basis of the claim; or (3) alleges that the foreign investor has breached its obligations under the IIA, domestic law, and investment contract or any other instrument binding on the claimant.[126] This provision draws on existing State practice as well as research from other organisations[127] to try and increase the availability of counterclaims for host States.

125 UNCITRAL Working Group III, 'Possible reform of investor-State dispute settlement (ISDS): Draft provisions on procedural and cross-cutting issues'(26 July 2023) UN Doc No. A/CN.9/WG.III/WP.231.

126 ibid 6.

127 UNCITRAL Working Group III, 'Possible reform of investor-State dispute settlement (ISDS): Annotations to the draft provisions on procedural and cross-cutting issues' (31 July 2023) UN Doc No. A/CN.9/WG.III/WP.232; UNCITRAL Working Group III (n 125) 3.

Hence, Draft Provision 11(1) sets out the requirement of a direct relationship between the counterclaim and the subject matter of the claim found in Article 46 ICSID Convention and the ICSID Arbitration Rules. The provision additionally draws from recent State practice where provisions expressly require arbitral tribunals to recognise both factual and legal connections between originating claims and counterclaims. Finally, Draft Provision 11(1)(c) establishes a connection if a host State alleges a breach of a foreign investor obligation in its counterclaim. Consequently, the terms of Draft Provision 11(1) encompass a much wider range of permissible connections than currently exist in IIAs, foreign investment legislation or arbitral practice.

If host States were to include provisions drafted in similar terms to Draft Provision 11(1) in their IIAs or foreign investment legislation, it is more likely that counterclaims based on international law would demonstrate a connection to the originating claim. A connection is more likely to exist based on Draft Provision 11(1) because it counters much of the arbitral practice that precludes the existence of a nexus between an originating claim and a counterclaim based on international law. Each subclause of Draft Provision 11(1) could assist a host State to establish the requisite connection. The first subclause, based on the ICSID Convention and the ICSID Arbitration Rules, could influence the interpretation of the UNCITRAL arbitration rules. Article 19(3) UNCITRAL Arbitration Rules (1976) specifies that there must be a contractual connection between originating claims and counterclaims. A similar requirement has been transposed into the application of Article 21(3) UNCITRAL Arbitration Rules (2010) even though this Article no longer refers to the need for a contractual relationship. Hence, by permitting a connection when there is a direct relationship between the subject matter of the claim and the counterclaim, the first subclause of Draft Provision 11(1) could relax the strict interpretation that arbitral tribunals have given to Article 21(3) UNCITRAL Arbitration Rules (2010). The second subclause gives greater recognition to factual connections between claims and counterclaims. As discussed above, expressly referring to factual connections means that arbitral tribunals must adopt a wider definition of a dispute. The third subclause of Draft Provision 11(1) prevents arbitral tribunals from requiring that a counterclaim is founded on a reciprocal legal obligation sourced from the same legal instrument as the originating claim. The third subclause of Draft Provision 11(1) significantly expands the types of legal relationships that can generate a counterclaim by removing the need for a nexus and only requiring a host State to base its counterclaim on a binding foreign investor obligation.[128] Thus, the third subclause of Draft provision 11(1) overcomes many of the restrictions identified in arbitral practice that centre on the legal source of the counterclaim. Each subclause of Draft Provision 11(1) has the potential to broaden how an arbitral tribunal defines a dispute and gives effect to the good administration of justice. Yet, by presenting these types of connection in the alternative, this provision appreciably expands what amounts to a dispute for the purposes of finding a connection between a claim and a counterclaim. In turn, the scope of what gives effect to the good administration of justice is enlarged to the same extent. Thus, Draft Provision 11(1) substantially improves the chances that an arbitral tribunal will be able to identify a connection between an originating claim and a counterclaim based on international law.

The terms of Draft Provision 11(1) are innovative and do not affect existing IIAs and foreign investment legislation. In the absence of provisions in similar terms, it is acknowledged that even those IIAs that extend the definition of a dispute are unlikely to significantly change arbitral practice to permit counterclaims based on international law. Therefore, host States will need to guide arbitral practice more closely by introducing legal argumentation that is based on the policies that underpin the good administration of justice.[129] The vague content and flexible nature of the good administration of justice provides host States with the opportunity to influence arbitral practice through legal argumentation. Based on how the good administration of justice has been applied in relation to counterclaims, host States should focus their legal argumentation on how the counterclaim based on international law enhances the effectiveness and efficiency of the investment arbitration whilst not prejudicing the foreign investor. The precise factors that should underpin the legal argumentation will vary depending on what considerations apply to each individual investment dispute. Nevertheless, expressly highlighting the significance of these factors may enable host States to justify counterclaims that are not based on the same legal order. For example, based on existing treaty provisions and arbitral

128 UNCITRAL Working Group III, Possible reform of investor-State dispute settlement (ISDS): Annotations to the draft provisions on procedural and cross-cutting issues (n 127) 7.

129 Host States can introduce legal argumentation to supplement a provision that generates a wider definition of a dispute or independently of this form of provision. In the absence of a provision, legal argumentation will need to additionally address how an arbitral tribunal defines a dispute, which may be more challenging to address by legal argumentation alone.

practice, an IIA and a contract would normally be viewed as different elements of the legal framework governing an investment. Hence, a treaty claim would preclude a counterclaim founded on a contract on the basis that the obligations that form the basis of the claim and the counterclaim must be derived from the same legal source. In this instance, a host State could argue that a connection between investment claims and contractual counterclaims exists by emphasising that failing to hear the claim and the counterclaim together could result in the duplication of resources and inconsistent outcomes.[130] In response, arbitral tribunals should be more willing to find a nexus between claims and counterclaims without requiring the claims to have a reciprocal legal relationship. Relying on the good administration of justice in this way has the potential to permit counterclaims based on international law because the beneficial impact of hearing both claims together in investment arbitration takes priority over the legal order that underpins the claims. This approach may also permit arbitral tribunals to find a connection when counterclaims are based on domestic law irrespective of whether they give effect to principles of international law. Legal argumentation will not guarantee that every counterclaim will be heard, however, arguing that a connection exists in this manner increases that chances that counterclaims that are currently overlooked may be considered. Therefore, references to the good administration of justice can be used to justify a wider range of counterclaims, including counterclaims based on international law.

The use of the good administration of justice in this way supplements existing arbitral practice. Yet, there are some limitations that cannot be overcome by referring to the good administration of justice. The need for a contractual connection in Article 19(3) UNCITRAL Arbitration Rules (1976) does not provide arbitral tribunals with the ability to apply the good administration of justice in the proposed manner. Thus, host States should avoid selecting the UNCITRAL Arbitration Rules (1976) if they wish to establish counterclaims in response to investment claims. Additionally, domestic legislation that does not directly relate to the investment will continue to be excluded based on the application of the principles set out in *Amco* v. *Indonesia*. Finally, there may be instances where arbitral tribunals exercise their judgment to exclude counterclaims because they are not efficient or are not in the interests of the disputing parties. Despite these limitations, by enhancing the significance of the good administration of justice when asserting that a nexus between claims and counterclaims exists, host States can increase the type of counterclaims that arbitral tribunals can address. In turn, this increases the likelihood

130 Provided that all the legal instruments allow the dispute resolution forum to hear the claim (Steingruber (n 31) 629).

that counterclaims based on international law will be heard in investment arbitration.

3.5 Preliminary Conclusions

For an arbitral tribunal to proceed to hear a counterclaim in investment arbitration, there must be a nexus between the originating claim and the counterclaim. The need for a nexus encourages arbitral tribunals to give effect to the good administration of justice by excluding unrelated counterclaims.

Whether a counterclaim is considered to be related to a claim is contingent on how arbitral tribunals define a dispute. Whilst ICSID AF arbitral practice is still evolving, ICSID arbitral practice and UNCITRAL arbitral practice primarily seek to identify legal connections which shows that arbitral tribunals rely on definitions of disputes that are framed in terms of competing legal claims. Arbitral practice has also required that counterclaims are based on reciprocal obligations that arise from the same legal source. Based on these criteria, counterclaims will only possess a sufficient nexus if they are based on the same legal instrument as the originating claim. The continued application of considerations that are relevant to contract claims in arbitral practice limits what amounts to a legal connection.

Arbitral practice presents challenges for host States that seek to present counterclaims based on international law. Counterclaims based on international law are likely to rely on legal principles drawn from different legal sources that originate from different legal orders. Thus, counterclaims based on international law will appear to be unrelated to originating claims when a legal connection is used as the reference point. Host States are likely to struggle to use other factors to demonstrate that a connection exists between a claim and a counterclaim based on international law. Arbitral practice has denied connections when counterclaims are based on domestic legislation and has predominantly overlooked factual connections between claims and counterclaims even though these connections can give effect to the good administration of justice. Hence, arbitral practice has applied a modified version of the good administration of justice, and in so doing, has prevented the operation of counterclaims based on international law.

To encompass counterclaims based on international law, host States need to encourage arbitral tribunals to adopt wider definitions of disputes to capture more relationships between claims and counterclaims. Host States can seek to alter arbitral practice by including provisions in IIAs and in foreign investment legislation that dictate how arbitral tribunals should identify a connection.

This type of provision can be supplemented by legal argumentation that emphasises the policies that underpin the good administration of justice so that arbitral tribunals focus less on the legal foundation of the counterclaim and more on ensuring that investment arbitration is effective and equitable. Although host States cannot dictate how arbitral tribunals use their powers to give effect to the good administration of justice, they can increase the chances of more connections being captured in arbitral practice, which would permit a greater number of counterclaims based on international law.

CHAPTER 4

Applicable Law and Counterclaims

4.1 Introduction

An arbitral tribunal must identify the substantive laws that it can refer to (known as the applicable law)[1] before it evaluates a claim on the merits.[2] If the applicable law does not encompass the substantive law that underpins a claim, an arbitral tribunal will not be able to proceed to resolve the dispute with reference to that law.[3]

An arbitral tribunal ascertains the applicable law by referring to party consent and the applicable arbitration rules.[4] Party consent is the primary means of selecting the applicable law,[5] however, host States frequently fail to specify the applicable law when consenting to investment arbitration.[6] Thus, when presented with a counterclaim based on international law, an arbitral tribunal will most probably only refer to the arbitration rules to determine the applicable law. Counterclaims based on international law will need an arbitral tribunal

1 In relation to the ICSID Convention, see Andrea K Bjorklund and Lukas Vanhonnaeker, 'Article 42' in Julien Fouret, Rémy Gerbay and Gloria M Alvarez (eds), *The ICSID Convention, Regulations and Rules: A Practical Commentary* (Edward Elgar Publishing 2019) 349; Dafina Atanasova, 'Applicable Law Provisions in Investment Treaties' (2019) 10 Journal of International Dispute Settlement 396, 399.

2 Taida Begic, *Applicable Law in International Investment Disputes* (Eleven International Publishing 2005) 3; Yas Banifatemi, 'The Law Applicable in Investment Treaty Arbitration' in Katia Yannaca-Small (ed), *Arbitration under International Investment Agreements: A Guide to the Key Issues* (Oxford University Press 2010) 191.

3 Melissa Ordonez, 'States' Counterclaims: how hard is it to counterattack in international investment arbitration?' (2019) 22 International Arbitration Law Review 27, 31.

4 Banifatemi (n 2) 191; Eric De Brabandere, *Investment Treaty Arbitration as Public International Law: procedural aspects and implications* (Cambridge University Press 2014) 124.

5 Giuditta Cordero Moss, 'Arbitration and Private International Law' (2008) 11 International Arbitration Law Review 153, 153; De Brabandere (n 4) 123.

6 Lucy Reed, Jan Paulsson and Nigel Blackaby, *Guide to ICSID Arbitration* (2nd edn, Kluwer Law International 2011) 71; Bjorklund and Vanhonnaeker (n 1) 353; Emmanuel Gaillard and Yas Banifatemi, 'The Meaning of "and" in Article 42(1), Second Sentence, of the Washington Convention: The Role of International Law in the ICSID Choice of Law Process' (2003) 18 ICSID Review – Foreign Investment Law Journal 375, 379; Massimo V Benedettelli, 'Determining the Applicable Law in Commercial and Investment Arbitration: Two Intertwined Road Maps for Conflicts-Solving' (2022) 37 ICSID Review – Foreign Investment Law Journal 687, 692; Banifatemi (n 2) 197.

 | DOI:10.1163/9789004420953_005

to refer to substantive principles of international law sourced from beyond IIL. Arbitration rules tend to favour the application of domestic legal systems[7] and limit the circumstances in which arbitral tribunals can refer to international law.[8] Arbitral tribunals must additionally classify the law and apply it to each element of a claim.[9] Consequently, there is a risk that arbitral tribunals may not be permitted to include principles of international law sourced from beyond IIL within the applicable law, or alternatively, may fail to apply them to a counterclaim. This chapter examines how host States can use party consent to direct an arbitral tribunal so that international law sourced from beyond IIL forms part of the applicable law of an investment dispute. It argues that host States should draft applicable law clauses in IIAs and foreign investment legislation that specify the applicable law and set out in what circumstances an arbitral tribunal should apply international law to a counterclaim.

To expand on this argument, the chapter proceeds in three sections. The first section considers how arbitral tribunals determine the applicable law and illustrates the extent to which international law can form part of the applicable law of an investment dispute (Section 4.2). The chapter then examines how arbitral tribunals have identified and characterised the applicable law in the context of counterclaims (Section 4.3). The section highlights that, in the absence of party consent, arbitral tribunals have limited opportunities to include international law as part of the applicable law in an investment dispute. Arbitral tribunals are either not given the interpretative scope to include international law as part of the applicable law or they must apply international law in a subsidiary manner to domestic law. Yet, these barriers can be overcome when host States include the applicable law in the terms of their party consent. Hence, host States potentially risk undermining the operation of counterclaims based on international law by failing to use party consent to specify the applicable law. Finally, the chapter discusses how host States can give full effect to counterclaims based on international law by using applicable law clauses that direct arbitral tribunals to include international law as part of the applicable law and specify how arbitral tribunals should apply international

7 Andrea Steingruber, 'Counterclaims: a Critical Analysis of Article 6 of the 2019 The Hague Resolution of the Institut de Droit International on the "Equality of Parties before International Investment Tribunals"' (2020) 35 ICSID Review – Foreign Investment Law Journal 595, 644.

8 Virtus Chitoo Igbokwe, 'Determination, Interpretation and Application of Substantive Law in Foreign Investment Treaty Arbitrations' (2006) 23 Journal of International Arbitration 267, 279–280.

9 Zachary Douglas, *The International Law of Investment Claims* (Cambridge University Press 2009) 44–46.

law to a counterclaim (Section 4.4). The chapter concludes with a summary of the findings (Section 4.5).

4.2 Determining the Applicable Law

An arbitral tribunal determines the applicable law in investment arbitration by interpreting party consent and the applicable arbitration rules.[10] Party consent governs the applicable law of an investment dispute. However, a host State's choice of law may not be comprehensive.[11] In the event that gaps arise, the arbitration rules guide arbitral tribunals to the most relevant sources of law. Once the applicable law has been identified, an arbitral tribunal must then evaluate the appropriateness of these legal sources for each claim in the investment dispute. In light of this process, this section highlights the extent to which international law can form part of the applicable law of an investment dispute.

The applicable law of an investment dispute is first determined by party consent.[12] Party consent is established when a host State's standing offer to arbitrate in an IIA or in foreign investment legislation is accepted by foreign investor.[13] A foreign investor accepts a standing offer to arbitrate when it commences investment arbitration proceedings.[14] The foreign investor's acceptance mirrors the terms of the standing offer, which includes any applicable

10 Banifatemi (n 2) 191; De Brabandere (n 4) 124.

11 Moss (n 5) 153; Andrea K Bjorklund, 'Applicable law in International Investment Disputes' in Chiara Giorgetti (ed), *Litigating International Investment Disputes: A practitioner's guide* (Brill 2014) 274.

12 Moss (n 5) 153; De Brabandere (n 4) 123.

13 Stefan Dudas, 'Treaty Counterclaims under the ICSID Convention' in Crina Baltag (ed), *ICSID Convention after 50 Years: Unsetttled Issues* (Kluwer Law International 2017) 395; Guiguo Wang, 'Consent in Investor-State Arbitration: A Critical Analysis' (2014) 13 Chinese Journal of International Law 335, 336; Konstanze Von Papp, 'Biting the Bullet or Redefining Consent in Investor-State Arbitration: Pre-Arbitration Requirements After *BG Group v Argentina*' (2015) 16 Journal of World Investment and Trade 695, 699; Dafina Atanasova, Adrián Martínez Benoit and Josef Ostřanský, 'The Legal Framework for Counterclaims in Investment Treaty Arbitration' (2014) 31 Journal of International Arbitration 357, 366; Hanno Wehland, 'Jurisdiction and Admissibility in Proceedings under the ICSID Convention and the Additional Facility Rules' in Crina Baltag (ed), *ICSID Convention After 50 Years: Unsetttled Issues* (Kluwer Law International 2017) 239; Andrea Steingruber, *Consent in International Arbitration* (Oxford University Press 2012) 206.

14 De Brabandere (n 4) 125.

law clause contained in the IIA or foreign investment legislation.[15] Therefore, a host State can determine the applicable law of an investment dispute by incorporating an applicable law clause into the terms of its standing offer.

An arbitral tribunal must interpret the terms of any applicable law clause to determine the intention of the disputing parties.[16] The rules of treaty interpretation set out in Articles 31–33 VCLT apply to an applicable law clause in an IIA.[17] The rules encompass the principle of systemic integration, which is set out in article 31(3)(c) VCLT. Systemic integration enables a treaty interpreter to refer to principles of international law external to the treaty being interpreted to ensure that international law is understood and applied in a coherent manner across different legal regimes.[18] Consequently, arbitral tribunals may interpret an applicable law clause in an IIA to include principles of international law sourced from beyond IIL. In contrast, applicable law clauses set out in foreign investment legislation are subject to variable interpretation methods including principles of statutory interpretation, rules of treaty interpretation and the international law on unilateral declarations by States.[19] Therefore, it remains unclear to what extent principles of international law sourced from beyond IIL can be referred to by an arbitral tribunal when an applicable law clause is set out in foreign investment legislation.

Despite the ability of host States to specify the applicable law, applicable law clauses are not common in IIAs and are rarely found in foreign investment

15 Pierre Lalive and Laura Halonen, 'On the Availability of Counterclaims in Investment Treaty Arbitration' (2011) II Czech Yearbook of International Law 141, 150; Douglas (n 9) 258.

16 The disputing parties are the host State and the foreign investor. The foreign investor is deemed to have consented to an applicable law clause despite not being able to influence the terms of the host State's offer.

17 Reed, Paulsson and Blackaby (n 6) 73; W Michael Reisman and Mahnoush J Arsanjani, 'Applicable Law under the ICSID Convention: The Tortured History of the Interpretion of Article 42' in Meg Kinnear and others (eds), *Building International Investment Law: The First 50 Years of ICSID* (Kluwer Law International 2015) 29; Bjorklund and Vanhonnaeker (n 1) 367.

18 Campbell McLachlan, 'The Principle of Systemic Integration and Article 31(3)(c) of the Vienna Convention' (2005) 54 International and Comparative Law Quarterly 279. See Bjorklund (n 11) 282.

19 Romesh Weeramantry, *Treaty Interpretation in Investment Arbitration* (Oxford University Press 2012) 167. The variation in wording may contribute to the diverse interpretations. See Michele Potestà, 'The Interpretation of Consent to ICSID Arbitration Contained in Domestic Investment Laws' (2011) 27 Arbitration International 149, 154–160. For a full discussion, see Section 2.3.

legislation.[20] In the absence of an applicable law clause, the arbitral tribunal must identify the applicable law in its entirety.[21] Even when an applicable law clause is included in an IIA, it is not usually comprehensive. Applicable law clauses in IIAs often refer to the IIA as a source of applicable law.[22] Frequently, the IIA is supplemented by the 'rules of international law' or '(general) principles of international law'.[23] Should an applicable law clause in an IIA refer to domestic law,[24] which is less common,[25] it is often limited to host State domestic law.[26] As a result, applicable law clauses do not provide detailed guidance to arbitral tribunals. When host States frame the applicable law in general terms, arbitral tribunals must fill any gaps in the coverage of the selected laws to give full effect to the disputing parties' intentions.[27] How arbitral tribunals undertake this process influences the degree to which international law may form part of the applicable law of an investment dispute.

Arbitration rules guide an arbitral tribunal when it needs to fill gaps in the applicable law. However, the arbitration rules were drafted on the basis that arbitral tribunals are resolving contractual disputes.[28] Hence, the arbitration rules tend to direct arbitral tribunals to domestic legal systems, and more specifically the host State's domestic law, because the host State's legal system is likely to have the closest connection to a contractual claim.[29] Arbitral tribunals are still able to refer to international law, however, the arbitration rules often frame international law as a supplementary source of law.[30] The distinction

---

20 Reed, Paulsson and Blackaby (n 6) 71; Bjorklund and Vanhonnaeker (n 1) 353; Gaillard and Banifatemi (n 6) 37; Benedettelli (n 6) 69; Banifatemi (n 2) 197.

21 ICSID Convention Article 42(2) does not permit an arbitral tribunal to make a finding of *non liquet*.

22 See Atanasova (n 1) 409; Banifatemi (n 2) 197. In these instances, a counterclaim is not possible unless the IIA contains reciprocal obligations (*Spyridon Roussalis v. Romania* ICSID Case No ARB/06/1, Award, 7 December 2011 [871]).

23 Atanasova (n 1) 409; Bjorklund and Vanhonnaeker (n 1) 364; Gaillard and Banifatemi (n 6) 377; Banifatemi (n 2) 197.

24 Atanasova (n 1) 411.

25 ibid 408, 411.

26 ibid 411.

27 Benedettelli (n 6) 692.

28 Steingruber, 'Counterclaims: a Critical Analysis of Article 6 of the 2019 The Hague Resolution of the Institut de Droit International on the "Equality of Parties before International Investment Tribunals"' (n 7) 633. In relation to the ICSID Convention, see Bjorklund and Vanhonnaeker (n 1) 349.

29 Steingruber, 'Counterclaims: a Critical Analysis of Article 6 of the 2019 The Hague Resolution of the Institut de Droit International on the "Equality of Parties before International Investment Tribunals"' (n 7) 644.

30 See Section 4.3 below.

between domestic law and international law in the arbitration rules becomes significant because, when identifying the applicable law, arbitral tribunals must navigate the hybrid structure of IIL.

IIL functions by relying on interactions between international law and domestic law.[31] Consequently, to substantiate a claim in IIL, an arbitral tribunal will frequently need to refer to different legal orders.[32] For example, investment disputes based on investment protection standards invoke international law as the foundation of a claim.[33] Investment protection standards are sourced either in an IIA or in foreign investment legislation that refers to international standards. However, whether an obligation has been breached will usually require an arbitral tribunal to examine domestic law, either in the form of domestic legislation or contractual provisions, to determine whether the host State's conduct has breached the investment protection standard.[34] In some instances, an arbitral tribunal will need to refer to domestic law to evaluate whether the investment protection standard applies. For example, when determining whether the foreign investor's investment is covered by the IIA, the arbitral tribunal will need to refer to domestic law to identify the asset owned by the foreign investor before deciding if it falls within the definition of investment in an IIA.[35] Thus, when applying IIL, arbitral tribunals must consider the interrelationship between international law and domestic law.

Further, arbitral tribunals may use international law and domestic law for different purposes. Both international law and domestic law can be used as a primary source of law to determine the substance of the claim, or as a secondary source of law in support of a claim. For instance, arbitral tribunals are likely to refer to secondary sources of law like principles of contractual interpretation or the rules of treaty interpretation to ascertain the content of the relevant laws.[36] As the arbitration rules do not provide a strict hierarchy between

31 Monique Sasson, *Substantive Law in Investment Treaty Arbitration: The Unsettled Relationship Between International Law and Municipal Law* (Kluwer Law International 2010) xxvi; Igbokwe (n 8) 285; Laurence Boisson de Chazournes, 'The Blurring of the Line Between Contract-Based and Treaty-Based Investment Arbitration' (2019) 1 ITA in Review 94, 98; Banifatemi (n 2) 204; Tomoko Ishikawa, *Corporate Environmental Responsibility in Investor-State Dispute Settlement: The Unexhausted Potential of Current Mechanisms* (Cambridge University Press 2022) 120.

32 Douglas (n 9) 44; Sasson (n 31) xxvi; Benedettelli (n 6) 691.

33 Douglas (n 9) 81; Bjorklund and Vanhonnaeker (n 1) 366.

34 Igbokwe (n 8) 285; Boisson de Chazournes (n 31) 102; De Brabandere (n 4) 127.

35 Sasson (n 31) xxix-xxx; Reed, Paulsson and Blackaby (n 6) 71; Igbokwe (n 8) 285; De Brabandere (n 4) 127.

36 Atanasova (n 1) 404.

these sources of law,[37] and the terms of party consent infrequently set out this relationship,[38] arbitral tribunals must characterise the law to identify which legal order it belongs to and to determine its applicability to each aspect of the dispute.[39] Where a claim is made up of elements that draw from different legal orders, an arbitral tribunal will need to 'depecage'[40] each source of law to the appropriate part of the claim.[41] Therefore, an arbitral tribunal's characterisation of the law as either international law or domestic law will determine whether the legal obligation forms part of the applicable law, and if so, whether it is a primary or supplementary source of law.[42]

The characterisation process undertaken by an arbitral tribunal can determine the extent to which substantive principles of international law sourced from beyond IIL form part of the applicable law in any given investment dispute. Nevertheless, characterising the law as either international or domestic is not necessarily problematic for counterclaims based on international law. For an arbitral tribunal to give effect to counterclaims based on international law, international law sourced from beyond IIL can be sourced in the applicable law either directly or indirectly. If international law forms part of the applicable law, an arbitral tribunal can support a counterclaim by directly referring to principles of international law. If domestic law is included in the applicable law, any principles of international law mirrored in domestic law can be applied to the counterclaim.[43] Hence, international law can also be indirectly applied to a counterclaim. The distinction between characterising a legal principle as being sourced from either international law or domestic law becomes significant if the arbitral tribunal does not refer to international law and the principles of international law have not been implemented in the domestic

37 Douglas (n 9) 44.

38 ibid.

39 ibid 45–46.

40 Depecage refers to applying different laws to different aspects of a case. See Bjorklund and Vanhonnaeker (n 1) 367; Bjorklund (n 11) 277–278.

41 Ibrahim F J Shihata and Antonio R Parra, 'Applicable Substantive Law in Disputes Between States and Private Foreign Parties: The Case of Arbitration under the ICSID Convention' (1994) 9 ICSID Review – Foreign Investment Law Journal 183, 189; Bjorklund and Vanhonnaeker (n 1) 355.

42 Bjorklund and Vanhonnaeker (n 1) 367; Benedettelli (n 6) 720; Banifatemi (n 2) 207. For a discussion of characterisation, see Hege Elisabeth Kjos, *Applicable Law in Investor-State Arbitration: The Interplay between National and International Law* (Oxford University Press 2013) 106–111.

43 The extent to which domestic law captures principles of customary international may vary from State to State (Kate Parlett, 'Claims under Customary International Law in ICSID Arbitration' (2016) 31 ICSID Review – Foreign Investment Law Journal 439, 445).

law. In this instance, the priority granted to domestic law by the arbitration rules could potentially exclude the principles of international law from the applicable law.

Given that a wide range of legal principles could apply to a counterclaim based on international law, it is desirable for a host State to ensure that international law, domestic law and any relevant contracts form part of the applicable law of the investment dispute. This formulation permits arbitral tribunals to refer to a wider range of sources of law that can give effect to all elements of a counterclaim. However, even if all of these sources are included, the arbitral tribunal will decide which law is applied to each aspect of a claim as part of the characterisation process.[44] Thus, the role that principles of international law sourced from beyond IIL can potentially play in counterclaims is contingent on how an arbitral tribunal characterises the counterclaim.

In conclusion, host States can specify the applicable law using applicable law clauses, but these provisions are rare and are not comprehensive. Therefore, arbitral tribunals are conferred with the power to determine the applicable law to the extent that party consent does not apply and are guided by the applicable arbitration rules. Arbitration rules tend to favour the application of the host State's domestic law, which can be problematic given IIL's hybrid structure. However, because principles of international law can be directly and indirectly sourced in the applicable law, their potential scope of application is increased. Nonetheless, arbitral tribunals still need to characterise the law and apply it to an investment dispute. As a result, the extent to which substantive principles of international law sourced from beyond IIL apply is subject to an arbitral tribunal's characterisation of the counterclaim. Hence, it is necessary to review arbitral practice to identify the extent to which international law does form part of the applicable law of investment disputes.

4.3 Applicable Law and Arbitration Rules

Party consent and arbitration rules direct arbitral tribunals to the sources of law that comprise the applicable law of an investment dispute. This section reviews arbitral practice to identify how arbitral tribunals determine the applicable law with an emphasis on disputes involving counterclaims. It argues that, in the absence of party consent, arbitral tribunals have limited opportunities to include international law as part of the applicable law because the

44 Benedettelli (n 6) 719.

arbitration rules minimise the circumstances in which international law can be considered. Thus, the arbitration rules have the potential to unduly limit the application of substantive principles of international law sourced from beyond IIL, which could restrict the use of counterclaims based on international law. However, these limitations can be overcome if host States set out the applicable law in the terms of their party consent. To substantiate these arguments, this section discusses arbitral practice based on the ICSID Convention and ICSID Arbitration Rules, the ICSID AF Arbitration Rules and the UNCITRAL Arbitration Rules before analysing how arbitral practice that determines the applicable law can impact counterclaims based on international law.

4.3.1 *ICSID Convention and ICSID Arbitration Rules*

In ICSID arbitral practice, Article 42(1) ICSID Convention governs how arbitral tribunals ascertain the applicable law. This provision is comprised of two sentences. The first sentence deals with instances where the parties have chosen the applicable law and the second sentence applies when there is an absence of a choice of law.[45] Arbitral tribunals are directed to consider different factors under each sentence of Article 42(1) ICSID Convention. Therefore, an arbitral tribunal must ascertain whether a choice of law has been made and apply Article 42(1) ICSID Convention appropriately.

When the disputing parties have made a choice of law, the arbitral tribunal is directed to the applicable law clause. The first sentence of Article 42(1) ICSID Convention gives effect to party consent[46] by requiring that an arbitral tribunal apply 'such rules of law as may be agreed by the parties'. Thus, when the disputing parties select the applicable law, the arbitral tribunal must interpret

45 Shihata and Parra (n 41) 188, 191; Bjorklund and Vanhonnaeker (n 1) 351–352.

46 AFM Maniruzzaman, 'International Commercial Arbitration: The Conflict of Laws Issues in Determining the Applicable Substantive Law in the Context of Investment Agreements' (1993) 40 Netherlands International Law Review 201, 233; Aron Broches, *Selected Essays: World Bank, ICSID and Other Subjects of Public and Private International Law* (Martinus Nijhoff 1995) 182–183, 184; Okezie Chukwumerije, 'International Law and Article 42 of the ICSID Convention' (1997) 14 Journal of International Arbitration 79, 83, 85; Christoph Schreuer, *The ICSID Convention: A Commentary* (Cambridge University Press 2001) 553, 558–559; Richard H Kriendler, 'The Law Applicable to International Investment Disputes' in Norbert Horn (ed), *Arbitrating Foreign Investment Disputes: Procedural and Substantive Legal Aspects* (Kluwer Law International 2004) 402; Begic (n 2) 5, 11, 13; Annie Leeks, 'The Relationship Between Bilateral Investment Treaty Arbitration and the Wider Corpus of International Law: The ICSID Approach' (2007) 65 University of Toronto Faculty of Law Review 1, 10; Banifatemi (n 2) 191, 192; Yavaslau Kryvoi, *International Centre for Settlement of Investment Disputes* (Kluwer Law International 2010) 61.

their intention[47] with reference to precise terms used by the disputing parties. In *Urbaser* v *Argentina*,[48] Article X(5) Spain-Argentina BIT provided that the applicable law was the BIT.[49] However, the applicable law clause also permitted reference to be made to either another treaty in force between the Parties, the host State's domestic law or 'general principles of international law',[50] provided that the BIT was connected to, or referred to, these sources of law.[51] Given that party consent in the BIT was not limited to claims based on rights directly set out in the BIT,[52] and that Article VII(1) of the BIT permitted the disputing parties to refer to agreements entered into by the Contracting Parties that were more favourable,[53] the arbitral tribunal concluded that the applicable law extended to international law sourced from beyond the BIT.[54] The arbitral tribunal's interpretation of the applicable law clause aligns with the disputing parties' intentions. An arbitral tribunal is bound by the terms of the applicable law clause and cannot extend the terms of party consent. Consequently, whilst party consent encompassed international law in this dispute, arbitral tribunals may be restricted by applicable law clauses drafted in narrower terms.

Arbitral tribunals may also determine if the disputing parties have inferred a choice of law. When a choice of law is inferred, arbitral tribunals are not bound by the text of an applicable law clause and can consider a range of factors to support their conclusions. Nonetheless, arbitral tribunals need to ensure that the surrounding circumstances support their conclusion.[55] Hence, arbitral tribunals have referred to provisions set out in domestic legislation permitting ICSID arbitration,[56] the terms of IIAs conferring ICSID with jurisdiction,[57]

---

47 Banifatemi (n 2) 199.

48 *Urbaser S.A. and Consorcio de Aguas Bilbao Biskaia, Bilbao Biskaia Ur Partzuergoa v. Argentine Republic* ICSID Case No ARB/07/26, Award, 8 December 2016.

49 ibid [1188].

50 ibid.

51 ibid.

52 ibid [1191].

53 ibid [1192].

54 ibid.

55 Shihata and Parra (n 41) 190; Chukwumerije (n 46) 92–93; Banifatemi (n 2) 198.

56 Schreuer (n 46) 574–576. See, for example, Joachim Delaney and Daniel Barstow Magraw, 'Procedural Transparency' in Peter T Muchlinski, Federico Ortino and Christoph Schreuer (eds), *The Oxford Handbook of International Investment Law* (Oxford University Press 2008).

57 Schreuer (n 46) 581–583. It has been argued that the invocation of dispute resolution provisions in a treaty implicitly permits the arbitral tribunal to refer to rules of general international law to supplement the treaty (Antonio R Parra, 'Applicable Substantive Law in ICSID Arbitrations Initiated Under Investment Treaties' (2001) 16 ICSID Review – Foreign

and the submissions of the disputing parties[58] to identify the applicable law. Thus, whilst an arbitral tribunal can infer the applicable law, its choice must be based on the surrounding evidence.

If the disputing parties have not selected the applicable law, an arbitral tribunal must consider specific sources of law based on the second sentence of Article 42(1) ICSID Convention. The second sentence directs an arbitral tribunal to 'apply the law of the Contracting State party to the dispute (including its rules on the conflict of laws) and such rules of international law as may be applicable'. As a result, the second sentence of Article 42(1) ICSID Convention is comprised of two elements: (1) a default choice of host State law; and (2) a supplementary role for international law.[59] Therefore, it is necessary to consider the impact of each element on the content of the applicable law.

An arbitral tribunal must apply domestic law to an investment dispute in the absence of party consent.[60] When identifying which domestic law should be applied, the second sentence of Article 42(1) ICSID Convention prioritises host State law[61] because it is most likely to have the closest connection to the investment that is the subject of the dispute.[62] Nonetheless, the provision also requires an arbitral tribunal to apply the host State's conflict of laws rules to identify if another domestic legal system is more appropriate.[63] The application of the conflict of laws rules will direct an arbitral tribunal to the most closely connected domestic legal system if it is not host State law. The significance of primarily focusing on host State law is evidenced by the decisions in *Burlington* v *Ecuador*[64] and *Perenco* v *Ecuador*.[65] In *Burlington* v *Ecuador*, the host State presented two counterclaims, one relating to environmental damage

---

Investment Law Journal 20, 21; Boisson de Chazournes (n 31) 102; c.f. Igbokwe (n 8) 281–283).

58 Schreuer (n 46) 577–581.

59 Regarding the potential impact of this language, see Gaillard and Banifatemi (n 6) 410.

60 ibid 376.

61 Schreuer (n 46) 596.

62 Maniruzzaman (n 46) 233; Schreuer (n 46) 599. As to the reasons why, see Bjorklund and Vanhonnaeker (n 1) 357. The adoption of host State law is subject to the operation of conflict of laws rules, therefore, if another domestic legal system is more closely connected to the investment, that law is to be applied instead (Chukwumerije (n 46) 95; Schreuer (n 46) 606; Begic (n 2) 106).

63 See Shihata and Parra (n 41) who suggest that the law of another State may be appropriate, when for example 'the investment involved takes the form of commercial loan' (191).

64 *Burlington Resources Inc. v. Republic of Ecuador* ICSID Case No ARB/08/5, Decision on Counterclaims, 7 February 2017.

65 *Perenco Ecuador Limited v. Republic of Ecuador* ICSID Case No ARB/08/6, Interim Decision on the Environmental Counterclaim, 11 August 2015.

and one relating to damage to infrastructure. Ecuador asserted that the relevant law for the environmental counterclaims was Ecuadorian tort law, but also relied on principles set out in the production sharing contracts.[66] The arbitral tribunal relied on the second sentence of Article 42(1) ICSID Convention, and decided to apply Ecuadorian law (consisting primarily of tort law, but also the production sharing contracts) to the counterclaim unless any particular matters called for the arbitral tribunal to refer to international law.[67] Hence, the arbitral tribunal prioritised host State law in accordance with the second sentence of Article 42(1) ICSID Convention. The arbitral tribunal in *Perenco* v *Ecuador* addressed counterclaims that mirrored those in *Burlington* but made no reference to Article 42(1) ICSID Convention.[68] The arbitral tribunal identified Ecuador's public law framework that governed the environment[69] and the production sharing contracts that governed operations in the oil fields in question[70] as comprising the applicable law. The arbitral tribunal's discussion suggests that the arbitral tribunal was applying the host State law based on the second sentence of Article 42(1) ICSID Convention. Thus, the second sentence of Article 42(1) ICSID Convention requires that an arbitral tribunal gives primacy to host State law when this law can govern a dispute.

Although an arbitral tribunal is clearly directed to host State law as the applicable domestic law, an arbitral tribunal is given more latitude regarding the role of international law.[71] The second sentence of Article 42(1) ICSID Convention enables an arbitral tribunal to have recourse to international law[72] when it 'may be applicable'.[73] The traditional interpretation given to this provision is to limit the role of international law to fill a lacuna in domestic law,

66 *Burlington Resources Inc. v. Republic of Ecuador* (n 64) [73].

67 ibid [74].

68 *Perenco Ecuador Limited v. Republic of Ecuador, Interim Decision on the Environmental Counterclaim* (n 65) [65].

69 ibid [65]–[107].

70 ibid [108]–[114].

71 Igbokwe (n 8) 279.

72 For the purposes of ICSID Convention Article 42(1), international law refers to those sources of law referred to in United Nations, Statute of the International Court of Justice, 18 April 1946, Article 38(1) (Statute of the ICJ) (ICSID, 'Report of the Executive Directors on the Convention on the Settlement of Investment Disputes Between States and Nationals of other States' <https://icsid.worldbank.org/rules-regulations/convention/report/section-one> accessed 22 February 2023). ICSID practice has also extended this to consideration of prior decisions and soft law instruments such as United Nations General Assembly Resolutions (Schreuer (n 46) 616–617, 618; Kryvoi (n 46) 66–67).

73 For an example of when an arbitral tribunal has considered it to be applicable, see *Ioan Micula and others v. Romania II* ICSID Case No ARB/14/29, Award, 5 March 2020 [348].

or alternatively to correct domestic law that is in violation with principles of international law.[74] Consequently, to ensure that host State law (or the law to be applied under the host State's conflict of laws rules) is in compliance with international law, both legal systems should be applied to the dispute before the ICSID tribunal.[75] International law will only be referred to if domestic law is in conflict with international law or domestic law does not address the legal question.[76] A more recent view is that both domestic law and international law should be applied with equal weight.[77] This requires an ICSID tribunal to consider the issue in dispute and undertake a process of classifying each aspect of the dispute to determine whether domestic or international law should apply.[78] In accordance with this approach, domestic law and international law interact in a complementary manner.[79] The divergence in approaches to the relationship between domestic law and international law within the second sentence of Article 42(1) ICSID Convention remains contentious, with ICSID

74 Maniruzzaman (n 46) 234, 235; Chukwumerije (n 46) 98; Schreuer (n 46) 623; Gaillard and Banifatemi (n 6) 375; Begic (n 2) 155; Andrea Giardina, 'International Investment Arbitration: Recent Developments as to the Applicable Law and Unilateral Recourse' (2006) 5 The Law and Practice of International Courts and Tribunals 29, 30; Leeks (n 46) 18; Banifatemi (n 2) 201–202; Ivar Alvik, 'The Hybrid Nature of Investment Treaty Arbitration – Straddling the National/International Divide' in Christoffer Erikson and Marius Emberland (eds), *The New International Law – An Anthology* (Martinus Nijhoff Publishers 2010) 95; Shihata and Parra (n 41) 192; De Brabandere (n 4) 125. See for example, Suzanne Spears, 'Making Way for the Public Interest in International Investment Agreements' in Chester Brown and Kate Miles (eds), *Evolution in Investment Treaty Law and Arbitration* (Cambridge University Press 2011) para 10.1.2.

75 Schreuer (n 46) 631; Begic (n 2) 106. See W Michael Reisman, 'The Regime for Lacunae in the ICSID Choice of Law Provision and the Question of Its Threshold' (2000) 15 ICSID Review – Foreign Investment Law Journal 362 who limits the application of international law to *jus cogens* provisions c.f. Reisman and Arsanjani (n 17) who view a dispute based on IIA as a choice of international law as the applicable law.

76 See *Klöckner Industrie-Anlagen GmbH v United Republic of Cameroon* ICSID Case No ARB/81/2, Decision on Annulment, 3 May 1985 [69]; *Amco Asia Corporation v. Republic of Indonesia* ICSID Case No ARB/81/1, Decision on Annulment, 16 May 1986 [20]–[22]. See Bjorklund and Vanhonnaeker (n 1) 362; Gaillard and Banifatemi (n 6) 389–393; Benedettelli (n 6) 692.

77 See for example, *Azurix Corp v. The Argentine Republic* ICSID Case No ARB/01/12, Award, 14 July 2006 [66]–[67]; Organisation for Economic Co-operation and Development, *International Investment Law: Understanding Concepts and Tracking Innovations* (Organisation for Economic Co-operation and Development Publishing 2008) para 441; Bjorklund and Vanhonnaeker (n 1).

78 *Wena Hotels Ltd v. Arab Republic of Egypt* ICSID Case No ARB/98/4, Annulment Proceeding, 5 February 2002 [40]–[41]. See Gaillard and Banifatemi (n 6) 403–411; Banifatemi (n 2) 203; Douglas (n 9) 45–52.

79 Alvik (n 74) 96.

arbitral tribunals applying both variably.[80] Consequently, the extent to which international law can be considered to fall within the applicable law of an ICSID tribunal in the absence of any agreement between the parties remains dependent on the arbitral tribunal's interpretation of 'applicable' in the second sentence of Article 42(1) ICSID Convention. As a result, the second sentence of Article 42(1) ICSID Convention confers arbitral tribunals with no choice regarding the primacy of host State law but grants more flexibility in relation to the supplementary function of international law in the applicable law.

Although Article 42(1) ICSID Convention enables investment arbitrators to identify the applicable law of an investment dispute, it does not dictate how an arbitral tribunal should proceed to characterise each element of the investment dispute before applying the law.[81] Therefore, this process is left to an arbitral tribunal's judgment.[82] The process of characterising claims as either being based in international law or domestic law and identifying the corresponding laws is not usually problematic.[83] Nonetheless, there is the risk that a principle of international law may be sourced in either domestic law or international law. If an arbitral tribunal classifies the claim and the law as belonging to different legal orders, then some principles of international law may be overlooked if they are only sourced in the one legal order. Hence, it is not guaranteed that the inclusion of a principle of international law in the applicable law will result in it being applied to a claim in the expected manner.

In short, ICSID arbitral tribunals are directed to different sources when determining the applicable law of a dispute. The sources and methods of identifying the law that arbitral tribunals can use varies based on the degree to which the disputing parties have exercised party autonomy to decide the applicable law and the terms of Article 42(1) ICSID Convention. An arbitral tribunal's ability to include international law in the applicable law becomes less certain the more vague the disputing parties are when identifying the applicable law. Thus, if international law is not chosen by the disputing parties as forming part of the applicable law, there is a risk it could be excluded and host State law will apply instead. Even if international law does form part of

80 See Benedetta Cappiello, 'Applicable Law in Investment Arbitration' in Julian Chaisse, Leïla Choukroune and Sufian Jusoh (eds), *Handbook of International Investment Law and Policy* (Springer 2021) 1133. For a discussion of the approaches, see Sasson (n 31).

81 Douglas (n 9) 129.

82 See ibid 42; Bjorklund and Vanhonnaeker (n 1) 368–369. As to the limits of an arbitral tribunal's discretion see *Venezuela Holdings B.V. et. al. v Bolivarian Republic of Venzuela* ICSID Case No, ARB/07/27, Decision on Annulment, 9 March 2017 [181].

83 See Bjorklund and Vanhonnaeker (n 1) 365–367.

the applicable law, an arbitral tribunal may exercise its judgment not to apply international law depending on how it has characterised the claim and the law.

4.3.2 *ICSID Additional Facility Arbitration Rules*

In ICSID AF arbitral practice, arbitral tribunals determine the applicable law in accordance with Article 54(1) ICSID AF Arbitration Rules (2006) and Rule 68(1) ICSID AF Arbitration Rules (2022). The ICSID AF Arbitration Rules point arbitral tribunals to varied sources of law when ascertaining the applicable law.

When the disputing parties have chosen the applicable law, arbitral tribunals must apply the disputing parties' choice. Both versions of the ICSID AF Arbitration Rules require an arbitral tribunal to initially refer to party consent to determine the applicable law.[84] Thus, arbitral tribunals must comply with any applicable law clause.[85] For example, the ICSID AF arbitral tribunals in *Gold Reserve Inc.* v *Venezuela*[86] and *Rusoro Mining* v *Venezuela*[87] were bound to apply the BIT together with applicable rules of international law[88] because this was the law specified in the applicable law clause in the Canada-Venezuela BIT.[89] Although these awards addressed originating claims (rather than counterclaims) the decisions evidence that when party consent is present, an arbitral tribunal must interpret the applicable law clause.

In the absence of party consent, arbitral tribunals are directed to domestic law and international law when ascertaining the applicable law. How these sources of law are applied depends on whether the 2006 or the 2022 edition of the ICSID AF Arbitration Rules have been selected. Article 54(1) ICSID AF

---

84 ICSID AF Arbitration Rules (2006) Article 54(1) and ICSID AF Arbitration Rules (2022) Rule 68(1).

85 The choice of law may also be sourced in a contractual provision. In *Lao Holdings N.V. v Laos*, the arbitral tribunal applied a choice of law that was contained in a deed of settlement (*Lao Holdings N.V. v. Lao People's Democratic Republic I* ICSID Case No ARB(AF)/12/6, Interim Ruling on Issues Arising Under the Deed of Settlement, 19 December 2014 [32]). When interpreting this provision and applying the law, the arbitral tribunal stressed that the arbitration remained treaty based and did not transform the arbitration into international commercial arbitration (*Lao Holdings N.V. v. Lao People's Democratic Republic I* ICSID Case No ARB(AF)/12/6, Decision on the Merits of Claimants Second Material Breach Application, 15 December 2017 [105]).

86 *Gold Reserve Inc. v. Bolivarian Republic of Venezuela* ICSID Case No ARB(AF)/09/1, Award, 22 September 2014.

87 *Rusoro Mining Ltd. v. Bolivarian Republic of Venezuela* ICSID Case No ARB(AF)/12/5, Award, 22 August 2016.

88 *Gold Reserve Inc. v. Bolivarian Republic of Venezuela* (n 86) [533]; *Rusoro Mining Ltd. v. Bolivarian Republic of Venezuela* (n 87) [349].

89 Article VII(7) provides that 'A tribunal established under this Article shall decide the issues in dispute in accordance with this Agreement and applicable rules of international law'.

Arbitration Rules (2006)[90] requires the arbitral tribunal to use conflict of laws rules to initially identify the applicable law, which the arbitral tribunal can supplement with any rules of international law that it deems relevant. Consequently, like ICSID arbitration, the requirement that an arbitral tribunal apply conflict of laws rules limits the applicable law to domestic law in the first instance. However, unlike ICSID arbitration, this provision does not assume that the host State will have the closest connection. Therefore, this provision requires an arbitral tribunal to apply conflict of laws rules to identify the most appropriate legal system. Despite the potential for varied results, in practice, the host State is likely to have the closest connection to the investment dispute. Hence, the arbitral tribunal is most likely to reach the same result as would be found in ICSID arbitration, which is that host State law will be applied.

The ICSID AF Arbitration Rules (2006) grant an ICSID AF arbitral tribunal more interpretative scope when considering the role of international law. International law[91] plays a secondary function to domestic law and is only applied when it is 'applicable'. The use of this term mirrors the language of Article 42(1) ICSID Convention. Should ICSID AF arbitral tribunals draw from ICSID arbitral jurisprudence when interpreting Article 54(1) ICSID AF Arbitration Rules (2006), divergent approaches regarding when international law can be invoked may arise. ICSID arbitration has taken conflicting views as to whether international law should only play a supplementary role to domestic law or whether international law and domestic law should be given equal weight as part of the applicable law (see Section 4.3.1).[92] Thus, how arbitral tribunals will exercise their judgment is uncertain. Nonetheless, international law is granted a more limited role compared to domestic law and arbitral tribunals can potentially exercise their judgment to limit the role of international law even further.

---

90 This provision applies to substantive disputes and not to jurisdictional issues (*Strabag SE, Raiffeisen Centrobank AG and Syrena Immobilien Holding AG v. Republic of Poland* ICSID Case No ADHOC/15/1, Partial Award on Jurisdiction, 4 March 2020 [8.106] c.f. *Lao Holdings N.V. v. Lao People's Democratic Republic I* (n 85) [32]). This interpretation is based on the phrase 'as applicable to the substance of the dispute' found in both ICSID AF Arbitration Rules (2006) Article 54 and ICSID Convention Article 42.

91 The arbitral tribunal in *Gold Reserve Inc.* v *Venezuela*, in obiter, interpreted the reference to 'such rules of international law as may be applicable' in the absence of party choice as being those sources identified in Article 38 Statute of the ICJ (n 72)(*Gold Reserve Inc. v. Bolivarian Republic of Venezuela* (n 86) [575]).

92 See Gaillard and Banifatemi (n 6); Monique Sasson, 'The Applicable Law and the ICSID Convention' in Crina Baltag (ed), *ICSID Convention after 50 Years: Unsettled Issues* (Kluwer Law International 2017).

Arbitral tribunals are conferred with more latitude under Rule 68(1) ICSID AF Arbitration Rules (2022). Rule 68(1) ICSID AF Arbitration Rules (2022) provides that an arbitral tribunal shall apply the law it 'determines' to be applicable and any rules of international law it 'considers' to be applicable. As a result, arbitral tribunals have more flexibility as to how they identify the applicable law because they do not have to comply with a specific methodology to identify the law. Arbitral tribunals are likely to identify domestic law based on the closest connection to the investment dispute, however, they do not need to apply conflict of laws rules to identify the applicable domestic law. Whether international law is considered applicable may depend on how arbitral tribunals understand the role of international law in investment disputes. It is more likely that international law will apply if it is understood as possessing equal weight to domestic law. Consequently, Rule 68(1) ICSID AF Arbitration Rules (2022) confers arbitral tribunals with greater power to decide the applicable law but does not mean that the power will be exercised to include more principles of international law.

How an ICSID AF arbitral tribunal uses principles of international law sourced from the applicable law is contingent on the characterisation process. Arbitral tribunals exercise their judgment to characterise a claim and apply the law.[93] Whilst principles of international law can be sourced in domestic law and international law, whether they are applied to an investment dispute will depend on whether an arbitral tribunal has classified a claim as domestic or international in nature. Therefore, it is not certain that principles of international law sourced from either domestic law or international will be applied an investment dispute.

In conclusion, the ICSID AF Arbitration Rules direct arbitral tribunals to applicable law clauses when disputing parties have chosen the applicable law. In the absence of a choice of law, when applying Article 54(1) ICSID AF Arbitration Rules (2006), the arbitral tribunal must apply conflict of laws rules and will only refer to international law if the arbitral tribunal considers that it is applicable to a dispute. In accordance with Rule 68(1) ICSID AF Arbitration Rules (2022), an arbitral tribunal has more flexibility regarding how it identifies the applicable law, including the extent to which it considers international law to be relevant to the dispute. Further, all ICSID AF arbitral tribunals are free to characterise the law and apply it to different elements of the dispute as they see fit. Thus, given that ICSID AF arbitral tribunals are able to exercise

93 Douglas (n 9) 45–46.

their judgment regarding the significance of international law, there is a risk that international law may not form part of the applicable law to the dispute.

4.3.3 *UNCITRAL Arbitration Rules*

The UNCITRAL Arbitration Rules (1976) and the UNCITRAL Arbitration Rules (2010) differ in their approaches to identifying the applicable law. Nonetheless, both give effect to party autonomy before providing a means of ascertaining the applicable law in the absence of party choice. To consider how arbitral tribunals determine the applicable law, the UNCITRAL Arbitration Rules (1976) and the UNCITRAL Arbitration Rules (2010) will be considered in turn.

The disputing parties are permitted to select the law that applies to the substance of the dispute in accordance with Article 33(1) UNCITRAL Arbitration Rules (1976). A choice of law may be express or implied, but it must be unambiguous.[94] Further, the disputing parties may choose the law at any time, including during the arbitration proceedings.[95] When the disputing parties designate the law, the arbitral tribunal must interpret that choice.[96] For example, Article 1131(1) NAFTA dictates that investment disputes are to be resolved in accordance with NAFTA and any applicable rules of international law.[97] To comply with this choice, arbitral tribunals will apply the terms of NAFTA and international law to the extent necessary to give effect to the IIA.[98] Hence, once the disputing parties have made a clear choice of law, the scope of the applicable law is constrained by that choice.

---

94 David D Caron and Lee Caplan, *The UNCITRAL Arbitration Rules: A Commentary* (Oxford University Press 2013) 112–113; Clyde Croft, Christopher Kee and Jeff Waincymer, *A Guide to the UNCITRAL Arbitration Rules* (Cambridge University Press 2013) 399.

95 Caron and Caplan (n 94) 113. See for example, *Chevron Corporation (U.S.A.) and Texaco Petroleum Corporation (U.S.A.) v. Republic of Ecuador II* PCA Case No 2009–23, First Partial Award on Track I, 17 September 2013: 'The 1995 Settlement Agreement contained no express provision for applicable law(s), dispute settlement or forum selection. It is nonetheless common ground between the Parties (together with their respective expert witnesses) that Ecuadorian law applies to its interpretation and effect, that agreed approach being here confirmed by the Tribunal for the purpose of these arbitration proceedings under Article 33 of the UNCITRAL Arbitration Rules' ([29]).

96 Banifatemi (n 2) 199.

97 North American Free Trade Agreement (adopted 17 December 1992, entered into force 1 January 1994) 32 ILM 289, 605.

98 See for example, *Methanex Corporation v. United States of America* UNCITRAL, Final Award, 3 August 2005, Part II Chapter B [8]; *Eli Lilly and Company v. Government of Canada* ICSID Case No UNCT/14/2, Final Award, 16 March 2017 [103]; *Ulysseas, Inc. v. Ecuador* PCA Case No 2009–19, Final Award, 12 June 2012, [111]; *National Grid P.L.C. v. Argentina Republic* UNCITRAL, Award, 3 November 2008 [87]; *Romak S.A. v. Republic of Uzbekistan* PCA Case No 2007–07/AA280, Award, 26 November 2009 [166].

In the absence of a selection, the arbitral tribunal must apply domestic law to the investment dispute.[99] Article 33(1) UNCITRAL Arbitration Rules (1976) directs an arbitral tribunal to 'apply the law determined by the conflict of laws rules which it considers applicable'. The reference to the conflict of laws rules restricts an arbitral tribunal to applying law from one domestic legal system.[100] The preference for domestic law reflects that the UNCITRAL Arbitration Rules (1976) were drafted for commercial disputes that were likely to be founded on contractual relationships.[101] To identify the domestic law, an arbitral tribunal may refer to the conflict of laws rules of the State with the closest connection, a closest connection test, domicile, or use each approach cumulatively.[102] The arbitral tribunal then applies the conflict of laws rules to identify the applicable law. The way an arbitral tribunal should identify the applicable law based on Article 33(1) UNCITRAL Arbitration Rules (1976) requires an arbitral tribunal to focus on domestic law rather than international law.

Disputing parties are conferred with more flexibility with their choice of law under the UNCITRAL Arbitration Rules (2010). If the disputing parties have selected the applicable law, an arbitral tribunal must still interpret their choice.[103] Yet, Article 35(1) UNCITRAL Arbitration Rules (2010) permits an arbitral tribunal to apply 'rules of law' (rather than 'the law') that have been selected by the disputing parties. As a result, the law does not have to be drawn from a national legal system,[104] granting the disputing parties more flexibility with their choice of law. Given that the applicable law does not need to be drawn from a domestic legal system, if there is no choice of law, the arbitral tribunal is not bound to use conflict of laws rules to determine the applicable law.[105] Instead, it 'shall apply the law which it determines to be appropriate'. Consequently, by removing the need to use conflict of laws rules,[106] an arbitral

99 Croft, Kee and Waincymer (n 94) 395.

100 ibid 396–397.

101 The contractual origins of the UNCITRAL Arbitration Rules (1976) are particularly evident in Article 33(3) UNCITRAL Arbitration Rules (1976) which requires the arbitral tribunal (whether or not the parties have selected the applicable law) to 'decide in accordance with the terms of the contract' and to consider 'usages of the trade' that may apply to the transaction. See *Chevron Corporation (U.S.A.) and Texaco Petroleum Corporation (U.S.A.) v. Republic of Ecuador II* (n 95) [75].

102 See Doug Jones, 'Choosing the Law or Rules of Law to Govern the Substantive Rights of the Parties' (2014) 26 Singapore Academy of Law Journal 911. See also Moss (n 5) 163–164.

103 Banifatemi (n 2) 199.

104 Caron and Caplan (n 94) 118.

105 ibid.

106 This change reflects that investment arbitration may not always focus on a contractual dispute. To reflect that investment arbitration may not be based on a contract, UNCITRAL

tribunal can exercise its judgment regarding how it identifies the applicable law.[107] Thus, international law can more readily be included in the applicable law,[108] especially because more than one type of law can be applied.[109] Therefore, the UNCITRAL Arbitration Rules (2010) provide an arbitral tribunal with more latitude when determining the applicable law in investment arbitration and potentially permit greater recourse to international law.

Nonetheless, in the absence of a choice of law, the arbitral tribunal has to decide whether it is appropriate for international law to form part of the applicable law. No methodology is given to assist the arbitral tribunal in making this determination and whether international law is relevant will depend on the characterisation of the dispute. In this regard, the award in *South American Silver Limited* v *Bolivia*[110] is instructive. The foreign investor was a mining company that acquired 10 mining concessions in areas populated by indigenous communities.[111] In 2010, the foreign investor was accused by the indigenous communities of polluting sacred sites, threatening members of the indigenous communities and raping women from the communities.[112] Following violent clashes and serious conflict between the indigenous communities and the foreign investor's employees,[113] Bolivia took ownership of the mining concessions,[114] which gave rise to the investment dispute. Hence, the background to the dispute raised legal questions regarding the extent to which the arbitral tribunal should refer to principles of human rights and indigenous rights law.

The IIA did not contain an applicable law clause.[115] Therefore, it was left to the arbitral tribunal to determine the applicable law. The arbitral tribunal did not want to emphasise or downplay the significance of the IIA with regards to the applicable law.[116] The issue arose as to which principles of international law formed part of the applicable law. The parties disagreed regarding which rules of interpretation applied to the IIA, and in particular, whether the IIA could be

---

Arbitration Rules (2010) Article 35(3) makes the need for the arbitral tribunal to refer to the contract conditional on the existence of a contract. Despite this change, the arbitration rule is not intended to regulate investment treaties (Caron and Caplan (n 94) 127).

107 Moss (n 5) 153, 164; Bjorklund (n 11) 272; Cappiello (n 80) 1128.

108 Caron and Caplan (n 94) 114, 116, 124.

109 Croft, Kee and Waincymer (n 94) 395.

110 *South American Silver Limited v. Plurinational State of Bolivia* PCA Case No 2013–15, Award, 22 November 2018.

111 ibid [89], [104].

112 ibid [114].

113 ibid [152]–[162].

114 ibid [163].

115 ibid [207].

116 ibid.

interpreted to include instruments setting out human rights and indigenous rights based on systemic integration set out in Article 31(3)(c) VCLT.[117] Whilst the tribunal recognised the applicability of the principle of systemic integration as part of the rules of treaty interpretation, it sought to apply systemic integration cautiously so as to prevent it from exceeding the arbitral tribunal's jurisdictional limits.[118] The arbitral tribunal ultimately rejected the inclusion of human rights and indigenous rights based on systemic integration on the grounds that Bolivia:

> has not justified why the Tribunal must apply in this particular case various rules that do not constitute customary law, nor has it shown that either of Bolivia or the United Kingdom are parties to the human rights treaties invoked. The Respondent also fails to explain how these rules conflict with the Treaty or why they should prevail over its provisions.[119]

The arbitral tribunal decided to exclude human rights and indigenous rights from the applicable law based on its characterisation of the dispute. International law was understood to consist of those principles of international law that assist with the application of the IIA. Thus, when examining each element of the claim, and the law needed to resolve each aspect of the claim, the arbitral tribunal did not ultimately consider the human rights and indigenous rights obligations to be related to the claim. Hence, the characterisation process can exclude international law sourced from beyond IIL if the host State does not explicitly set out how the principles of international law are relevant to the claim being made and how they should be applied by the arbitral tribunal.

In conclusion, the UNCITRAL Arbitration Rules require arbitral tribunals to take different approaches when ascertaining the applicable law. Based on the UNCITRAL Arbitration Rules (1976), arbitral tribunals have limited choice when identifying the applicable law. However, the commercial origins of the rules favour the application of domestic law and are more likely to preclude international law. In contrast, the UNCITRAL Arbitration Rules (2010) are less prescriptive, which enables arbitral tribunals to refer to principles of international law. Yet, arbitral tribunals retain the ability to exercise their judgment when characterising and applying the law. Consequently, they may opt to exclude international law sourced from beyond IIL as part of the applicable law.

117 ibid [209]–[210].

118 ibid [216].

119 ibid [217].

4.3.4 *Analysis of Arbitral Practice*

Arbitral practice conducted in accordance with the ICSID Convention and the ICSID Arbitration Rules, the ICSID AF Arbitration Rules and the UNCITRAL Arbitration Rules show that the arbitration rules determine how arbitral tribunals should discern the applicable law. In general terms, the arbitration rules: (1) require an arbitral tribunal to refer to domestic law; or (2) grant arbitral tribunals the ability to refer to international law as a subsidiary source of the applicable law. However, the arbitration rules give priority to party consent, meaning that arbitral tribunals must give effect to any host State choice regarding the content of the applicable law. This section examines how the interplay of the arbitration rules, party consent and the characterisation of claims may impact the viability of counterclaims based on international law by examining whether international law sourced from beyond IIL is likely to form part of the applicable law.

An arbitral tribunal must refer to domestic law when the arbitration rules require it to apply conflict of laws rules to determine the applicable law. This situation arises under the ICSID Convention, the ICSID AF Arbitration Rules (2006) and the UNCITRAL Arbitration Rules (1976). Conflict of laws rules direct arbitral tribunals to the domestic law that is most closely connected to the investment dispute. The use of conflict of laws rules as the preferred methodology to identify the applicable law can exclude principles of international law sourced from beyond IIL from the applicable law. This is because conflict of laws rules give primacy to domestic law. Domestic law is frequently more detailed than international law and is more likely to address the legal issues in dispute.[120] Consequently, international law is likely to only play a supplementary role,[121] and in these instances, arbitral tribunals will exercise their judgment when deciding whether international law forms part of the applicable law. Thus, a host State will be able invoke any principles of international law found in the applicable domestic laws to support a counterclaim. However, a host State cannot be certain that an arbitral tribunal will refer to international law, and if it does, whether it will include principles of international law sourced from beyond IIL. Therefore, a host State cannot ensure that an arbitral tribunal will refer to principles of international law sourced from beyond IIL to support a counterclaim unless the specific principles have been implemented in the applicable domestic law.

120 Gaillard and Banifatemi (n 6) 394; Benedettelli (n 6) 711.

121 See Benedettelli (n 6) 711 on the need for gap filling.

Despite the primary focus on domestic law as the applicable law, arbitral tribunals can refer to international law in limited circumstances when determining the applicable law of an investment dispute. This situation arises when the arbitration rules permit an arbitral tribunal to apply international law when it is 'appropriate' or 'applicable' in the circumstances. Arbitral tribunals are conferred with this power when, in the absence of party consent, they (1) select the applicable law under the UNCITRAL Arbitration Rules (2010) and the ICSID AF Arbitration Rules (2022); and (2) determine whether international law should supplement the applicable law in ICSID, ICSID AF and UNCITRAL arbitrations. The way that these arbitration rules are phrased does not necessarily mean that principles of international law will be excluded from the applicable law. However, the language adopted to guide an arbitral tribunal in these situations is vague and may lead to different arbitral understandings of what is appropriate or applicable in an investment dispute. In both contexts there could be implications for counterclaims based on principles of international law sourced from beyond IIL. For example, when identifying the applicable law, an arbitral tribunal might determine that the most appropriate or applicable domestic legal system is not that of the host State. If a host State is relying on principles of international law sourced from beyond IIL, and the other State has not domestically implemented these principles, the host State would not be able to establish the counterclaim. In this situation, a host State would need to ensure that the arbitral tribunal additionally considered international law to form part of the applicable law so that the relevant principles of international law could be directly applied to the claim. However, an arbitral tribunal may not consider principles of international law sourced from beyond IIL as being applicable or appropriate to an investment dispute. Whilst most arbitral tribunals will identify host State law as the applicable domestic law, this example illustrates that in the absence of party consent, the host State cannot compel an arbitral tribunal to apply host State law or international law that supports the operation of a counterclaim based on international law. Therefore, even though arbitral tribunals can refer to international law in some instances, host States may lose control over aspects of their counterclaim that rely on principles of international law sourced from beyond IIL.

Arbitral practice has focused on the interpretation of arbitral rules. However, the arbitration rules only guide an arbitral tribunal to identify the applicable law in the absence of party consent. If there is an applicable law clause or an inferred choice of law, arbitral tribunals are restricted to identifying and interpreting the disputing parties' choice of law.[122] Hence, subject to an arbitral tribunal's interpretation, applicable law clauses provide host States with a means to ensure that the relevant principles of international law form part of the applicable law. Thus, the failure of host States to include applicable law clauses in IIAs and foreign investment legislation increases the likelihood that international law sourced from beyond IIL will be excluded from the applicable law.

No matter how the applicable law is identified, arbitral tribunals are not directed by either party consent or the applicable arbitration rules when they characterise and apply the law to a claim. Should an arbitral tribunal characterise a claim in a particular way, it may not identify a role for principles of international law sourced from beyond IIL as illustrated by the decision in *South American Silver Limited* v *Bolivia*. In this dispute, the arbitral tribunal characterised the dispute to exclude human rights and indigenous rights and understood international law as a means of giving effect to the IIA. Understanding principles of international law in this way is not unusual,[123] but in taking this approach, the arbitral tribunal minimised the role of systemic integration. The role of systemic integration in treaty interpretation is circumscribed and should not be seen a simple way of integrating new legal obligations into treaties.[124] Nonetheless, this award highlights that arbitral tribunals may exercise their judgment to frame claims in investment disputes as being solely governed by IIL and principles of international law that give effect to investment protection standards despite the existence of mechanisms that enable reference to principles of international sourced from beyond IIL. Host States are not able to dictate how arbitral tribunals characterise claims and laws that apply to a claim. Therefore, when arbitral tribunals are conferred with the ability to exercise their judgment, there remains a high risk that principles of international law sourced from beyond IIL will be excluded from the applicable law. The exclusion of principles of international law sourced from beyond IIL prevents counterclaims based on international law from being able to function.

---

122 Banifatemi (n 2) 199.

123 Although Petersmann suggests that interpretations of these terms can capture principles sourced from beyond IIL (Ernst-Ulrich Petersmann, 'Human Rights in International Investment Law and Adjudication: Legal Methodology Questions' in Julian Chaisse, Leïla Choukroune and Sufian Jusoh (eds), *Handbook of International Investment Law and Policy* (Springer 2021) 1714).

124 See for example, Johannes Hendrik Fahner and Matthew Happold, 'The Human Rights Defence in International Investment Arbitration: Exploring the Limits of Systemic Integration' (2019) 68 International and Comparative Law Quarterly 741.

In conclusion, whether the applicable law is governed by party consent or arbitration rules, an arbitral tribunal could exclude principles of international law sourced from beyond IIL from the applicable law. Thus, host States need to direct how arbitral tribunals identify and apply the applicable law of an investment dispute as much as possible to ensure that international law forms part of the applicable law and that international law is not limited to those principles that give effect to IIAs and investment protection standards. Otherwise, host States cannot ensure the operation of counterclaims based on international law.

4.4 Tailoring Applicable Law Provisions to Counterclaims

Party consent is the most effective way for host States to direct an arbitral tribunal when it determines the applicable law of an investment dispute.[125] Host States can exercise party consent by including applicable law clauses in their standing offers. However, host States do not prioritise applicable law clauses when formulating standing offers to arbitrate.[126] Hence, by overlooking applicable law clauses entirely,[127] or adopting broadly drafted or incomplete applicable law clauses,[128] host States risk counterclaims based on international law failing. This section argues that host States need to make greater use of party consent and include detailed applicable law clauses in standing offers to arbitrate.[129] Not only should applicable law clauses identify the applicable law in detail, but they should also set out in what circumstances the law should be applied. By focusing their full attention on applicable law clauses, host States can maximise the operation of counterclaims based on international law by ensuring that arbitral tribunals identify and apply principles of international law sourced from beyond IIL to the counterclaim.

125 Benedettelli (n 6) 717–718.

126 Host States rarely engage with applicable law in IIAs because applicable law clauses are often one of the last provisions to be drafted and frequently simultaneously address the arbitral tribunal's jurisdiction (Atanasova (n 1) 396).

127 Reed, Paulsson and Blackaby (n 6) 71; Bjorklund and Vanhonnaeker (n 1) 353; Gaillard and Banifatemi (n 6) 37; Benedettelli (n 6) 69; Banifatemi (n 2) 197.

128 Atanasova (n 1) 411.

129 See Paul E Trinel, 'Counterclaims and legitimacy in investment treaty arbitration' (2022) 38 Arbitration International 59, 75; Steingruber, 'Counterclaims: a Critical Analysis of Article 6 of the 2019 The Hague Resolution of the Institut de Droit International on the "Equality of Parties before International Investment Tribunals"' (n 7) 45.

Arbitral practice highlights that, in the absence of party consent, the arbitration rules minimise or exclude international law from the applicable law of an investment dispute. Party consent takes priority over the default application of the arbitration rules, but it is currently underused. Further, an arbitral tribunal's ability to characterise a claim may still prevent counterclaims based on international law no matter how the applicable law is determined. Yet, host States can direct arbitral tribunals to include international law as part of the applicable law through detailed applicable law clauses.

Applicable law clauses can specify the law that is to be applied to a specific type of claim or cause of action.[130] Provisions such as Article 21(14) Japan-Uruguay BIT (2015) illustrate how this can be achieved.[131] This provision initially contains a standard formulation which sets out that the applicable law is the BIT and applicable rules of international law.[132] However, it provides further guidance to arbitral tribunals in the event that the dispute relates to a written agreement between the parties regarding the investment. In this instance, the applicable law is the law specified in the written agreement, or other rules of law agreed upon by the disputing parties.[133] If the written agreement does not contain any choice of law, the arbitral tribunal is instructed to refer to such rules of international law as may be applicable together with the host State's conflict of laws rules.[134] Whilst this provision adopts language similar to that found in arbitration rules, the manner in which the provision is structured provides a model that could be used by host States to support counterclaims based on international law.

Host States could use applicable law clauses to specify that principles of international law sourced from beyond IIL should be applied in counterclaims. For example, the applicable law clause could set out that should a host State commence a counterclaim, the applicable law is comprised of written agreements, the host State's domestic law and international law consisting of treaty law, customary international law and any general principles of international

130 Atanasova (n 1) 419. See for example, Nicaragua-Taiwan Province of China FTA 2006 (adopted 23 June 2006, entered into force 1 January 2008); Japan-Uruguay BIT 2015 (adopted 26 January 2015, entered into force 14 April 2017); Australia-Republic of Korea FTA 2014 (adopted 8 April 2014, entered into force 12 December 2014); Japan-Switzerland Free Trade and Economic Partnership Agrement 2009 (adopted 19 February 2009, entered into force 1 September 2009).

131 This type of clause originated in US treaty practice (Atanasova (n 1) 413). See Bjorklund (n 11) 270.

132 Japan-Uruguay BIT 2015 (n 130) Article 21(14)(a).

133 ibid Article 21(14)(b)(i).

134 ibid Article 21(14)(b)(ii).

law required to give effect to treaty and customary international law. These sources of law capture principles of international law sourced from beyond IIL that can be applied as primary or supplementary sources of law in the investment dispute. If specific types of claims are anticipated, for example a counterclaim based on human rights obligations, an applicable law clause could set out that when a counterclaim is based on human rights, the arbitral tribunal is to apply certain human rights instruments (for example, the human rights treaties that bind the host State) as it deems relevant. Similar approaches could be adopted in relation to international labour standards, international environmental law or any other field of international law that that host State considers that it might wish to use in support of a counterclaim. Clauses that direct arbitral tribunals to consider sources of law that contain principles of international law beyond IIL require arbitral tribunals to actively consider these sources of law. Consequently, arbitral tribunals cannot overlook the relevance of these legal principles because they must act in accordance with party consent.

Should a host State take this approach, it would need to negotiate detailed applicable law clauses with its treaty partners or include applicable law clauses in foreign investment legislation. Current treaty negotiation practice does not prioritise applicable law clauses and may even merge their function with clauses that limit an arbitral tribunal's jurisdiction (see Section 2.4).[135] As a result, host States would need to make applicable law clauses a priority in treaty negotiations in future. A host State's negotiating expertise may also determine the extent to which it can secure this type of clause in an IIA (see Section 2.2).[136] Alternatively, host States may be able to include detailed applicable law provisions in foreign investment legislation. Regardless of the type of standing offer used, detailed applicable law clauses provide host States with the ability to ensure that principles of international law sourced from beyond IIL form part of the applicable law of counterclaims. In turn, arbitral tribunals must actively consider international law as part of the applicable law and apply it in the manner directed. Therefore, applicable law clauses provide a means of directing arbitral tribunals to international law in a way that increases the chances that it will form part of the applicable law of the investment dispute.

In summary, host States can rely on party consent and draft applicable law clauses that specify what law should apply to a counterclaim and in what

---

135 Atanasova (n 1) 418.

136 See Tarald Laudal Berge and Øyvind Stiansen, 'Negotiating BITS with Models: The Power of Expertise' (10th Annual Conference on the Political Economy of International Organizations, University of Bern, Switzerland, January 12–14, 2017).

circumstances an arbitral tribunal should refer to particular sources of law. Hence, party consent can minimise the risk that arbitral tribunals will overlook principles of international law sourced from beyond IIL and ensure that the applicable law gives effect to counterclaims based on international law.

4.5 Preliminary Conclusions

The applicable law of an investment dispute must extend to principles of international law sourced from beyond IIL for an arbitral tribunal to give effect to counterclaims based on international law. Arbitral practice highlights that, when the disputing parties do not choose the applicable law, arbitration rules guide arbitral tribunals towards using domestic law as the applicable law, and in some instances, confer arbitral tribunals with the opportunity to decide whether to apply international law to a claim. Whilst this does not exclude principles of international law sourced from beyond IIL being included in the applicable law, it also does not ensure that they will be included. Thus, there is a risk that arbitral tribunals will not consider principles of international law sourced from beyond IIL as forming part of the applicable law unless they are set out in an applicable law clause. Therefore, host States should rely on party consent to draft applicable law clauses, which take priority over the default application of the arbitration rules. Host States can draft detailed applicable law clauses that specify that principles of international law sourced from beyond IIL form part of the applicable law for counterclaims. Applicable law clauses can also direct arbitral tribunals on how to apply the law, minimising the risk that arbitral tribunals will characterise a claim in a way that excludes international law. This type of applicable law clause can ensure that principles of international law sourced from beyond IIL are included in the applicable law and encourages arbitral tribunals to give effect to counterclaims in investment arbitration based on international law.

CHAPTER 5

The Source of the Counterclaim

5.1 Introduction

To substantiate a counterclaim, the host State must first identify a legal obligation owed by the foreign investor to the host State.[1] It is only when the legal source underpinning the counterclaim has been identified that an arbitral tribunal can proceed to interpret and apply the law.[2]

A counterclaim based on international law requires the foreign investor to owe legal obligations to the host State.[3] It can be difficult to identify international laws that display this attribute because foreign investors do not possess international legal personality.[4] However, international law can bind foreign investors either directly or indirectly. When international law is framed in this way, foreign investors already owe some obligations to host States to comply with international law. Further, sources of law exist that have the potential to generate foreign investor obligations. Thus, it is possible to establish a counterclaim based on international law in investment arbitration. Nonetheless, international legal obligations are not always drafted with the requisite clarity to ensure that a counterclaim would be successful. Therefore, it is necessary to not only consider the source of the legal obligation, but also its potential enforceability against a foreign investor. To address these challenges, this chapter initially reviews different sources of international law to determine: (1) which sources of law can give rise to foreign investor obligations; (2) whether foreign investor obligations exist; and (3) whether these obligations are enforceable. The chapter then identifies the characteristics that laws should ideally possess if they are to provide an effective foundation for a counterclaim in investment arbitration. The chapter argues that host States should invoke law that binds a foreign investor, directly or indirectly links to international law, and contains precise legal obligations. Whilst sources that possess these attributes exist,

1 The law should fall within the scope of the applicable law (see Chapter 4).

2 See Chapter 6 on the merits of the counterclaim.

3 Yavaslau Kryvoi, 'Counterclaims in Investor-State Arbitration' (2012) 21 Minnesota Journal of International Law 216, 234.

4 For a discussion of how international investment law views foreign investors from the perspective of international legal personality, see Astrid Kjeldgaard-Pedersen, *The International Legal Personality of the Individual* (Oxford University Press 2018) 202–218.

 | DOI:10.1163/9789004420953_006

host States can additionally help to secure a foundation for counterclaims by tailoring provisions specifically for counterclaims. Arbitral tribunals will then be better placed to give effect to a host State's counterclaim.

To expand on this argument, the chapter proceeds in two sections. The first section considers the nature of the international legal obligation that provides the foundation for the counterclaim and reviews the potential sources of law that could give rise to a foreign investor obligation (Section 5.2). This section reviews treaty law, customary international law, *jus cogens*, and domestic law for legal obligations that can bind a foreign investor and discusses how soft law could influence the interpretation of these laws. Laws that host States could enforce against foreign investors can be found in express provisions in IIAs, domestic law that implements international obligations and investment contracts that contain provisions that address foreign investor misconduct. Further, other types of legal obligations can inform the interpretation of these laws and new interpretations of existing laws may create binding obligations for foreign investors in the future. The chapter then proceeds to identify the characteristics that laws should possess if counterclaims are to become viable in investment arbitration in the longer term (Section 5.3). The chapter concludes with a summary of the key findings (Section 5.4).

5.2 Suitable Legal Obligations

Foreign investors do not inherently possess international legal personality,[5] and therefore, are not automatically bound by rights or obligations in international law. Nonetheless, States can expressly or implicitly confer foreign investors with international legal personality.[6] Further, foreign investors are bound by the host State's domestic law that implements principles of international law.[7] Consequently, both international law and domestic law can potentially

5 Patrick Dumberry and Èrik Labelle-Eastaugh, 'Non-state actors in international investment law: The legal personality of corporations and NGOs in the context of investor-state arbitration' in Jean d'Aspremont (ed), *Participants in the International Legal System: Multiple Perspectives on Non-State Actors in International Law* (Routledge 2011) 365.

6 R Hansen, 'The International Legal Personality of Multinational Enterprises: Treaty, Custom and the Governance Gap' (2010) 10 Global Jurist 1, 13; Roland Portmann, *Legal Personality in International Law* (Cambridge University Press 2010) 82.

7 Monique Sasson, *Substantive Law in Investment Treaty Arbitration: The Unsettled Relationship Between International Law and Municipal Law* (Kluwer Law International 2010) 200; Audley Sheppard and Antony Crockett, 'Are Stabilization Clauses a Threat to Sustainable Development?' in Marie-Claire Cordonier Segger, Markus W Gehring and Andrew Newcombe (eds), *Sustainable Development in World Investment Law* (Kluwer Law International 2011) 344.

form the foundation of a counterclaim based on international law. However, the law that forms the basis of the counterclaim must create a right that is owed directly to the host State[8] and be drafted in terms that are precise enough for the host State to enforce.

Whilst some laws exist that meet these attributes, in general terms, arbitral tribunals may struggle to find laws that can form the basis of a counterclaim based on international law in investment arbitration. For example, in *Urbaser v Argentina*[9] the arbitral did not have jurisdiction over matters relating to Argentina's domestic law.[10] Consequently, international obligations that indirectly bound the foreign investor were excluded from the arbitral tribunal's remit. When sourcing international obligations that directly bound the foreign investor, the arbitral tribunal relied on soft law instruments[11] and international human rights law treaties,[12] neither of which create binding legal obligations on foreign investors. Despite this, the arbitral tribunal proceeded to identify that the foreign investor must respect the right to water[13] but eventually held that this obligation can only bind the foreign investor on the domestic plane.[14] Further analysis of the arbitral tribunal's reasoning is set out in Section 6.3, however, this decision has been criticised for finding that foreign investors owe an obligation to host States when the sources it refers to do not explicitly

8 See *Tethyan Copper Company Pty Limited v. Islamic Republic of Pakistan* ICSID Case No ARB/12/1, Decision on Jurisdiction and Liability, 10 November 2017 [1421]–[1446] addressing whether the rights were those of the Republic of Pakistan or the autonomous province Balochistan and whether a treaty claim based on a definition could give rise to an obligation owed to the Republic of Pakistan. See also *Chevron Corporation (U.S.A.) and Texaco Petroleum Corporation (U.S.A.) v. Republic of Ecuador II*, PCA Case No 2009–23, Second Partial Award on Track II, 30 August 2018 [7.37(3)]–[7.45].

9 *Urbaser S.A. and Consorcio de Aguas Bilbao Bizkaia, Bilbao Biskaia Ur Partzuergoa v. The Argentine Republic* ICSID Case No ARB/07/26, Decision on Jurisdiction, 19 December 2012; *Urbaser S.A. and Consorcio de Aguas Bilbao Biskaia, Bilbao Biskaia Ur Partzuergoa v. Argentine Republic* ICSID Case No ARB/07/26, Award, 8 December 2016.

10 *Urbaser S.A. and Consorcio de Aguas Bilbao Bizkaia, Bilbao Biskaia Ur Partzuergoa v. The Argentine Republic*, Decision on Jurisdiction (n 9) [251].

11 Universal Declaration of Human Rights (adopted 10 December 1948) UNGA Res 217 A(III) (UDHR); United Nations' General Assembly Resolution 64/292 (3 August 2010) A/RES/64/292; International Labor Office's Tripartite Declaration of Principles concerning Multilateral Enterprises and Social Policy (of 1977, as amended in 2006) Article 8.

12 ICESCR in addition to CESCR, 'General Comment no 15' on 'The Right to Water (arts. 11 and 12 of the International Covenant on Economic, Social and Cultural Rights)' (20 January 2003) UN Doc E/C.12/2002/11.

13 *Urbaser S.A. and Consorcio de Aguas Bilbao Biskaia, Bilbao Biskaia Ur Partzuergoa v. Argentine Republic*, Award (n 9) [1199].

14 ibid [1206]–[1210].

create this type of obligation.[15] In part, the novel approach taken by the arbitral tribunal was in response to the lack of international obligations that bind foreign investors. Thus, *Urbaser* v *Argentina* highlights the difficulties of trying to find foreign investor obligations in international law, especially when an arbitral tribunal has limited jurisdiction. Nonetheless, it may be possible to locate foreign investor obligations when a wider range of sources of international law are considered.

This section reviews, in turn, sources of international law to identify which types of obligations directly and indirectly bind foreign investors. Rather than focusing on specific obligations (the applicability of which will vary from counterclaim to counterclaim) the section examines the attributes of each potential source of law that could provide the basis of a counterclaim. In relation to each source, the section identifies whether: (1) the source of law can generate foreign investor obligations; (2) foreign investor obligations exist; and (3) any existing obligations are enforceable. It also addresses sources of law that could influence the interpretation of foreign investor obligations. The section argues that express provisions in IIAs, domestic law that implements international obligations and investment contracts can generate foreign investor obligations that provide a foundation for a counterclaim based on international law. Additionally, there is potential for customary international human rights law to form the basis of counterclaims in the future and soft law obligations could influence the interpretation of all these sources. Nonetheless, the section also asserts that whichever source is used, host States must ensure that foreign investor obligations are drafted precisely enough to ensure that they are enforceable.

5.2.1 *Treaty Law*

Treaty obligations only bind States party to the treaty.[16] Yet, States can directly confer rights and obligations on non-State actors through treaty provisions.[17]

15 See Patrick Abel, 'Counterclaims Based on International Human Rights Obligations of Investors in International Investment Arbitration: Fallacies and Potentials of the 2016 ICSID *Urbaser v. Argentina* Award' (2018) 1 Brill Open Law 61; Edward Guntrip, '*Urbaser v Argentina*: The Origins of a Host State Human Rights Counterclaim in ICSID Arbitration?' (*EJIL:Talk!*, 10 February 2017) <https://www.ejiltalk.org/urbaser-v-argentina-the-origins-of-a-host-state-human-rights-counterclaim-in-icsid-arbitration/> accessed 17 January 2023; Edward Guntrip, 'Private Actors, Public Goods and Responsibility for the Right to Water in International Investment Law: An Analysis of *Urbaser v Argentina*' (2018) 1 Brill Open Law 37.

16 *Certain German Interests in Polish Upper Silesia* (Merits) PCIJ Rep Series A No 7, 5, 29.

17 Hansen (n 6) 13; Portmann (n 6) 82.

For example, treaties in IIL and international human rights law create rights for non-State actors that are opposable to the State[18] and international criminal law treaties create binding obligations for individuals.[19] The ability of a State to confer rights and obligations on non-State actors using a treaty provides a means by which foreign investors can owe obligations to host States, and consequently, could form the legal foundation of a counterclaim. However, international law regimes that govern the main types of foreign investor misconduct (such as international environmental law, international labour standards and international human rights law) only place obligations on States.[20] Whilst IIAs also only bind States, they contain provisions that are enforceable by foreign investors.[21] Given that IIAs are directed towards foreign investors,

---

18 See Ole Spiermann, 'Individual Rights, State Interests and the Power to Waive ICSID Jurisdiction Under Bilateral Investment Treaties' (2004) 20 Arbitration International 179, 185; Kate Parlett, *The Individual in the International Legal System: continuity and change in international law* (Cambridge University Press 2011) 335.

19 International criminal law treaties create binding obligations on individuals for serious violations of both international humanitarian law and international human rights law (see for example Rome Statute of the International Criminal Court (adopted 17 July 1998, entered into force 1 July 2002) 2187 UNTS 90). It is highly unlikely that foreign investor misconduct would meet the legal threshold of international crimes such as genocide or apartheid. As a result, international criminal law has been excluded from the scope of this book.

20 In relation to international environmental law, see Catherine Redgwell, 'International Environmental Law' in Malcolm D Evans (ed), *International Law* (5th edn, Oxford University Press 2018) 680–682; Daniel Bodansky, Jutta Brunnée and Ellen Hey, 'International Environmental Law: Mapping the Field' in Daniel Bodansky, Jutta Brunnée and Ellen Hey (eds), *The Oxford Handbook of International Environmental Law* (Oxford University Press 2008) 8–10; in relation to international labour standards, see International Labour Organization, 'Introduction to International Labour Standards: Conventions and Recommendations' <https://www.ilo.org/global/standards/introduction-to-international-labour-standards/conventions-and-recommendations/lang--en/index.htm> accessed 5 April 2023; in relation to international human rights law, see Office of the High Commissioner for Human Rights, 'Instruments and Mechanisms: International Human Rights Law' <https://www.ohchr.org/en/instruments-and-mechanisms/international-human-rights-law> accessed 5 April 2023. Foreign investors have a duty to respect these rights in many corporate social responsibility instruments. However, corporate social responsibility instruments do not create binding legal obligations for the foreign investor (see Section 5.2.5).

21 See *SGS Société Générale de Surveillance S.A. v. Republic of the Philippines* ICSID Case No ARB/02/6, Decision of the Tribunal on Objections to Jurisdiction, 29 January 2004 [154]. It remains unclear whether by initiating a claim the investor is conferred with a procedural or a substantive right (see Zachary Douglas, 'The Hybrid Foundations of Investment Treaty Arbitration' (2003) 74 British Yearbook of International Law 151, 162–164; Anthea Roberts, 'Power and Persuasion in Investment Treaty Interpretation: The Dual Role of States' (2010) 104 American Journal of International Law 179, 184–185).

there is greater scope to include provisions that create foreign investor obligations in IIAs. Therefore, this section considers the extent to which treaty obligations sourced from regimes beyond IIL are transposed into IIAs and examines the enforceability of this type of provision. The section argues that provisions in IIAs that draw from regimes beyond IIL can form the foundation of a counterclaim based on international law in investment arbitration if they create precise obligations for foreign investors.

A host State is likely to struggle to establish a counterclaim based on many IIAs because the majority of IIAs do not contain foreign investor obligations. Some IIAs and Model BITs refer to international legal obligations sourced from beyond IIL but fail to generate foreign investor liability. These provisions may require States to 're-affirm',[22] use 'best endeavours',[23] or 'strive'[24] to comply with obligations drawn from international environmental law, international human rights law and international labour standards. Alternatively, provisions may set out obligations that prevent States from lowering environmental or labour standards to attract or maintain FDI.[25] These types of provisions create State obligations[26] and are therefore ineffective for the purposes of establishing a counterclaim. Further, the language adopted is aspirational which makes these provisions difficult to enforce.[27] Consequently, the majority of IIAs do not generate foreign investor liability and cannot form the foundation of a counterclaim based on international law.

Conversely, the latest generation of IIAs contain provisions that seek to address the impact of foreign investor misconduct.[28] These provisions integrate obligations sourced from beyond IIL into the IIA. In general terms, the latest Model BITs and IIAs often impose substantive obligations on foreign

22 European Free Trade Association (EFTA)-Costa Rica-Panama FTA (adopted 24 June 2013, entered into force 19 August 2014), Articles 9.5 and 9.6; Netherlands Model BIT 2019, Article 7(2); ECOWAS Supplementary Act A/SA.3/12/08 Adopting Community Rules on Investment and the Modalities for their Implementation with ECOWAS, Article 20(1).

23 PAIC Article 24.

24 EFTA-Costa Rica-Panama FTA (n 22) Article 9.7; Netherlands Model BIT 2019 (n 22) Article 6(2).

25 For example, PAIC (n 23) Articles 34(1) and 37(2), ECOWAS (n 22) Article 20(3); Morocco-Nigeria BIT (adopted 3 December 2016, not yet in force) Article 15(2) and (3) (labour); Netherlands Model BIT 2019 (n 22) Article 6(2) (environment and labour).

26 Jorge E Viñuales, 'Investor Diligence in Investment Arbitration: Sources and Arguments' (2017) 32 ICSID Review – Foreign Investment Law Journal 346, 355.

27 ibid.

28 See Tomoko Ishikawa, *Corporate Environmental Responsibility in Investor-State Dispute Settlement: The Unexhausted Potential of Current Mechanisms* (Cambridge University Press 2022) 50–53.

investors relating to environmental law, labour standards, human rights, corruption[29] and corporate social responsibility.[30] For example, provisions in recent Model BITs and IIAs refer to the need for foreign investors to undertake environmental and social impact assessments[31] and comply with environmental management standards.[32] More progressive innovations include provisions regulating practices that can generate violations of international law, such as land grabbing[33] (which can affect indigenous rights), socio-cultural values[34] (which can link to cultural rights), and equality[35] (which can affect the prohibition on discrimination). Significantly, these provisions generate enforceable foreign investor obligations that can form the foundation of a counterclaim in investment arbitration.

These provisions are enforceable against foreign investors because of the way in which they are drafted. Whilst the language used in Model BITs and IIAs varies, some common elements can be identified. First, these provisions adopt mandatory (rather than aspirational) language, and thus, establish enforceable obligations. Second, the obligations are directed at the foreign investor. Hence, rather than requiring the State to give effect to the provisions, the foreign investor is directly responsible for compliance. Finally, many of the provisions refer to domestic laws and international instruments that the foreign investor must comply with.[36] In some instances, reference is made to

29 SADC Model Bilateral Investment Treaty Template Article 15; PAIC (n 23) Article 20(1)(e) on labour standards, Article 24 on human rights; ECOWAS (n 22) Article 27(1)(a) on the environment; Morocco-Nigeria BIT (n 25) Article 13 on the environment, Article 15(1) on labour rights, Article 17 on corruption; Netherlands Model BIT 2019 (n 22) Article 6(6) on international law on the environment, labour rights and human rights and Article 7(1) on domestic law on human rights, the environment and labour rights; Belgium-Luxembourg Economic Union Model BIT 2019, Article 18(1).

30 ECOWAS (n 22) Article 16; PAIC (n 23) Article 22; Netherlands Model BIT 2019 (n 22) Article 7(2) and (5), Belgium-Luxembourg Economic Union Model BIT 2019 (n 29) Article 18(2) and (3); Belarus-India BIT (adopted 24 September 2018, entered into force 5 March 2020) Article 11(2) and (3). See also Brazil Model Cooperation and Facilitation Investment Agreement 2015, Articles 14–16.

31 SADC, 'SADC Model Bilateral Investment Treaty Template with Commentary' <https://www.iisd.org/itn/wp-content/uploads/2012/10/sadc-model-bit-template-final.pdf> accessed 5 April 2023, Article 13; ECOWAS (n 22) Article 27(1)(b); Morocco-Nigeria BIT (n 25) Article 14; Belarus-India BIT (n 30) Article 14.

32 SADC Model Bilateral Investment Treaty Template (n 29) Article 14.

33 PAIC (n 23) Article 23(2).

34 ibid Article 20(1)(b).

35 ECOWAS (n 22) Article 38.

36 Belgium-Luxembourg Economic Union Model BIT 2019 (n 29) Article 18(1); Netherlands Model BIT 2019 (n 22) Article 7(1); Belarus-India BIT (n 30) Article 12(1); SADC Model Bilateral Investment Treaty Template (n 29) Article 15.

obligations set out in the host State's international agreements, while others refer to specific legal instruments. Consequently, the scope of the obligations sourced from beyond IIL can be identified by referring to the relevant legal instrument(s). The binding nature and specificity of these provisions enhance their enforceability and create a workable foundation for a counterclaim in investment arbitration.

Despite the potential of these provisions, two factors may limit their ability to form the foundation of a counterclaim in investment arbitration. First, in many of the instruments adopting foreign investor obligations, host States have not consented to investment arbitration or counterclaims,[37] or alternatively, an offer of investment arbitration is combined with host State[38] or home State jurisdiction[39] over investment claims. As a result, even if an enforceable foreign investor obligation is present, as set out in Chapter 2, it can only form the foundation of a counterclaim in investment arbitration if host States consent to investment arbitration and counterclaims. Despite this limitation, the way in which these provisions are drafted provides a potential foundation for counterclaims based on international law in investment arbitration.

A second limitation is that the provisions in Model BITs only set out the desired position of one negotiating party, and consequently, are subject to change. Modifications may be made during the drafting of the Model BIT. For example, following consultations, Article 12 of the Draft India Model BIT 2015, which, amongst other things, obliged foreign investors to be bound by human rights (Article 12.1(v)) was removed from the Final India Model BIT 2015.[40] Alterations may also be made to a Model BIT during the negotiations between the contracting States when reaching an agreement. Despite the potential for the terms of Model BITs to be varied, either before or during negotiations, the Morocco-Nigeria BIT evidences that it is possible to conclude BITs that contain foreign investor obligations.[41] This BIT creates binding foreign investor obligations in relation to the environment, human rights and labour standards.[42] The

37 Morocco-Nigeria BIT (n 25) Article 27; ECOWAS (n 22) Article 33.

38 SADC Model Bilateral Investment Treaty Template (n 29) Article 17; ECOWAS (n 22) Article 17.

39 SADC Model Bilateral Investment Treaty Template (n 29) Article 19(2); ECOWAS (n 22) Article 18(5) and 29; Netherlands Model BIT 2019 (n 22) Article 7(4).

40 Article 12 was removed from the 'India Model BIT (March 2015)' <https://www.mygov.in/sites/default/files/master_image/Model%20Text%20for%20the%20Indian%20Bilateral%20Investment%20Treaty.pdf> accessed 5 April 2023. See Grant Hanessian and Kabir Duggal, ' The Final 2015 Indian Model BIT: Is This the Change the World Wishes to See?' (2017) 32 ICSID Review – Foreign Investment Law Journal 216.

41 Morocco-Nigeria BIT (n 25).

42 ibid Article 18.

ability of Morocco and Nigeria to implement these clauses in a negotiated BIT (albeit yet to enter into force) is supported by the wider investment policies adopted by African regional bodies that set out similar standards.[43] Thus, in the correct political setting, it is feasible for States to negotiate and conclude IIAs with foreign investor obligations which can form the foundation of a counterclaim in investment arbitration.

In summary, although treaties bind States, IIAs can contain foreign investor obligations. States have included provisions in recent IIAs that create foreign investor obligations by referring to legal standards sourced from beyond IIL and adopting precise language to make the obligations enforceable. Consequently, provisions in IIAs that create this type of foreign investor obligation can form the foundation of a counterclaim in investment arbitration.

5.2.2 *Customary International Law*

Customary international law is established through State practice and *opinio juris*.[44] As States are central to its creation, customary international law traditionally only binds States[45] and cannot create obligations that bind foreign investors. Nonetheless, the position in relation to customary human rights law obligations has become less certain. Hence, this section argues that foreign investors could potentially become bound by customary international human rights law obligations.

Principles of customary international human rights law are most frequently established based on the provisions of the Universal Declaration of Human Rights of 1948 (UDHR).[46] Many provisions in the UDHR were transposed into

---

43 See Makane Moïse Mbengue and Stefanie Schacherer, 'The 'Africanization' of International Investment Law: The Pan-African Investment Code and the Reform of the International Investment Regime' (2017) 18 The Journal of World Investment and Trade 414; Makane Moïse Mbengue, 'Africa's Voice in the Formation, Shaping and Redesign of International Investment Law' (2019) 34 ICSID Review – Foreign Investment Law Journal 455. See also Niccolò Zugliani, 'Human Rights in International Investment Law: The 2016 Morroco-Nigeria Bilateral Investment Treaty' (2019) 68 International and Comparative Law Quarterly 761; Okechukwu Ejims, 'The 2016 Morocco-Nigeria Bilateral Investment Treaty: More Practical Reality in Providing a Balanced Investment Treaty?' (2019) 34 ICSID Review – Foreign Investment Law Journal 62.

44 See for example, *Continental Shelf* (*Libyan Arab Jamahiriya/Malta*) (Judgment) [1985] ICJ Rep 13, 29; *Jurisdictional Immunities of the State* (*Germany v. Italy; Greece intervening*) (Judgment) [2012] ICJ Rep 99, 122–123.

45 Kate Parlett, 'Claims under Customary International Law in ICSID Arbitration' (2016) 31 ICSID Review – Foreign Investment Law Journal 439, 446.

46 LB Sohn, 'The Human Rights Law of the Charter' (1977) 12 Texas International Law Journal 129, 133; Andrew J Cunningham, 'The European Convention on Human Rights, Customary International Law and the Constitution' (1994) 43 International and Comparative Law

the ICCPR and ICESCR.[47] Those obligations that appear in the UDHR and either the ICCPR or ICESCR have often been accepted as having customary status because the widespread adoption of the ICCPR and ICESCR is taken to indicate that most States consider themselves legally bound by these obligations.[48] Therefore, it is possible to identify customary international human rights law obligations. However, these obligations need to bind foreign investors to form the foundation of a counterclaim based on international law.

There have been several attempts to claim that the UDHR is binding on non-State actors (such as foreign investors) based on the text of the UDHR. The opening paragraph of the UDHR refers to the role of 'every individual and every organ of society' in promoting respect for human rights.[49] Although this paragraph suggests a shared obligation amongst all actors to comply with the UDHR's content, the obligations set out in the UDHR's operative paragraphs

---

Quarterly 537, 542; Hurst Hannum, 'The Status of the Universal Declaration of Human Rights in National and International Law' (1995/1996) 25 Georgia Journal of International and Comparative Law 287, 322–325. This position has been accepted by the ICJ. Judge Tanaka's dissenting opinion in *South West Africa Second Phase* (Judgment) [1966] ICJ Rep 6 clarified the role of the UDHR in the formation of customary international law by stating that it 'constitute[s] evidence of the interpretation and application of the relevant Charter provisions' (293). Vice-President Ammoun's Separate Opinion in *Legal Consequences for States of the Continued Presence of South Africa in Namibia (South West Africa) notwithstanding Security Council Resolution 276 (1970)* (Advisory Opinion) [1971] ICJ Rep 16 identified that the right to equality was a binding customary norm (76). See also *United States Diplomatic and Consular Staff in Tehran* (Judgment) [1980] ICJ Rep 3 where the ICJ inferred the binding nature of principles drawn from the UDHR when it stated that 'Wrongfully to deprive human beings of their freedom and to subject them to physical restraint in conditions of hardship is in itself manifestly incompatible with the principles of the Charter of the United Nations, as well as with the fundamental principles enumerated in the Universal Declaration of Human Rights' (34).

47 Dinah Shelton, 'Commentary and Conclusions' in Dinah Shelton (ed), *Commitment and Compliance: The Role of Non-Binding Norms in the International Legal System* (Oxford University Press 2000) 449; Adam McBeth, *International Economic Actors and Human Rights* (Routledge 2010) 18.

48 C.f. Arthur M Weisburd, 'The Effect of Treaties and Other Formal International Acts on the Customary Law of Human Rights' (1995/1996) 25 Georgia Journal of International and Comparative Law 99, 113 who denies the ICCPR a customary basis in 1966 due the lack of an enforcement mechanism for the rights set out within the instrument.

49 See Jordan J Paust, 'The Other Side of Right: Private Duties under Human Rights Law' (1993) 5 Harvard Human Rights Journal 51, 53; Carlos M Vázquez, 'Direct vs. Indirect Obligations of Corporations Under International Law' (2005) 43 Colombia Journal of Transnational Law 927, 942; Jennifer A Zerk, *Multinationals and Corporate Social Responsibility: Limitations and Opportunities in International Law* (Cambridge University Press 2006) 77; McBeth (n 47) 60.

are clearly directed at States.[50] Further, Article 29(1) UDHR refers to everyone having 'duties to the community in which alone the free and full development of his personality is possible'. Despite the reference to the role of individuals in fulfilling the UDHR's aims, Article 29(1) UDHR also fails to set out specific obligations for non-State actors.[51] Therefore, it is doubtful whether the UDHR can singularly establish binding obligations for non-State actors like foreign investors.

The transfer of human rights obligations from the UDHR to the ICCPR and ICESCR does not fundamentally alter this position. Customary international human rights law obligations that can additionally be sourced in the ICCPR and ICESCR are unlikely to bind foreign investors because the obligations set out in these treaties only bind States. Any customary obligations based on these treaty provisions will mirror the same approach. Consequently, it is difficult to identify a customary international law obligation that directly binds a foreign investor and can form the basis of a counterclaim in investment arbitration.

Despite this general position, recent jurisprudence suggests that foreign investors can be bound by customary international human rights law. In *Urbaser* v *Argentina*[52] (which is discussed at length in Section 6.3) the arbitral tribunal held that foreign investors owe a duty not to interfere in the human rights of others, based in part on the UDHR.[53] However, in *Nevsun Resources* v *Araya*,[54] the Canadian Supreme Court indicated that Nevsun might be directly bound by customary international human rights law. This domestic case centred on three Eritrean workers who had been conscripted to the military and were required to work in Nevsun's mine.[55] They argued that Nevsun was bound by the customary prohibitions on slavery, forced labour and inhuman conduct.[56] In a preliminary ruling, Nevsun argued that these claims should be struck out on the basis that Nevsun was not bound by customary international law. The Court held that the prohibitions relied upon were established in customary international law.[57] The majority additionally found that it was not 'plain and obvious' that customary international law obligations could not

50 Jan Arno Hessbruegge, 'Human Rights Violations Arising from Conduct of Non-State Actors' (2005) 11 Buffalo Human Rights Law Review 21, 35.

51 ibid.

52 *Urbaser S.A. and Consorcio de Aguas Bilbao Biskaia, Bilbao Biskaia Ur Partzuergoa v. Argentine Republic*, Award (n 9).

53 ibid [1196].

54 *Nevsun Resources Ltd v Araya* [2020] 1 SCR 166.

55 ibid [3].

56 ibid [60].

57 ibid [77]–[84].

directly bind private individuals.[58] The majority considered that international law had become 'human-centric' to the extent that corporations should not be excluded from these obligations by virtue of their status alone, given that the norms were 'obligatory, definable and universal'.[59] The decisions in *Urbaser* and *Nevsun* deviate from classic understandings of the effect of customary international law and do not definitively establish that customary international law binds foreign investors. However, they are indicative of a potential shift in how some dispute resolution fora may understand which actors are bound by customary international human rights law. A more permissive approach could permit counterclaims in investment arbitration based on customary international human rights law in the future.[60]

The ability to establish a counterclaim in investment arbitration based on customary international human rights law will, in part, depend on whether the obligation is enforceable. Although the content and scope of each human right differs, should the customary obligation mirror those found in international human rights law treaties, existing treaty body and State practice can assist in determining the scope of the obligation. The content of these obligations will need to be adapted to take into account that a foreign investor must fulfil the obligation rather than a State.[61] However, many customary international human rights law obligations will be specific enough for an arbitral tribunal to apply the human rights obligation to a foreign investor.[62] Thus, referring to an established body of international human rights law can enable arbitral tribunals to enforce customary international human rights law against a foreign investor as part of counterclaim procedures in investment arbitration.

In summary, customary international law usually only binds States. However, in relation to international human rights law, customary obligations have the potential to bind foreign investors. Recent decisions have looked beyond traditional rationales that exclude non-State actors from customary international human rights law to establish that foreign investors could potentially be bound

58 ibid [104]–[111].

59 ibid [113].

60 For a discussion on the prospects of such an approach, see Siddharth Aatreya, '"Private" Breaches of International Law: Lessons from Domestic Courts for International Investment Law' (*OpinioJuris*, 4 March 2020) <http://opiniojuris.org/2020/03/04/private-breaches-of-international-law-lessons-from-domestic-courts-for-international-investment-law/> accessed 5 April 2023.

61 Karsten Nowrot, *The Other Side of Rights in the Processes of Constitutionalizing International Investment Law: Addressing Investors' Obligations as a New Regulatory Experiment* (Heft 21 Rechtswissenschaftliche Beiträge der Hamburger Sozialökonomie, 2018) 16.

62 See for example, the customary rights at issue in *Nevsun Resources Ltd v Araya* (n 54).

by certain customary international human rights law obligations. Additionally, these obligations may be enforceable given that the specific content of the rights can be ascertained with reference to treaty obligations. Therefore, although it is not a widespread practice yet, these decisions generate the possibility that customary international human rights law could be used to establish a counterclaim in investment arbitration in the future.

5.2.3 Jus Cogens

Jus cogens norms possess characteristics that differ from standard treaty and customary obligations in international law. Thus, it is necessary to examine the utility of norms being classified as *jus cogens* for counterclaims in investment arbitration. *Jus cogens* norms are fundamental legal obligations in international law from which no derogation is permitted.[63] Hence, *jus cogens* norms are deemed to take priority over other conflicting norms in international and domestic law.[64] In the context of treaty law, this position stems from Articles 53 and 64 VCLT, which provide that *jus cogens* obligations prevail over inconsistent treaty obligations.[65] Outside the remit of the VCLT, the exact foundation for *jus cogens* operating in this way is unclear, and has been variably sourced from natural law, necessity, international public order, and the development of constitutional principles.[66] Arbitral tribunals have not excluded *jus cogens* obligations from taking priority over IIL,[67] however, there is no real benefit to a norm possessing *jus cogens* status when establishing a counterclaim in investment arbitration. This is because a counterclaim is an independent

63 See ILC, 'First Report on *jus cogens*' by Dire Tladi, Special Rapporteur' (8 March 2016) UN Doc A/CN4/693, 15–16.

64 Dan Dubois, 'The Authority of Peremptory Norms in International Law: State Consent or Natural Law?' (2009) 78 Nordic Journal of International Law 133, 135, 137; Olivier De Schutter, *International Human Rights Law* (Cambridge University Press 2010) 65; McBeth (n 39) 20; Dinah Shelton, 'Normative Hierarchy in International Law' (2006) 100 The American Journal of International Law 291, 305.

65 ILC (n 63) 15–16.

66 ibid 23; Shelton, 'Normative Hierarchy in International Law' (n 64); Andrea Bianchi, 'Human Rights and the Magic of *Jus Cogens*' (2008) 19 European Journal of International Law 491, 505. Different attitudes towards the status of *jus cogens* norms are identified in Helene Ruiz Fabri, 'Enhancing the Rhetoric of *Jus Cogens*' (2012) 23 European Journal of International Law 1049, 1052–1053.

67 See for example, *Methanex Corporation v. United States of America* UNCITRAL, Final Award, 3 August 2005, Part V Chapter C [14]; *Continental Casualty Company v. Argentine Republic* ICSID Case No ARB/03/9, Award, 5 September 2008 [261]; *EDF International S.A., SAUR International S.A. and León Participaciones Argentinas S.A. v. Argentine Republic* ICSID Case No ARB/03/23, Award, 11 June 2012 [909].

claim.[68] Therefore, questions of priority do not arise because the foreign investor's claim and the host State's counterclaim are considered separately and the norms are not in direct conflict. Further, *jus cogens* norms still originate from treaty and customary international law.[69] Thus, as outlined in Sections 5.2.1. and 5.2.2 above, the obligation would still need to directly bind a foreign investor and clearly set out the foreign investor's obligations to the host State. If these attributes are present a counterclaim can be established. The norm's *jus cogens* status becomes a secondary consideration that could only be used to highlight the gravity of the foreign investor's misconduct. As a result, *jus cogens* obligations cannot independently provide a foundation for a counterclaim in investment arbitration.

5.2.4 *Domestic Law*

International law can indirectly bind foreign investors when domestic law sets out international obligations. Domestic law may reflect international obligations when host States implement international law into their domestic legal frameworks.[70] Additionally, domestic contract law can give effect to obligations in investment contracts that require foreign investors to comply with international law.[71] This section contends that domestic law that uses either of these means to give effect to international law has the potential to provide a foundation for a counterclaim in investment arbitration.

When a foreign investor operates within a host State's jurisdiction, it is bound by the host State's domestic law.[72] Consequently, foreign investors are bound by any international legal principles that are domestically implemented into host State law. As a result, host States can regulate a foreign investor using domestic law frameworks that give effect to principles of international law. The means by which international law will be implemented into domestic law will

68 Kryvoi (n 3) 220.

69 Shelton, 'Normative Hierarchy in International Law' (n 64) 297; see also Prosper Weil, 'Towards Relative Normativity in International Law' (1983) 77 The American Journal of International Law 413 425; Carlo Focarelli, 'Promotional *Jus Cogens*: A Critical Appraisal of *Jus Cogens*' Legal Effects' (2008) 77 Nordic Journal of International Law 429, 444.

70 For a general discussion of how domestic implementation may take place, see Gleider Hernández, *International Law* (2nd edn, Oxford University Press 2022) Chapter 4.

71 As to the role of domestic law in contract interpretation, see Yuliya Chernykh, *Contract Interpretation in Investment Treaty Arbitration: A Theory of the Incidental Issue* (Brill 2022) Chapter 2.

72 Sasson (n 7) 200; Sheppard and Crockett (n 7) 344. See Andrea Carlevaris, 'The Conformity of Investments with the Law of the Host State and the Jurisdiction of International Tribunals' (2008) 9 Journal of World Investment and Trade 35 [98].

depend on the constitution of the host State.[73] Treaty obligations will generally either bind a State directly[74] or will need to be incorporated into domestic legislation.[75] Customary international law usually automatically binds States, however, the extent to which custom forms part of domestic law may be limited by the State's constitutional principles.[76] Whether based on treaty provisions or customary international law, a State may need to reframe the international obligations so that they create direct obligations on non-State actors. By framing the obligations in this way, the likelihood that the obligation is enforceable against a foreign investor is increased, which makes the international obligations more suited for use in counterclaims in investment arbitration.

To establish the counterclaim in investment arbitration, the host State will need to identify and correlate the domestic legal provisions with the international obligation to show that it is sourced in international law. For example, in *Perenco* v *Ecuador*,[77] the arbitral tribunal recognised that Ecuador's domestic environmental laws flowed from the concept of sustainable development that originated in the 1992 Rio Declaration on the Environment and Development.[78] Thus, provided that the link to international law can be established, it is arguable that a domestic law that gives effect to an international law obligation can form the basis of a counterclaim.

Investment contracts, although not forming part of domestic law, can bind foreign investors based on the host State's domestic contract law. Therefore, if an investment contract requires a foreign investor to comply with international law, the contractual provision can form the foundation of a counterclaim in investment arbitration.[79] It is unclear how many investment contracts currently contain this type of provision given that many remain unpublished,[80]

---

73 Hernández (n 70) 86.

74 This is a monist approach. See ibid 87.

75 This is a dualist approach. See ibid. States are under an obligation to enforce international human rights law on the domestic plane. This comprises the 'fulfil' element of the 'respect', 'protect' and 'fulfil' framework that applies to international human rights law obligations. See McBeth (n 47) 45; Hernández (n 70) 91.

76 This is regardless of whether a monist or dualist conception of national and public international law is adopted by a state. See Hernández (n 70) 95; see also Parlett, 'Claims under Customary International Law in ICSID Arbitration' (n 45) 444–445.

77 *Perenco Ecuador Limited v. Republic of Ecuador* ICSID Case No ARB/08/6, Interim Decision on the Environmental Counterclaim, 11 August 2015.

78 ibid [331].

79 Ishikawa (n 28) 149.

80 Barnali Choudhury, 'Human Rights Provisions in International Investment Treaties and Investor-State Contracts' in Julian Scheu and others (eds), *Investment Protection, Human Rights, and International Arbitration in Extraordinary Times* (Nomos 2022) 103.

however, there is evidence that the practice of including foreign investor obligations in investment contracts that govern misconduct is increasing.[81] To be enforceable, the clause must precisely set out the foreign investor's obligations. An example of how a clause can be drafted in this way can be seen in the concession contract between Liberia and Firestone Liberia, which provides:

> Except as explicitly provided in this Agreement, Firestone Liberia Inc. shall be subject to Law as in effect from time to time, including with respect to labor, environmental health and safety, customs and tax matters, and shall conduct itself in a manner consistent with Liberia's obligations under international treaties and agreements in so far as those have the effect of Law in Liberia.[82]

By explicitly setting out the domestic and international law that binds the foreign investor, the provision can be easily enforced, either by direct reference to international law or to domestic law that mirrors the international legal obligations.[83] Consequently, contractual provisions in these terms could form the foundation of a counterclaim in investment arbitration.

In short, domestic law provides two potential sources of foreign investor obligations that could permit a counterclaim in investment arbitration. International law can be implemented in the host State's domestic law which binds the foreign investor. Additionally, provisions in investment contracts can require the foreign investor to comply with international law or domestic law that gives effect to international law. In both cases, the provisions can be made to be enforceable against the foreign investor.

5.2.5 *Soft Law*

Soft law does not create binding obligations for States or for foreign investors. As a result, soft law cannot be invoked as the sole basis for a counterclaim in investment arbitration. Nonetheless, soft law obligations could be used to supplement a counterclaim that is based on other legal grounds.

---

81 Laurence Boisson de Chazournes, 'The Blurring of the Line Between Contract-Based and Treaty-Based Investment Arbitration' (2019) 1 ITA in Review 94, 103. See Choudhury (n 80) 103–107.

82 Amended and Restated Concession Agreement between the Republic of Liberia and Firestone Liberia Inc. Art 30.1 in Zachary Douglas, 'The enforcement of environmental norms in investment treaty arbitration' in Pierre-Marie Dupuy and Jorge E Viñuales (eds), *Harnessing Foreign Investment to Promote Environmental Protection: Incentives and Safeguards* (Cambridge University Press 2013) 434–435.

83 ibid 435.

Soft law is playing an increasing role in the field of corporate social responsibility. Consequently, the conduct of corporate foreign investors is likely to be shaped by soft law in the form of corporate social responsibility initiatives.[84] In this regard, the influence of the United Nations Guiding Principles on Business and Human Rights (UNGPs)[85] is significant. The UNGPs create a framework in which States retain the duty to protect against human rights violations, but corporations have a responsibility to respect human rights. Thus, corporations should avoid infringing the human rights of others[86] by complying with domestic laws and respecting internationally recognised human rights[87] to the greatest extent possible in the circumstances.[88] Further, corporations should avoid causing, or contributing to, adverse human rights impacts[89] by identifying human rights risks in advance.[90] Therefore, the UNGPs create non-binding expectations regarding the conduct of corporate foreign investors.

Although the UNGPs are not binding, the responsibility to respect in the UNGPs has started to inform the scope of corporate duties. In *Urbaser* v *Argentina*,[91] the arbitral tribunal relied on the UNGPs to establish that foreign investors owed a duty not to interfere in the human rights of others (discussed further in Section 6.3).[92] In a domestic context, in *Milieudefensie et al.* v. *Royal Dutch Shell plc.*,[93] the District Court of the Hague held that under Book 6 Section 162 of the Dutch Civil Code, corporations are under a duty of care to reduce carbon dioxide emissions.[94] The duty of care was based, in part, on the corporate responsibility to respect human rights set out in the UNGPs, which the Court considered to be a well-established and widely accepted principle.[95]

---

84 David Kinley and Junko Tadaki, 'From Talk to Walk: The Emergence of Human Rights Responsibilities for Corporations at International Law' (2004) 44 Virginia Journal of International Law 931, 952.

85 Office of the High Commissioner for Human Rights, 'Guiding principles on business and human rights: implementing the United Nations "Protect, Respect and Remedy" framework (2011)' <https://www.ohchr.org/sites/default/files/documents/publications/guidingprinciplesbusinesshr_en.pdf> accessed 5 April 2023.

86 ibid Principle 11.

87 ibid Principle 23.

88 ibid Principle 23 Commentary.

89 ibid Principle 13.

90 ibid Principle 11; Principle 15.

91 *Urbaser S.A. and Consorcio de Aguas Bilbao Biskaia, Bilbao Biskaia Ur Partzuergoa v. Argentine Republic*, Award (n 9).

92 ibid [1199].

93 *Milieudefensie et al. v. Royal Dutch Shell plc* ECLI:NL:RBDHA:2021:5339 C/09/571932/ HA ZA 19–379.

94 ibid [4.4.1]–[4.4.3] and [5.3].

95 ibid [4.4.11]–[4.4.21].

Hence, even though the UNGPs are not legally binding, they can be used to guide the interpretation of other legal standards. Although the UNGPs are only beginning to be used in this way, these decisions evidence how soft law can potentially play a role in informing how legal obligations are constructed. Thus, soft law could play an interpretative role when other international obligations are used as the basis of counterclaims in investment arbitration.

5.3 The Desirable Characteristics of the Legal Obligation

Foreign investors do not inherently possess international legal personality, and therefore, are not traditionally bound by international law. Consequently, arbitral tribunals may find it difficult to identify sources of law that can form the foundation of a counterclaim based on international law. However, a review of the key sources of international law highlights that it is possible to establish counterclaims based on international law in investment arbitration. To provide a foundation for a counterclaim, the legal obligation must bind the foreign investor and flow from the foreign investor to the host State. Obligations that meet this criterion can be created by: (1) introducing foreign investor obligations in IIAs based on international obligations sourced from different legal regimes; (2) implementing international obligations into domestic legal frameworks; and (3) including obligations in investment contracts that require foreign investors to comply with international law. Foreign investor obligations currently exist in these forms and can already provide a foundation for counterclaims in investment arbitration. Although the law is still nascent, recent jurisprudence hints that customary international human rights law might also have the potential to form the foundation of a counterclaim in the future. As a result, it is possible to identify foreign investor obligations that can form the foundation of a counterclaim based on international law.

The obligation must also be sufficiently precise so that it can be enforced against a foreign investor. To be enforceable, foreign investor obligations should adopt mandatory language and be drafted precisely enough to indicate the scope of the obligation. The way foreign investor obligations are being drafted in the latest generation of Model BITs and IIAs and investment contracts creates binding obligations for foreign investors. When international law is transposed into domestic law, host States may need to reframe international obligations so that non-State actors bear the responsibility. Nonetheless, when setting out the responsibilities, many foreign investor obligations do refer to international agreements or domestic laws. Thus, the content of the obligation can be ascertained based on how provisions have been understood in the legal regime in which they are sourced. Further, soft law obligations, such as the UNGPs, can inform how legal standards are being interpreted, providing additional guidance to foreign investors and investment arbitrators. Hence, it is possible to identify enforceable foreign investor obligations that can provide the foundation for counterclaims based on international law in investment arbitration.

Nevertheless, while it is possible to identify foreign investor obligations that can give rise to counterclaims in investment arbitration, the characteristics identified above only address the minimum requirements to establish a counterclaim. To provide a clear foundation for counterclaims in investment arbitration, it is desirable that host States enhance foreign investor obligations by tailoring legal provisions specifically for counterclaims. This requires host States to draft foreign investor obligations with more precision. For example, if a host State is seeking to make a procedural obligation enforceable against a foreign investor, it should specify clear and detailed processes that the foreign investor should follow. The steps must be outlined in a way that makes it clear to foreign investors what procedures must be employed and allow an arbitral tribunal to identify whether the foreign investor has complied with the processes. When substantive obligations are imposed on foreign investors, the scope of the obligation should be made clear in the provision rather than solely relying on arbitral tribunals referring to other fields of law. The provisions relied upon by the host State should specify whether the obligations apply in in the pre-establishment, post-establishment and post-operation phases of the investment project. If obligations differ during these different stages, this should be made clear. If there are any ambiguities when an investment tribunal applies the obligations that bind the foreign investor, the uncertainty could undermine the host State's counterclaim. Consequently, by setting out precisely what the foreign investor needs to do, the foreign investor obligation is more enforceable, which increases the chances of a host State being successful on the merits when a foreign investor's conduct is in breach of the obligation.

For a counterclaim to succeed on the merits, it must bind the foreign investor and be sufficiently precise to be enforceable. Foreign investor obligations that possess these attributes already exist. Nonetheless, foreign investor obligations can provide a more secure foundation for counterclaims by setting out the foreign investor's obligations in detail. More detailed provisions permit arbitral tribunals to identify the source and scope of the foreign investor's obligations more readily.

5.4 Preliminary Conclusions

To establish a counterclaim, a host State must identify an enforceable legal obligation owed by the foreign investor to the host State. As foreign investors do not have international legal personality, they are not automatically bound by international law. Despite this limitation, foreign investors can be bound by provisions in IIAs, international law that has been implemented in domestic law, and provisions in investment contracts. Further, soft law can be used by arbitral tribunals to provide interpretative guidance. Therefore, host States can invoke law that directly or indirectly links to international law as the foundation of their counterclaim. Host States must additionally ensure that the foreign investor obligations are drafted with sufficient precision to be enforceable against a foreign investor. Many of the foreign investor obligations already refer to legal instruments with well-established interpretations that can guide foreign investors and arbitral tribunals. Nonetheless, where host States need foreign investors to undertake specific conduct, this should be set out as explicitly as possible. Arbitral tribunals will then be able to easily identify the source of law and scope of the foreign investor's obligations in international law.

CHAPTER 6

The Merits of the Counterclaim

6.1 Introduction

The merits stage of a counterclaim determines whether the foreign investor has breached its obligations to the host State. Once the legal foundation of the counterclaim has been identified (see Chapter 5) the host State will present legal arguments to the arbitral tribunal based on its interpretation of the law and the facts of the dispute.[1] The foreign investor can defend the counterclaim by presenting legal arguments that challenge the host State's legal and factual claims.[2] The arbitral tribunal must then evaluate the evidence before it, interpret the legal obligation that forms the basis of the counterclaim and apply the law to the evidence.[3] If the arbitral tribunal determines that the foreign investor breached its legal obligations, the host State's counterclaim will succeed.

The adjudicative process is not a precise art and the outcome of an investment dispute is influenced by many variables. Hence, multiple factors may determine whether a counterclaim in investment arbitration is successful on the merits. Nevertheless, counterclaims in investment arbitration that are based on international law present one significant challenge for host States and arbitral tribunals – the law that forms the foundation of a counterclaim based on international law is highly likely to be sourced from beyond IIL. Investment arbitrators are primarily experts in IIL.[4] Consequently, there is a risk that investment arbitrators will not interpret and apply laws sourced from beyond IIL consistently with how they are understood in the legal regime from which they are sourced. Further, each arbitral tribunal that is presented with a counterclaim based on the same legal principle could take a unique approach, resulting in conflicting interpretations of the legal principle within investment arbitration. If investment arbitrators generate inconsistent interpretations of

1 Barton Legum, 'An Overview of Procedure in an Investment Treaty Arbitration' in Katia Yannaca-Small (ed), *Arbitration under International Investment Agreements: A Guide to the Key Issues* (2nd edn, Oxford University Press 2018) 110–111.

2 ibid.

3 ibid 111.

4 Milanka Kostadinova, 'Aspects of Procedure for Institution of Proceedings and Establishment of Tribunals in Investment Treaty Arbitration' in Katia Yannaca-Small (ed), *Arbitration under International Investment Agreements: A Guide to the Key Issues* (2nd edn, Oxford University Press 2018) 139.

 | DOI:10.1163/9789004420953_007

international legal principles across different legal regimes, and within investment arbitration, the jurisprudence regarding a single legal obligation could become inconsistent and unpredictable. At the level of individual disputes, host States would be required to take a risk when presenting a counterclaim based on international law given the lack of clarity regarding the content of the law. If a lack of legal coherence becomes prevalent in arbitral practice, host States may lose trust in investment arbitration more generally, which could undermine investment arbitration's legitimacy.

This chapter addresses how host States and investment arbitrators can minimise inconsistent decision-making when a counterclaim is based on international law. The chapter argues that, when investment arbitrator expertise is combined with the legal structures that underpin international law and investment arbitration, arbitral tribunals may produce inconsistent interpretations of law sourced from beyond IIL at the merits stage of a counterclaim. Inconsistent interpretations of the law make counterclaims risky for host States because they produce unpredictable outcomes and unpredictability can undermine investment arbitration's legitimacy. To enhance investment arbitration's legitimacy, host States can encourage arbitral tribunals to produce consistent awards by including interpretative provisions in IIAs and foreign investment legislation. However, the best way of mitigating the risk of incoherent decision-making is if arbitral tribunals refer to experts to guide them on the law underpinning counterclaims. Yet, arbitral tribunals may not be able or willing to appoint experts in every dispute. Therefore, host States will need to consider whether investment arbitration is the most desirable dispute resolution forum in which to bring a claim for foreign investor misconduct and should evaluate the risks of commencing a counterclaim based on international law in investment arbitration on a claim-by-claim basis.

To expand on these arguments, the chapter proceeds in four sections. The chapter initially examines how consistent decision-making contributes to the legitimacy of a legal system and outlines how arbitral tribunals might create conflicting interpretations of international legal principles sourced from beyond IIL when resolving counterclaims (Section 6.2). The chapter then identifies the extent to which conflicting interpretations have arisen when arbitral tribunals have considered counterclaims based on international law at the merits stage (Section 6.3). It proceeds to address how host States can minimise the risk of conflicting interpretations when arbitral tribunals are required to interpret legal obligations sourced from beyond IIL (Section 6.4). Although host States can use interpretative provisions in IIAs and foreign investment legislation to guide arbitral tribunals, this section asserts that arbitral tribunals should, where possible, appoint legal experts to inform their interpretation of legal principles sourced from beyond IIL to improve consistency in decision-making and to enhance investment arbitration's legitimacy. Given that the use of experts cannot be guaranteed, the final section of the chapter addresses the factors that host States should consider when deciding to proceed with a counterclaim based on international law in investment arbitration (Section 6.5). The chapter closes by outlining the key findings (Section 6.6).

6.2 Legitimacy and Inconsistent Decision-Making

Consistency is often cited as being a desirable attribute of a legal system.[5] When decision-making is inconsistent it generates conflicting interpretations of the law which can reduce trust in a legal system and diminish its legitimacy.[6] Arbitral tribunals may struggle to produce consistent interpretations of legal principles sourced from beyond IIL because of international law's fragmented structure and the *ad hoc* nature of investment arbitration. This section argues that these factors could result in arbitral tribunals reaching inconsistent decisions. Not only does inconsistency have the potential to make counterclaims based on international law unpredictable for host States but it could also undermine investment arbitration's legitimacy.

Consistent decision-making generates certainty regarding the scope of the law. Certainty contributes to social stability[7] because when the law is certain, legal outcomes are predictable[8] and subjects of the law can plan their actions

5 Christoph Schreuer, 'Coherence and Consistency in international investment law' in Roberto Echandi and Pierre Sauvé (eds), *Prospects in International Investment Law and Policy* (Cambridge University Press 2013) 391.

6 Julian Arato, Chester Brown and Federico Ortino, 'Parsing and Managing Inconsistency in Investor-State Dispute Settlement' (2020) 21 Journal of World Investment and Trade 336, 340; Susan D Franck, 'The Legitimacy Crisis in Investment Treaty Arbitration: Privatizing Public International Law Through Inconsistent Decisions' (2005) 73 Fordham Law Review 1521, 1584.

7 Christian J Tams, *An Appealing Option? The Debate about an ICSID Appellate Structure* (Essays in Transnational Economic Law No 57, 2006) 17.

8 Katharina Diel-Gligor, *Towards consistency in international investment jurisprudence: a preliminary ruling system for ICSID arbitration* (Brill 2017) 121; August Reinisch, 'The challenge of fostering greater coherence in international investment law' in Roberto Echandi and Pierre Sauvé (eds), *Prospects in International Investment Law and Policy* (Cambridge University Press 2013) 236–237; Tams (n 7) 18; Franck (n 6) 1584; Thomas Schultz, 'Against Consistency in Investment Arbitration' in Zachary Douglas, Joost Pauwelyn and Jorge E Viñuales (eds), *The Foundations of International Investment Law: Bringing Theory into Practice* (Oxford University Press 2014) 297.

based on the law.[9] For example, should a dispute arise, predictable legal outcomes can assist disputing parties to reach a settlement[10] or can lead to more efficient dispute resolution by setting clear expectations.[11] Thus, consistency makes the law reliable.[12] Nonetheless, legal systems require a certain degree of inconsistency to function. Hence, whilst consistency is viewed as being beneficial, some inconsistent decision-making is not inherently problematic.[13] For instance, inconsistency enables decision-makers to operate with autonomy because they are empowered to reach different conclusions.[14] Further, divergent understandings of the law enable it to be flexible so that it can develop and respond to new challenges.[15] Therefore, a limited degree of inconsistent decision-making within a legal system can be expedient. Thus, legal systems must balance[16] these competing considerations by permitting decision-makers to reach varied decisions within a range of permissible outcomes.[17]

If decision-makers do not strive to achieve this balance, they can produce conflicting interpretations of the law. A conflicting interpretation is a legal interpretation of the same rule or standard that generates a different outcome that cannot be justified based on the characteristics of the claim.[18] When

9 Arato, Brown and Ortino (n 6) 341, 342; Irene M Ten Cate, 'The Costs of Consistency: Precedent in Investment Treaty Arbitration' (2013) 51 Columbia Journal of Transnational Law 418, 452; Franck (n 6) 1584.

10 See Arato, Brown and Ortino (n 6) 341.

11 Tams (n 7) 1; Anders Nilsson and Oscar Englesson, 'Inconsistent Awards in Investment Treaty Arbitration: Is an Appeals Court Needed?' (2013) 30 Journal of International Arbitration 561, 575.

12 Franck (n 6) 1584.

13 Arato, Brown and Ortino (n 6) 339.

14 Cate (n 9) 458, 467; Giovanni Zarra, 'The Issue of Incoherence in Investment Arbitration: Is There Need for a Systemic Reform?' (2018) 17 Chinese Journal of International Law 137, 157.

15 Arato, Brown and Ortino (n 6) 339; Zarra (n 14) 157; Cate (n 9) 450.

16 Cate (n 9) 450.

17 Every legal provision permits a range of feasible interpretations (Eleni Methymaki and Antonios Tzanakopolous, 'Masters of Puppets? Reassertion of Control through Joint Investment Treaty Interpretation' in Andreas Kulick (ed), *Reassertion of control over the investment treaty regime* (Cambridge University Press 2017) 158–159).

18 This definition is based on UNCITRAL Working Group III, 'Report of Working Group III (Investor-State Dispute Settlement Reform) on the Work of Its Thirty-Fifth Session (New York, 23–27 April 2018)' (14 May 2018) UN Doc A/CN.9/935 [21]. Franck outlines that inconsistent decisions can occur in three situations. First, different conclusions can be drawn about the same standard in the same treaty. Second, different tribunals under different treaties can come to different conclusions about disputes involving the same facts, related parties and similar investment rights. Finally, different tribunals under different treaties consider disputes regarding a similar commercial situation and similar rights but will reach different conclusions (Franck (n 6) 1545–1546).

decision-making is this inconsistent outcomes may be perceived to be arbitrary,[19] which can undermine the rule of law.[20] Subjects of the law may perceive dispute resolution processes to be unreliable and ineffective,[21] and trust and faith in the legal system can become eroded.[22] Thus, conflicting interpretations can impact the legitimacy of a legal system.[23]

There are two types of conflicting interpretations that affect counterclaims based on international law that have the potential to result in unpredictable outcomes and detrimentally impact investment arbitration's legitimacy. First, at the level of international law, an arbitral tribunal may interpret a legal principle differently from how it is understood in the legal regime from which it is sourced. This form of inconsistency can be attributed to the fragmentation of international law. Fragmentation refers to the process where, as each legal regime in international law becomes more specialised, its legal framework becomes more distinctive, and the body of law becomes increasingly sophisticated.[24] Consequently, it becomes progressively more difficult for specialists in one field of international law to interpret and apply law from other specialist regimes that may be relevant to a given situation.[25] The degree of specialism exhibited in IIL (and concomitantly the expertise of investment arbitrators) can limit the ability of arbitral tribunals to easily interpret and apply principles sourced from other regimes in international law (including international environmental law, international labour law and international human rights law). Hence, should a host State introduce counterclaims based on international law sourced from beyond IIL there is the risk that the arbitral tribunal will not be able to interpret these legal principles consistently with how they are understood in that specialist field. From the perspective of a host State, this is problematic because the counterclaim is likely to rely on an interpretation of the foreign investor's obligation that is accessible and accepted in the regime from which it is sourced. This understanding of the legal principle may not be applied by the arbitral tribunal that hears the dispute. Therefore, the outcome of the counterclaim based on international law is likely to be unpredictable. Unpredictable outcomes may prevent host States from being able to take

19 Cate (n 9) 455.

20 Diel-Gligor (n 8) 118; Schultz (n 8) 297; Arato, Brown and Ortino (n 6) 341; Franck (n 6) 1584.

21 C.f. Cate (n 9) and Schultz (n 8) who both advocate for correct decisions above consistency.

22 Arato, Brown and Ortino (n 6) 340.

23 Diel-Gligor (n 8) 122; Cate (n 9) 455; Schultz (n 8) 297.

24 ILC, 'Fragmentation of International Law: Difficulties Arising from the Diversification and Expansion of International Law' (13 April 2006) UN Doc A/CN4/L682, 10.

25 See ibid.

informed decisions regarding whether to commence a counterclaim based on international law and when a counterclaim should be pursued or settled. Should inconsistent decision-making become a regular concern, host States may lose trust in investment arbitration when disputes involve counterclaims that are based on international law. In the longer term, host State mistrust has the potential to undermine investment arbitration's legitimacy.

The second type of inconsistency occurs within investment arbitration and arises when two arbitral tribunals interpret the same rules or standards to reach different conclusions that cannot be justified based on the characteristics of the claim.[26] The cause of this type of inconsistency can, in part, be attributed to IIL's decentralised framework.[27] Investment obligations are set out in a large network of IIAs. Although substantive commonalities exist in IIAs,[28] the language adopted in IIAs is frequently indeterminate[29] and the intentions of the State parties may vary between IIAs.[30] Consequently, arbitral tribunals will not necessarily reach the same conclusion in every dispute because each IIA represents a different compromise between the States party to the IIA. Additionally, investment arbitration does not operate in a structural hierarchy and does not rely on strict rules of precedent.[31] Given that investment

26 Frequently cited examples of when arbitral tribunals have done this are *SGS Société Générale de Surveillance S.A. v. Islamic Republic of Pakistan* ICSID Case No ARB/01/13, Award on Jurisdiction, 6 August 2003; *SGS Société Générale de Surveillance S.A. v. Republic of the Philippines* ICSID Case No ARB/02/6, Decision of the Tribunal on Objections to Jurisdiction, 29 January 2004; *CMS Gas Transmission Company v. Argentine Republic* ICSID Case No ARB/01/8, Award, 12 May 2005; *LG&E Energy Corp., LG&E Capital Corp. and LG&E International Inc. v. Argentine Republic* ICSID Case No ARB/02/1, Decision on Liability, 3 October 2006; *CME Czech Republic B.V. v. Czech Republic* UNCITRAL, Partial Award, 13 September 2001; *CME Czech Republic B.V. v. Czech Republic* UNCITRAL, Final Award, 14 March 2003; *Ronald S. Lauder v. Czech Republic* UNCITRAL, Final Award, 3 September 2001.

27 Cate (n 9) 425. See Yas Banifatemi, 'Consistency in the interpretation of substantive investment rules: is it achievable?' in Roberto Echandi and Pierre Sauvé (eds), *Prospects in International Investment Law and Policy* (Cambridge University Press 2013) 202–204.

28 Nilsson and Englesson (n 11) 562.

29 Arato, Brown and Ortino (n 6) 346; Tams (n 7) 17; Zarra (n 14) 167–168; Franck (n 6) 1584; Cate (n 9) 454.

30 Tams (n 7) 18; Reinisch (n 8) 237.

31 Nilsson and Englesson (n 11) 562; Cate (n 9) 438; Zarra (n 14) 156. Although arbitral tribunals are not bound by precedent, they may seek to achieve some level of consistency (see *AES Corporation v. Argentine Republic* ICSID Case No ARB/02/17, Decision on Jurisdiction, 26 April 2005 [23(d)] and [30] and *Saipem S.p.A. v. People's Republic of Bangladesh* ICSID Case No ARB/05/07, Decision on Jurisdiction and Recommendation on Provisional Measures, 21 March 2007 [67]). On the role of precedent, see Andrés Rigo Sureda, 'Precedent in Investment Treaty Arbitration' in Christina Binder and others (eds),

arbitrators' primary remit is to resolve investment disputes, arbitral tribunals are relatively free to produce awards that are tailored to each investment dispute.[32] As each dispute will display unique characteristics, interpretations and outcomes will mirror these variations. Further, the composition of each arbitral tribunal is established on an *ad hoc* basis. Not only are there a multiplicity of arbitral tribunals,[33] but there is also diversity in the investment arbitrators that make up each tribunal,[34] which can result in contrasting interpretations and decisions.[35] Consequently, varied interpretations and outcomes are to be expected in investment arbitration. However, when arbitral tribunals reach opposite conclusions based on the same law and facts, this can be particularly problematic for counterclaims based on international law. Not only does this generate similar challenges to those caused by fragmentation (such as preventing effective litigation strategies and generating mistrust from host States) but it may also exacerbate the impact of fragmentation. Arbitral tribunals could produce a series of decisions that potentially interpret legal principles from other regimes incorrectly and that are simultaneously inconsistent with each other. The creation of inconsistent interpretations of the law across legal regimes, and between arbitral tribunals, increases the complexity of how the law might be understood and undermines any form of predictability for host States. Hence, by generating differing interpretations of the same legal principle both within and across legal regimes, international law becomes even more fragmented. Both outcomes reduce the desirability of counterclaims in investment arbitration based on international law and could negatively affect investment arbitration's legitimacy.

In conclusion, conflicting interpretations can arise in investment arbitration across legal regimes due to the fragmentation of international law and arbitral tribunals can also produce contradictory decisions in similar disputes because of IIL's decentralised legal framework. When these forms of inconsistency are combined, the effects become magnified. Conflicting interpretations reduce the predictability of how arbitral tribunals will interpret counterclaims, which could not only increase the risks for host States that seek to rely on counterclaims based on international law but could also harm investment arbitration's legitimacy. Therefore, it is necessary to examine

International Investment Law for the 21st Century: Essay in Honour of Christophe Schreuer (Oxford University Press 2009).

32 See Zarra (n 14) 156–157.

33 Tams (n 7) 18–19; Cate (n 9) 450.

34 Tams (n 7) 19.

35 Schreuer (n 5) 398–399; Banifatemi (n 27) 202.

arbitral practice on counterclaims to determine the extent to which these forms of inconsistency are problematic.

6.3 Inconsistent Decision-Making in Arbitral Practice

Inconsistent decision-making can be difficult to evaluate because each dispute will introduce new variables. Nonetheless, by focusing on the impact of fragmentation and whether arbitral tribunals have produced conflicting interpretations of the same law, it is possible to identify whether these specific forms of inconsistency have arisen in arbitral practice addressing counterclaims based on international law. Only three arbitral tribunals have evaluated the merits of a counterclaim based on international law in investment arbitration. Given the limited number of awards, this section does not seek to extrapolate any trends from these decisions. It merely seeks to determine whether inconsistent interpretations have arisen, and if so, the form the inconsistency takes. To undertake this process, the three disputes (*Urbaser* v *Argentina*;[36] *Burlington* v *Ecuador*;[37] *Perenco* v *Ecuador*)[38] and the decision in *Aven* v *Costa Rica*[39] will be considered with reference to each type of inconsistency. This section argues that each award on the merits demonstrates some form of conflicting interpretation.

The first type of inconsistent decision-making that may arise in counterclaims based on international law results from the fragmentation of international law. The distinct legal frameworks that result from the fragmentation of international law make it challenging for investment arbitrators to correctly interpret the law sourced from beyond IIL that forms the foundation of the counterclaim. This type of inconsistency is evident in the *Urbaser* v *Argentina*

---

36 *Urbaser S.A. and Consorcio de Aguas Bilbao Biskaia, Bilbao Biskaia Ur Partzuergoa v. Argentine Republic* ICSID Case No ARB/07/26, Award, 8 December 2016.

37 *Burlington Resources Inc. v. Republic of Ecuador* ICSID Case No ARB/08/5, Decision on Liability, 14 December 2012; *Burlington Resources Inc. v. Republic of Ecuador* ICSID Case No ARB/08/5, Decision on Counterclaims, 7 February 2017.

38 *Perenco Ecuador Limited v. Republic of Ecuador and Empresa Estatal Petróleos del Ecuador* ICSID Case No ARB/08/6, Decision on Jurisdiction, 30 June 2011; *Perenco Ecuador Limited v. Republic of Ecuador* ICSID Case No ARB/08/6, Interim Decision on the Environmental Counterclaim, 11 August 2015; *Perenco Ecuador Limited v. Republic of Ecuador and Empresa Estatal Petróleos del Ecuador* ICSID Case No ARB/08/6, Decision on Claimant Application for Dismissal of Respondent Counterclaims, 18 August 2017; *Perenco Ecuador Limited v. Republic of Ecuador* ICSID Case No ARB/08/6, Award, 27 September 2019.

39 *David R. Aven and others v. Republic of Costa Rica* ICSID Case No UNCT/15/3, Final Award, 18 September 2018.

award.[40] In *Urbaser* v *Argentina*, a shareholder in a concessionaire that supplied water and sewerage services in Buenos Aires[41] commenced ICSID arbitral proceedings against Argentina for violations of the Spain-Argentina BIT.[42] It claimed that Argentina's emergency measures in response to Argentina's 2001–2 financial crisis caused the concession financial loss, which eventually led to it becoming insolvent.[43] Argentina counterclaimed, alleging that the concessionaire's failure to provide the necessary level of investment led to violations of the human right to water.[44] Thus, to resolve the dispute, the arbitral tribunal was required to interpret international human rights law.

The impact of the fragmentation of international law is evident in how the arbitral tribunal identified the foreign investor's obligations in international human rights law. Whilst initially recognising that corporations possess limited international legal personality,[45] the arbitral tribunal acknowledged that, in certain contexts,[46] corporations can be subjects of international law.[47] Hence, the arbitral tribunal proceeded to consider whether the foreign investor was a subject of international law in the context of this dispute. To establish whether there were human rights obligations for foreign investors associated with a right to water, the arbitral tribunal referred to the UDHR and the ICESCR.[48] The arbitral tribunal highlighted Articles 1, 21(2) and 25(1) of the UDHR and Articles 11(1) and 12 of the ICESCR as being applicable to the right to water.[49] However, when referring to these provisions, the arbitral tribunal conferred some of them with legal content or effects that do not align with how they are understood in the context of international human rights law. The arbitral

40 *Urbaser S.A. and Consorcio de Aguas Bilbao Biskaia, Bilbao Biskaia Ur Partzuergoa v. Argentine Republic* (n 36).

41 ibid [68]–[69].

42 ibid [34]–[35].

43 ibid.

44 ibid [36]–[37].

45 ibid [1194].

46 ibid [1195].

47 ibid.

48 In the context of the ICESCR, the arbitral tribunal additionally referred to interpretations of the right to water by the CESCR in General Comment No. 15 (CESCR, 'General Comment no 15' on 'The Right to Water (arts. 11 and 12 of the International Covenant on Economic, Social and Cultural Rights)' (20 January 2003) UN Doc E/C.12/2002/11) and United Nations' General Assembly Resolution 64/292 (3 August 2010) A/RES/64/292 that highlighted the fundamental nature of the right to water (*Urbaser S.A. and Consorcio de Aguas Bilbao Biskaia, Bilbao Biskaia Ur Partzuergoa v. Argentine Republic* (n 36) [1196]–[1197]).

49 *Urbaser S.A. and Consorcio de Aguas Bilbao Biskaia, Bilbao Biskaia Ur Partzuergoa v. Argentine Republic* (n 36) [1197].

tribunal cited Article 21(2) UDHR as being relevant to the right to water given its use of the term 'public service'.[50] Rather than referring to public services such as water and sewerage services, the provision is commonly understood as referring to the right to equal employment opportunities within a State's public or civil service.[51] This mistake indicates a lack of familiarity with the legal content associated with this human right. To make international human rights law binding on foreign investors, the arbitral tribunal relied on Articles 5(1) UDHR and Article 30 ICESCR.[52] Article 5(1) UDHR and Article 30 ICESCR are interpreted in international human rights law as 'abuse of rights' clauses.[53] Their impact in international human rights law is to prevent the deliberate misinterpretation of one human rights obligation to justify the violation of other rights.[54] Thus, these provisions govern how individuals can invoke rights and do not provide a legal foundation to create binding human rights obligations for corporations.[55] Nonetheless, based on these misinterpretations, the arbitral tribunal found that corporations have a legal duty to respect the right to water.[56] Hence, the arbitral tribunal justifies its conclusion based on a lack of understanding of the content of international human rights law, which may be attributable to the fragmentation of international law.

The arbitral tribunal also displays a misunderstanding of international human rights law's legal framework. This is evident when the arbitral tribunal seeks to allocate responsibility for the right to water between the foreign

---

50 ibid [1196].

51 See Committee on Civil and Political Rights (CCPR), CCPR General Comment No. 25: Article 25 (Participation in Public Affairs and the Right to Vote), The Right to Participate in Public Affairs, Voting Rights and the Right of Equal Access to Public Service (12 July 1996) CCPR/C/21/Rev.1/Add.7 [23], which addresses Article 25(c) ICCPR, which is phrased in similar terms to Article 21(2) UDHR.

52 *Urbaser S.A. and Consorcio de Aguas Bilbao Biskaia, Bilbao Biskaia Ur Partzuergoa v. Argentine Republic* (n 36) [1196], [1197].

53 Edward Guntrip, '*Urbaser v Argentina*: The Origins of a Host State Human Rights Counterclaim in ICSID Arbitration?' (*EJIL:Talk!*, 10 February 2017) <https://www.ejiltalk.org/urbaser-v-argentina-the-origins-of-a-host-state-human-rights-counterclaim-in-icsid-arbitration/> accessed 15 May 2023; Patrick Abel, 'Counterclaims Based on International Human Rights Obligations of Investors in International Investment Arbitration: Fallacies and Potentials of the 2016 ICSID *Urbaser v. Argentina* Award' (2018) 1 Brill Open Law 61, 80.

54 See Ben Saul, David Kinley and Jaqueline Mowbray, *The International Covenant on Economic, Social and Cultural Rights: Commentary, Cases and Materials* (Oxford University Press 2014) 263.

55 See Guntrip (n 53).

56 *Urbaser S.A. and Consorcio de Aguas Bilbao Biskaia, Bilbao Biskaia Ur Partzuergoa v. Argentine Republic* (n 36) [1199].

investor and the host State. International human rights law adopts a respect, protect, fulfil framework to capture the variety of ways in which a human rights violation may take place.[57] Based on this framework, States must not interfere with the enjoyment of the right (the duty to respect), give effect to and support the right by preventing third parties from infringing the right (the duty to protect) and take necessary action to ensure the right is enjoyed (the duty to fulfil).[58] When this framework was established, there was no need to clearly delineate these categories for the purposes of allocating responsibility because States were the only actors bound by international human rights law.[59] However, in *Urbaser* v *Argentina*, the arbitral tribunal sought to allocate these legal duties between the foreign investor and host State.[60] More specifically, the arbitral tribunal held that States are bound by the duty to protect,[61] but foreign investors and States are both bound by the duty to respect.[62] The division of the duty to respect in this way makes it difficult to determine whether a foreign investor or a host State (or both) should be held responsible for a human rights violation.[63] This is because when two actors can potentially be held legally responsible for human rights violations, whether an obligation is a breach of the duty to protect or respect depends on which perspective

---

57 In the context of the ICESCR, this was first given effect to in CESCR, 'General Comment no 12' on 'The Right to Adequate Food' (12 May 1999) UN Doc E/C.12/1999/5.

58 See Frédéric Mégret, 'Nature of Obligations' in Daniel Moeckli, Sangeeta Shah and Sandesh Sivakumaran (eds), *International Human Rights Law* (Oxford University Press 2010) 130–131; Christian Tomuschat, *Human Rights Between Idealism and Realism* (Oxford University Press 2014) 142.

59 See Edward Guntrip, 'Private Actors, Public Goods and Responsibility for the Right to Water in International Investment Law: An Analysis of *Urbaser v Argentina*' (2018) 1 Brill Open Law 37, 54.

60 *Urbaser S.A. and Consorcio de Aguas Bilbao Biskaia, Bilbao Biskaia Ur Partzuergoa v. Argentine Republic* (n 36) [1199]. Whilst soft law instruments, such as the UNGPs, require corporations to respect human rights, this does not create a legal obligation. See Guntrip, 'Private Actors, Public Goods and Responsibility for the Right to Water in International Investment Law: An Analysis of *Urbaser v Argentina*' (n 59) 49. For a discussion of the obligations, see Kevin Crow and Lina Lorenzoni Escobar, 'International Corporate Obligations, Human Rights and the *Urbaser* Standard: Breaking New Ground' (2018) 36 Boston University International Law Journal 87.

61 *Urbaser S.A. and Consorcio de Aguas Bilbao Biskaia, Bilbao Biskaia Ur Partzuergoa v. Argentine Republic* (n 36) [1205].

62 ibid [1207]–[1210]. See Guntrip, 'Private Actors, Public Goods and Responsibility for the Right to Water in International Investment Law: An Analysis of *Urbaser v Argentina*' (n 59) 52.

63 Guntrip, 'Private Actors, Public Goods and Responsibility for the Right to Water in International Investment Law: An Analysis of *Urbaser v Argentina*' (n 59) 54.

is adopted.[64] For example, in this award, if the foreign investor had failed to maintain a water supply service, the foreign investor would be preventing the local population from accessing water by its failure to act, thereby destroying the host State population's enjoyment of this right. This could be seen as violating the obligation to respect.[65] The same conduct could be viewed from the perspective that the host State had not taken sufficient action to ensure that the right of the local population to water was not being damaged or destroyed by the foreign investor. If framed in these terms, the insufficient level of investment would be classified as the State's failure to protect the human right to water.[66] Hence, it is not possible to easily allocate responsibility between the foreign investor and the host State. The arbitral tribunal's allocation of responsibility uses a mechanism that is well established in the context of international human rights law. However, it cannot be readily transposed to the context of foreign investor responsibility and fails to give effect to the arbitral tribunal's aims. Consequently, the arbitral tribunal has adopted elements of international human rights law out of context which may be due to the fragmentation of international law.

The decision of *Aven* v *Costa Rica*[67] demonstrates how the consequences of the fragmentation of international law may be compounded in IIL. This arbitral tribunal did not consider the merits of the counterclaim because the counterclaim did not meet the procedural requirements of the UNCITRAL Arbitration Rules.[68] Nonetheless, as part of the arbitral tribunal's reasoning, it embraced the position taken in *Urbaser* v *Argentina*. It referred to *Urbaser* v *Argentina* to support the view that foreign investors can be subjects of international law, especially when rights and obligations concern all States, which is the case with regards to environmental protection.[69] The arbitral tribunal identified that foreign investors could be subject to international environmental law based on Articles 10.9.3(c), 10.11 and 17 DR-CAFTA, which allow States to adopt environmental measures.[70] On this basis, the arbitral tribunal found

64 ibid.

65 ibid 55.

66 ibid.

67 *David R. Aven and others v. Republic of Costa Rica* (n 39).

68 ibid [744]–[747].

69 ibid [738]. See Debadatta Bose, '*David R Aven v Costa Rica*: The Confluence of Corporations, Public International Law and International Investment Law' (2020) 35 ICSID Review – Foreign Investment Law Journal 20, 22–25.

70 *David R. Aven and others v. Republic of Costa Rica* (n 39) [737]. However, the arbitral tribunal noted that these provisions did not impose an affirmative obligation on foreign investors and did not provide that any breach of domestic environmental laws would amount to a violation of the DR-CAFTA (ibid [743]).

that it had prima facie jurisdiction over the counterclaim (see Section 2.3.3). Thus, the premise for the arbitral tribunal's analysis remains contingent on *Urbaser* v *Argentina*, which relied on non-standard interpretations of international human rights law. The arbitral tribunal in *Aven* v *Costa Rica* applied a similar logic to international environmental law without fully considering the different legal structure of the regime and the nature of the obligations.[71] Consequently, the inconsistent application of law in one award could be replicated in later awards.[72] Hence, there is the potential for the consolidation of divergent understandings of the same legal principle across different legal regimes in international law.

The second type of inconsistency arises when arbitral tribunals reach contrasting conclusions when addressing the same (or a very similar) dispute. This form of inconsistency is evident in *Burlington* v *Ecuador*[73] and *Perenco* v *Ecuador*.[74] Burlington and Perenco were consortium partners in two oil exploration blocks in Ecuador's Amazon rainforest.[75] Burlington and Perenco had production sharing contracts with Ecuador.[76] After oil prices increased, Ecuador unsuccessfully tried to renegotiate the contracts.[77] Instead, Ecuador imposed a new tax regime on oil revenues.[78] Ecuador tried to further negotiate the terms of the contracts but Burlington and Perenco eventually abandoned the negotiations.[79] Ecuador terminated the contracts[80] and claimed for

71 The arbitral tribunal did identify that States bear most of the obligations in international environmental law, but it did not consider whether the logic of *Urbaser* v *Argentina* was transposable to international environmental law (ibid [737]). See Andrew Ling, 'Adjudicating State Counterclaims in ICSID Investor-State Arbitration' (2021) 57 Texas International Law Journal 103, 118.

72 C.f. *Bear Creek Mining Corporation v. Republic of Peru* ICSID Case No ARB/14/21, Partial Dissenting Opinion of Professor Philippe Sands QC, 30 November 2017 [10]–[11] where the principle of systemic integration referred to in *Urbaser* v *Argentina* was applied correctly.

73 *Burlington Resources Inc. v. Republic of Ecuador,* Decision on Liability (n 37).

74 *Perenco Ecuador Limited v. Republic of Ecuador,* Interim Decision on the Environmental Counterclaim (n 38).

75 *Burlington Resources Inc. v. Republic of Ecuador,* Decision on Liability (n 37) [15]; *Perenco Ecuador Limited v. Republic of Ecuador,* Decision on Jurisdiction (n 38) [13].

76 *Burlington Resources Inc. v. Republic of Ecuador,* Decision on Liability (n 37) [6]; *Perenco Ecuador Limited v. Republic of Ecuador,* Decision on Jurisdiction (n 38) [13].

77 *Burlington Resources Inc. v. Republic of Ecuador,* Decision on Liability (n 37) [28].

78 ibid [29]–[32]; *Perenco Ecuador Limited v. Republic of Ecuador,* Decision on Jurisdiction (n 38) [16]–[20].

79 *Burlington Resources Inc. v. Republic of Ecuador,* Decision on Liability (n 37) [39] – [50]; *Perenco Ecuador Limited v. Republic of Ecuador,* Decision on Jurisdiction (n 38) [21].

80 *Burlington Resources Inc. v. Republic of Ecuador,* Decision on Liability (n 37) [63]–[66].

overdue tax,[81] which resulted in Burlington and Perenco commencing separate investment claims against Ecuador.[82] Ecuador counterclaimed, alleging that Burlington and Perenco had polluted the environment and damaged oil extraction infrastructure.[83] Separate arbitral tribunals were established to resolve the disputes. Despite similar factual scenarios, the arbitral tribunals adopted different positions regarding the content of the applicable law of the counterclaims.

Both arbitral tribunals decided the counterclaim based on Ecuador's domestic environmental protection laws (which are derived from international environmental law).[84] Ecuador's environmental laws include the 2008 Ecuadorian Constitution which establishes a strict liability regime for environmental damage.[85] However, Burlington and Perenco entered the production sharing contracts in 2001 and 2002 respectively.[86] Therefore, both arbitral tribunals had to decide whether a strict liability or a fault-based regime applied prior to 2008. Ecuador presented expert evidence that environment damage gave rise to strict liability based on Ecuadorian case law that had applied since 2002.[87] The arbitral tribunals took opposing views regarding how these laws operated prior to 2008. The arbitral tribunal in *Perenco* v *Ecuador* found the applicable Ecuadorian law established a fault-based regime prior to 2008.[88] Consequently, it held that a rebuttable presumption exists that operators engaged in risky operations are responsible for damage.[89] Conversely, in *Burlington* v *Ecuador*,

81 ibid [56].

82 ibid [67]–[68]; *Perenco Ecuador Limited v. Republic of Ecuador*, Decision on Jurisdiction (n 38) [22].

83 *Burlington Resources Inc. v. Republic of Ecuador*, Decision on Counterclaims (n 37) [52],[79]; *Perenco Ecuador Limited v. Republic of Ecuador*, Interim Decision on the Environmental Counterclaim (n 38) [34]–[39].

84 *Perenco Ecuador Limited v. Republic of Ecuador*, Interim Decision on the Environmental Counterclaim (n 38) [81].

85 See *Burlington Resources Inc. v. Republic of Ecuador*, Decision on Counterclaims (n 37) [225]–[230]; *Perenco Ecuador Limited v. Republic of Ecuador*, Interim Decision on the Environmental Counterclaim (n 38) [319]–[320]. The 2008 Ecuadorian Constitution was influenced by the Rio Declaration on Environment and Development (concluded 13 June 1992) UN Doc. A/CONF.151/26 (vol. I) (*Perenco Ecuador Limited v. Republic of Ecuador*, Interim Decision on the Environmental Counterclaim (n 38) [331]).

86 *Burlington Resources Inc. v. Republic of Ecuador*, Decision on Liability (n 37) [14]; *Perenco Ecuador Limited v. Republic of Ecuador*, Decision on Jurisdiction (n 38) [13].

87 *Burlington Resources Inc. v. Republic of Ecuador*, Decision on Counterclaims (n 37) [90]; *Perenco Ecuador Limited v. Republic of Ecuador*, Interim Decision on the Environmental Counterclaim (n 38) [118]–[124].

88 *Perenco Ecuador Limited v. Republic of Ecuador*, Interim Decision on the Environmental Counterclaim (n 38) [357].

89 ibid [371]–[379].

the arbitral tribunal found the applicable Ecuadorian law prior to 2008 had established a strict liability regime in relation to oil fields,[90] which merely requires proof that economic activities had created a serious risk to the environment.[91] As *Burlington* v *Ecuador* was the later decision on this point, it noted the different decisions reached by the separate arbitral tribunals and recognised that it had difficulty in reaching the same conclusion to that in *Perenco*.[92] The opposing positions taken by these tribunals is problematic. Both arbitral tribunals were presented with the same evidence regarding the legal standards employed in Ecuador's domestic legal system, yet the *Perenco* arbitral tribunal imposed a different legal standard to the one applied by Ecuador's domestic courts.[93] It would be expected that arbitral tribunals would reach similar conclusions when presented with the same evidence regarding almost identical claims.

In summary, each award that has addressed the merits stage of a counterclaim displays conflicting interpretations of legal principles. The potential cause of the conflicting interpretations is either the fragmentation of international law or arbitral tribunals reaching opposing decisions in the same dispute. There is also a risk that inconsistent decision-making can influence legal outcomes in subsequent arbitral awards. The extent to which conflicting interpretations of the law are present in the few counterclaims that have been considered at the merits stage is concerning. Host States cannot be sure how obligations sourced from beyond IIL will be interpreted, which makes the law unpredictable and increases the risks associated with presenting counterclaims. Given the existence of conflicting interpretations in these awards, it becomes necessary to determine how conflicting interpretations can be minimised when arbitral tribunals address the merits of counterclaims based on international law.

---

90 *Burlington Resources Inc. v. Republic of Ecuador*, Decision on Counterclaims (n 37) [235]–[238], [247].

91 ibid [235]–[238].

92 ibid [248].

93 See James Harrison, 'Environmental Counterclaims in Investor-State Arbitration' (2016) 17 Journal of World Investment and Trade 479, 486; Jason Rudall, 'The Tribunal with a Toolbox: On *Perenco v Ecuador*, Black Gold and Shades of Green' (2020) 11 Journal of International Dispute Settlement 485, 495–496.

6.4 Means of Overcoming Conflicting Interpretations

Conflicting interpretations of the law generate unpredictable outcomes, which can reduce trust in a legal system and negatively impact its legitimacy.[94] Thus, investment arbitration's legitimacy could potentially be affected when arbitral tribunals reach conflicting interpretations when resolving counterclaims based on international law. Given this risk, arbitral tribunals should have an incentive to produce consistent decisions. Host States can capitalise on the need for legitimacy in investment arbitration by providing arbitral tribunals with guidance on how to interpret laws sourced from beyond IIL to avoid conflicting interpretations of the law. Host States can attempt to influence how arbitral tribunals interpret the law sourced from beyond IIL by drafting provisions in IIAs and in foreign investment legislation that contain interpretative guidance.[95] However, interpretative provisions drafted by host States will be of limited effect because they cannot prevent arbitral tribunals from producing inconsistent decisions caused by an arbitral tribunal's lack of familiarity with the substantive law. Therefore, this section argues that a more effective means of avoiding conflicting interpretations is for arbitral tribunals to appoint independent experts when interpreting law sourced from beyond IIL. Independent experts can provide more detailed guidance on law sourced from beyond IIL, which increases the chances of arbitral tribunals producing consistent decisions when they are presented with counterclaims based on international law. Nonetheless, independent experts can only be appointed in accordance with the applicable arbitration rules, which may preclude their use in some investment disputes.

Host States can guide how arbitral tribunals interpret the applicable law by setting out interpretative guidance in treaty provisions in IIAs or clauses in foreign investment legislation.[96] Host States can use interpretative guidance to set the parameters in which arbitral tribunals should interpret both international law and domestic law. For example, host States can specify that international legal principles from beyond IIL should be interpreted with reference to customary international law.[97] In relation to domestic law, host States can

94 Arato, Brown and Ortino (n 6) 340; Franck (n 6) 1584.

95 See Dafina Atanasova, 'Applicable Law Provisions in Investment Treaties' (2019) 10 Journal of International Dispute Settlement 396, 410.

96 ibid.

97 See China-Colombia BIT 2008 (adopted 22 November 2008, entered into force 2 July 2013) Article 9.11. This is one of the few examples of this type of clause (Atanasova (n 95) 410).

require the arbitral tribunal to apply 'the law that a domestic court or tribunal of proper jurisdiction would apply in the same case'.[98] Thus, host States can integrate interpretative provisions into their standing offer to arbitrate to pre-emptively determine the scope of legal obligations before a dispute arises.

Nevertheless, the guidance offered by interpretative provisions may not be effective in reducing conflicting interpretations in investment arbitration. A provision guiding an arbitral tribunal to interpret a legal principle using customary international law will not ensure consistent decision-making unless arbitral tribunals understand how customary international law is applied in that legal regime. A reference to the host State's domestic case law will not assist an arbitral tribunal that is unaccustomed with the host State's legal system. Arbitral tribunals will generally be unfamiliar with other specialist regimes in international law due to the fragmentation of international law.[99] The lack of detailed knowledge of these international legal regimes, and how these legal principles are implemented in domestic law, is likely to result in arbitral tribunals reaching divergent interpretations of the same legal principle. Hence, interpretative provisions cannot easily overcome conflicting interpretations caused by the fragmentation of international law.

Interpretative provisions are also unlikely to remedy conflicting interpretations that arise within investment arbitration. The legal framework governing investment disputes, to a certain degree, encourages inconsistent decision-making. Inconsistency results from IIL's decentralised structure,[100] the lack of precedent in investment arbitration[101] and the *ad hoc* composition of arbitral tribunals.[102] Thus, host States only have the power to limit the interpretative scope of the arbitral tribunal that is hearing their dispute. As each arbitral tribunal operates independently from one another, arbitral tribunals could apply interpretative guidance differently, potentially giving rise to conflicting interpretations within investment arbitration. Therefore, whilst interpretative guidance may assist a host State in relation to a singular dispute, the lack of

98 Morocco-United States of America FTA 2004 (adopted 15 June 2004, entered into force 1 January 2006) Article 10.21.3 with footnote 8. Regarding how these clauses have been constructed, see Atanasova (n 95) 414. Any interpretations of domestic law should align with a host State's international obligations. If they do not, the counterclaim will not be based on international law, and an arbitral tribunal may substitute the domestic law with the applicable international obligations.

99 See ILC (n 24) 10.

100 Cate (n 9) 425; Banifatemi (n 27) 202–204.

101 Nilsson and Englesson (n 11) 562; Cate (n 9) 438; Zarra (n 14) 156.

102 Tams (n 7) 18–19; Cate (n 9) 450.

systemic coherence in IIL and investment arbitration can still result in conflicting interpretations across multiple investment awards.

In short, interpretative guidance cannot fully overcome the impact of the fragmentation of international law or alter how IIL and investment arbitration function. Consequently, host States have limited control over how arbitral tribunals interpret and apply the law that underpins counterclaims based on international law. Fundamentally, it is arbitral tribunals that determine how the law is interpreted, the degree to which decision-making is consistent in investment arbitration, and ultimately, investment arbitration's legitimacy.

Given their influence over investment arbitration, arbitral tribunals should appoint legal experts to provide them with evidence on the legal principles that form the foundation of counterclaims based on international law. Legal experts can provide the expertise in international law sourced from beyond IIL that arbitral tribunals lack. Tribunal-appointed experts are preferred to party-appointed experts because party-appointed experts have not reduced the risk of inconsistent decision-making.[103] Further, arbitral tribunals are more likely to trust tribunal-appointed experts because arbitral tribunals must evaluate the reliability of the evidence presented by party-appointed experts more thoroughly.[104] Expert evidence can set out the scope of the legal obligations for the arbitral tribunal, which in turn, provides interpretative limitations for the arbitral tribunal and minimises the risk of conflicting interpretations of law sourced from beyond IIL. If arbitral tribunals consistently appoint experts when host States make counterclaims based on international law, the risk of conflicting interpretations between arbitral tribunals on the same point of law can also be reduced. Consistent decision-making would give host states more confidence in counterclaims in investment arbitration which would improve investment arbitration's legitimacy. Despite these potential benefits, the use of tribunal-appointed legal experts complicates investment arbitration proceedings. Therefore, it is necessary to address the practical implications of using tribunal-appointed legal experts in this way.

An arbitral tribunal must examine the applicable arbitration rules and the terms of party consent before appointing a legal expert. The UNCITRAL

---

103 As demonstrated by *Burlington* v *Ecuador* and *Perenco* v *Ecuador* in Section 6.3 above, evidence from party-appointed legal experts does not prevent conflicting interpretations.

104 Asaf Niemoj, 'The Limitations on Article 43 ICSID Convention: An (Un)limited Instrument of the Tribunal?' (2019) 34 ICSID Review – Foreign Investment Law Journal 697, 700; see Mèlida Hodgson and Melissa Stewart, 'Experts in Investor-State Arbitration: The Tribunal as Gatekeeper' (2018) 9 Journal of International Dispute Settlement 453, 455.

Arbitration Rules[105] and the ICSID AF Arbitration Rules[106] explicitly address the need for party consent before appointing an expert. In contrast, the position under the ICSID Convention and the ICSID Arbitration Rules (2006) is not as clear. Article 43 ICSID Convention permits arbitral tribunals to call on the parties to produce evidence[107] and to undertake site visits,[108] but is silent on an arbitral tribunal's power to appoint an independent expert.[109] The ICSID Arbitration Rules (2006) do not refer to tribunal-appointed experts when addressing how arbitral tribunals should address evidence.[110] In the absence of clear guidance, arbitral practice has generally permitted the appointment of independent experts.[111] Nevertheless, in *Abaclat* v *Argentina*,[112] the use of an arbitral tribunal-appointed independent expert in ICSID arbitration was tested when the host State objected to the independent expert's appointment. The majority took the view that an independent expert could be appointed based on arbitral practice relying, in part, on Article 43 ICSID Convention and Rule 34 ICSID Arbitration Rules (2006).[113] However, the dissenting arbitrator held that Article 43 ICSID Convention did not permit the appointment of independent experts in the absence of party consent.[114] Independent experts in all prior cases were appointed with the agreement of the disputing parties. Therefore, party consent, rather than the ICSID Convention and the ICSID Arbitration Rules (2006), may have provided the foundation for their appointment.[115] The issue has been resolved by Rule 39 ICSID Arbitration Rules (2022) which makes it clear that an arbitral tribunal can appoint an independent expert unless the parties agree otherwise. Hence, arbitral tribunals are conferred with the ability

105 UNCITRAL Arbitration Rules (1976) Article 27 and UNCITRAL Arbitration Rules (2010) Article 29.

106 ICSID AF Arbitration Rules (2006) Article 43(c) and ICSID AF Arbitration Rules (2022) Rule 49(1).

107 ICSID Convention Article 43(a).

108 ibid Article 43(b).

109 Niemoj (n 104) 700.

110 ICSID Arbitration Rules (2006) Rules 34–36. See Niemoj (n 104) 701.

111 See for example, *South American Silver Limited v. Plurinational State of Bolivia* PCA Case No 2013-15, Procedural Order No 2, 1 December 2014.

112 *Abaclat and others (formerly Giovanna a Beccara and others) v. Argentine Republic* ICSID Case No ARB/07/5, Procedural Order No 15, 20 November 2012.

113 ibid [12].

114 *Abaclat and others (formerly Giovanna a Beccara and others) v. Argentine Republic* ICSID Case No ARB/07/5, Dissenting Opinion to Procedural Order No 15, 20 November 2012, [26]–[27].

115 See Niemoj (n 104) 709.

to appoint independent experts, but any appointment is most likely to require an arbitral tribunal to address whether there is party consent to do so.

The need for party consent means that the disputing parties can prevent an arbitral tribunal from appointing an independent legal expert.[116] Host States will have a greater motivation to consent to tribunal-appointed independent experts because they will usually be subject to investment disputes on a more regular basis than foreign investors and are more likely to want to achieve consistent interpretations of the law. In contrast, foreign investors are less likely to consider the systemic issues in IIL and investment arbitration and may be more focused on their individual dispute. Hence, foreign investors may prevent an arbitral tribunal from appointing an independent expert. In the absence of independent experts, host States may seek to resolve disputes that would otherwise be heard as counterclaims in investment arbitration by commencing originating claims in domestic dispute resolution fora. The use of domestic dispute resolution fora generates risks for foreign investors (see Section 1.3), meaning that foreign investors may prefer to consent to the appointment of a tribunal-appointed legal expert in investment arbitration than resolve the dispute in the host State. Thus, whether party consent to independent legal experts is granted is likely to be context specific. Nonetheless, party consent may preclude arbitral tribunals from appointing independent legal experts in relation to every counterclaim based on international law.

The appointment of tribunal-appointed legal experts generates risks for the integrity of the investment arbitration proceedings. Legal experts should only present their expert opinion on the law but there is the possibility that they may engage with the adversarial aspects of the dispute.[117] Should a legal expert express their views on the outcome of the dispute, they are effectively fulfilling the role of either the disputing parties' advocates or the arbitral tribunal.[118] Disputing parties will generally want to retain control over what evidence they wish to present and the formation of legal argumentation surrounding their claim. Consequently, a legal expert that exceeds the boundaries of their role may undermine the disputing parties' litigation strategies and may have been

116 ICSID Arbitration Rules (2022) Rule 39 requires both disputing parties to withhold consent to the appointment of an independent expert.

117 Hodgson and Stewart (n 104) 454.

118 See Brooks W Daly and Fiona Poon, 'Technical and Legal Experts in International Investment Disputes' in Chiara Giorgetti (ed), *Litigating International Investment Disputes: a practitioner's guide* (Brill 2014) 338.

better appointed as a co-counsel.[119] An arbitral tribunal may also need to be wary of legal experts expressing their opinion on the outcome of a dispute because this could be perceived to be a delegation of their decision-making authority.[120] Hence, the arbitral tribunal must be able to evaluate the reliability of the evidence without potentially compromising the litigation strategies of the disputing parties and its own function.

To mitigate against these risks, the arbitral tribunal must ensure that the legal expert can effectively perform their role based on their expertise and experience. The arbitration rules are silent as to who qualifies as an expert and what qualities an independent expert should possess.[121] Therefore, arbitral tribunals should exercise their discretion carefully to ensure that the proposed expert is suitably qualified to provide the evidence that it needs.[122] An arbitral tribunal should consider the degree of experience that the expert has in presenting evidence to arbitral tribunals to minimise the risk of the expert acting as a legal advocate or investment arbitrator.[123] However, an expert's prior experience of providing similar evidence should not automatically be seen as compromising their independence.[124] Where the law sourced from beyond IIL is subject to competing interpretations, an arbitral tribunal may wish to appoint more than one expert to ensure that it is presented with different perspectives. Finally, an arbitral tribunal should consider additional factors that are relevant to the dispute, such as language skills[125] and the availability of the expert.[126] Each arbitral tribunal will need to balance these competing considerations to

119 See Nigel Blackaby and Alex Wilbraham, 'Practical Issues Relating to the Use of Expert Evidence in Investment Treaty Arbitration' (2016) 31 ICSID Review – Foreign Investment Law Journal 655, 661; Hodgson and Stewart (n 104) 455.

120 Giovanni De Berti, 'Experts and Expert Witnesses in International Arbitration: Adviser, Advocate or Adjudicator?' in Christian Klausegger and others (eds), *Austrian Yearbook of International Law* (C.H. Beck 2010) 61–62; Matthew W Swinehart, 'Reliability of Expert Evidence in International Disputes' (2017) 38 Michigan Journal of International Law 287, 307–308; Blackaby and Wilbraham (n 119) 664; Tomoko Ishikawa, *Corporate Environmental Responsibility in Investor-State Dispute Settlement: The Unexhausted Potential of Current Mechanisms* (Cambridge University Press 2022) 132.

121 UNCITRAL Arbitration Rules (2010) Article 29(2) only requires the expert to provide a description of his or her qualifications. See also IBA Guidelines on Conflicts of Interest in International Arbitration (2014) 3.4.3. See Hodgson and Stewart (n 104) 458; Daly and Poon (n 118) 336.

122 The arbitral tribunal should act as a gatekeeper (Hodgson and Stewart (n 104) 461).

123 See Daly and Poon (n 118) 350 regarding the use of law professors rather than practitioners to avoid this risk.

124 ibid 347–348.

125 ibid 341.

126 ibid.

ensure that the legal expert can provide the independent expertise needed for the specific counterclaim.

To maintain investment arbitration's adversarial nature, the disputing parties should be given the opportunity to object to the appointment of a proposed independent expert or challenge the expert's findings. The ICSID Arbitration Rules (2022) and ICSID AF Arbitration Rules (2022) require that an arbitral tribunal consult with the disputing parties regarding the appointment of an expert[127] and require party consent before an expert is instructed.[128] The UNCITRAL Arbitration Rules (2010)[129] mirror the International Bar Association (IBA) Rules on Evidence that permit parties to object to an expert after they receive a description of qualifications and independence from the arbitral tribunal.[130] In accordance with IBA Rules on Evidence, the disputing parties can only object to the appointment of a legal expert at a later stage if something new comes to light.[131] Therefore, in accordance with these arbitration rules, the disputing parties may be able to question the qualifications and independence of the tribunal-appointed experts. However, the ICSID Arbitration Rules (2006), the ICSID AF Arbitration Rules (2006) and the UNCITRAL Arbitration Rules (1976) are silent on the disputing parties' ability to object to the appointment of an expert. Nonetheless, it is common practice that the disputing parties can engage with the arbitral tribunal at various stages of the evidence gathering process. This can include formulating the terms of reference,[132] expressing an opinion on the report,[133] making written submissions on the expert's report,[134] and interrogating the expert at the hearing.[135] Consequently, even

127 ICSID Arbitration Rules (2022) Rule 39(2) and ICSID AF Arbitration Rules (2022) Rule 49(2). See Daly and Poon (n 118) 328.

128 ICSID Arbitration Rules (2022) Rule 39(1) and ICSID AF Arbitration Rules (2022) Rule 49(1).

129 UNCITRAL Arbitration Rules (2010) Article 29(2).

130 IBA Rules on the Taking of Evidence in International Arbitration (2020) Article 6(2). See also UNCITRAL Notes on Organizing Arbitral Proceedings (2016) para 102.

131 IBA Rules on the Taking of Evidence in International Arbitration (2020) Article 6(2).

132 ICSID Arbitration Rules (2022) Rule 39(2); ICSID AF Arbitration Rules (2022) Rule 49(2).

133 UNCITRAL Arbitration Rules (1976) Article 27(3); UNCITRAL Arbitration Rules (2010) Article 29(4); IBA Rules on the Taking of Evidence in International Arbitration (2020) Article 6(5). See *Perenco Ecuador Limited v. Republic of Ecuador*, Interim Decision on the Environmental Counterclaim (n 38) [588].

134 ICSID Arbitration Rules (2022) Rule 39(5); ICSID AF Arbitration Rules (2022) Rule 49(5); IBA Rules on the Taking of Evidence in International Arbitration (2020) Article 6(5). See *Perenco Ecuador Limited v. Republic of Ecuador*, Interim Decision on the Environmental Counterclaim (n 38) [588].

135 UNCITRAL Arbitration Rules (1976) Article 27(4); UNCITRAL Arbitration Rules (2010) Article 29(5); IBA Rules on the Taking of Evidence in International Arbitration (2020)

if the disputing parties cannot challenge the appointment of the legal expert, they can use these avenues to challenge any of the legal expert's findings.[136]

The introduction of external actors into investment arbitration inevitably complicates the dispute resolution process. Hence, a key drawback associated with using independent experts is the increase in delays and costs,[137] which may disincentivise some host States from proceeding with counterclaims. Nevertheless, any additional costs might be recovered if the counterclaim is successful and the host State is awarded compensation. Therefore, host States will need to determine on a case-by-case basis whether the additional burdens associated with tribunal-appointed legal experts provide sufficient advantages for the host State's counterclaim.

Although it may not be simple to appoint an independent expert, expert evidence on law sourced from beyond IIL can enhance the effectiveness of counterclaims based on international law. The evidence the legal expert provides can give arbitral tribunals a frame of reference so that the interpretation of the international legal principles is consistent with how the law is understood in the regime from which it is sourced. If arbitral tribunals consistently use legal experts (which remains subject to party consent) the risk of inconsistent interpretations between arbitral tribunals is reduced. The higher levels of consistent decision-making will enhance host State certainty regarding the content of the law and maintain their trust in investment arbitration. Yet, investment arbitrators may be reluctant to appoint independent experts on legal questions that they believe they are qualified to address. Thus, discussions surrounding the use of tribunal-appointed legal experts should be framed as being an issue of investment arbitration's legitimacy. In instances where arbitral tribunals lack the requisite expertise in a field of law, by highlighting the risk of inconsistent decision-making, host States can raise concerns about consistency and predictability, the function of the rule of law and ultimately the legitimacy of investment arbitration as justifications for the use of independent experts. Host States cannot be certain that these arguments will be

---

Article 6(6). The expert may not need to physically attend the hearing (UNCITRAL Arbitration Rules (2010) Article 28(4)).

136 See Ishikawa (n 120) 133.

137 This was a concern for the *Burlington* v *Ecuador* arbitral tribunal and was raised in *Perenco Ecuador Limited v. Republic of Ecuador*, Award (n 38) [489], [490] and *Perenco Ecuador Limited v. Republic of Ecuador*, Interim Decision on the Environmental Counterclaim (n 38) [593]–[594]. See Hiroko Yamamoto, Shreya Ramesh and Sebestian Seelmann-Eggebert, '*Perenco Ecuador v Republic of Ecuador Lessons from Perenco*: Tribunal-Appointed Experts and Avoiding Double Recovery' (2020) 35 ICSID Review – Foreign Investment Law Journal 459, 466; Daly and Poon (n 118) 323.

accepted. Nevertheless, these arguments provide a strong policy foundation for an arbitral tribunal to justify the appointment of an independent expert.

In summary, to reduce the likelihood of inconsistent decision-making in investment arbitration, host States can tailor provisions in IIAs to include interpretative guidance for arbitral tribunals. Yet, a more effective approach would be for arbitral tribunals to appoint independent experts to provide evidence regarding interpretations of legal principles sourced from beyond IIL. Whilst it is procedurally possible, arbitral tribunals must consider party consent and should be careful to appoint an appropriately qualified and experienced expert. Host States may have to accept delays and increased costs associated with introducing external parties into the dispute resolution process. Nonetheless, on balance, tribunal-appointed legal experts can help arbitral tribunals to achieve consistent interpretations of law sourced from beyond IIL, which will enhance host State trust in investment arbitration. However, whether an arbitral tribunal can use tribunal-appointed experts is not within host State control. Hence, if it is not possible for an arbitral tribunal to appoint experts, host States remain subject to the risks associated with inconsistent decision-making when a counterclaim based on international law reaches the merits stage.

6.5 Assessing the Desirability of Counterclaims in Investment Arbitration

Host States cannot prevent arbitral tribunals from producing unpredictable outcomes when resolving a counterclaim based on international law at the merits stage of the proceedings. Interpretative provisions in IIAs or foreign investment legislation do not adequately control how arbitral tribunals will interpret and apply the law. Further, host States do not possess the power to require an arbitral tribunal to appoint an independent expert to assist the arbitral tribunal to interpret international law. Thus, the potential for inconsistent decision-making remains. Consequently, this section argues that host States need to assess the desirability of using counterclaims based on international law in investment arbitration to seek redress for foreign investor misconduct on a claim-by-claim basis. While it is not possible to definitively determine in what circumstances a host State should bring a counterclaim based on international law in investment arbitration, host States should evaluate several factors.

Host States should consider the clarity of the law underpinning the counterclaim. Whether an arbitral tribunal is likely to produce an inconsistent interpretation of the law may be influenced by the substantive legal obligations that form the foundation of the counterclaim. The more complex the legal framework from which the obligations are sourced, the greater the chances that an arbitral tribunal will generate a conflicting interpretation of the law. Thus, in *Urbaser* v *Argentina*, the arbitral tribunal failed to consider the consequences of transplanting the respect, protect, fulfil framework from international human rights law into situations of shared responsibility. As a result, foreign investors may have a legal responsibility to respect human rights that is potentially indistinguishable from the host State's responsibility to protect human rights in relation to the same legal obligation. Yet, the law does not need to be complex to generate conflicting interpretations of the law. Again, in *Urbaser* v *Argentina*, the human rights obligations that were misinterpreted by the arbitral tribunal have well established meanings in international human rights law. It does not appear that interpretations of the provisions generated by international human rights law bodies were taken into account by the arbitral tribunal. In *Burlington* v *Ecuador* and *Perenco* v *Ecuador*, the arbitral tribunals reached conflicting decisions when deciding whether Ecuador's domestic law imposed a fault based or strict liability regime prior to 2008 when both tribunals were presented with the same evidence regarding how the law had been applied by Ecuador's domestic courts. Consequently, host States should be cognisant of the complexity of the legal framework from which the substantive legal obligation that underpins the counterclaim is sourced, whilst also recognising that any degree of unfamiliarity with the legal system could mean that an arbitral tribunal generates an inconsistent outcome.

Host States should additionally be aware of the composition of the arbitral tribunal. In the first instance, host States should determine the expertise of the investment arbitrators that comprise the arbitral tribunal. Investment arbitrators that do not have a background or training in public international law may be more likely to misunderstand and misapply the international law that forms the basis of the counterclaim. However, this generalisation will not always hold true, so host States should try to gain as much information as possible about how the investment arbitrator is likely to interpret and apply international law sourced from beyond IIL. As many investment arbitrators are repeatedly appointed to resolve investment disputes,[138] host States should review prior decisions of the investment arbitrators on the arbitral tribunal. Prior decisions can be useful to understand how investment arbitrators have applied international law before, or to expose how certain investment arbitrators understand

138 See Sergio Puig, 'Social Capital in the Arbitration Market' (2014) 25 European Journal of International Law 387.

the role of international law in investment arbitration more generally. In addition to an investment arbitrator's expertise, host States should also consider whether an investment arbitrator has a record of creative law-making. For example, the arbitral tribunal in *Urbaser* v *Argentina* presented novel interpretations of international human rights law, which might suggest that those investment arbitrators could produce novel interpretations of other legal obligations in the future. Once a host State has a sense of how the arbitral tribunal might act in relation to a counterclaim based on international law, it can decide how best to proceed.

When electing whether to commence a counterclaim based on international law in investment arbitration, host States should examine the availability of alternative dispute resolution fora to determine if there is a better forum in which to bring a claim against the foreign investor. Host States should consider several factors when deciding whether there are better dispute resolution fora in which to bring the claim. Logistically, bringing a claim outside of investment arbitration may result in a duplication of resources for the host State. A host State is likely to have to replicate evidence and present new legal argumentation in a different dispute resolution forum whilst defending legal proceedings in investment arbitration. New legal proceedings will take additional time and incur further costs. Nonetheless, the logistical drawbacks may be compensated for by the specialist expertise that can be found in different dispute resolution fora. If a claim against a foreign investor relies on law that is best interpreted and applied by decision-makers with specialist knowledge, another dispute resolution forum may be a better option. However, if the claim is based on international law, a host State may struggle to bring a claim directly against a foreign investor due to their lack of standing in many international dispute resolution fora. The option of commencing legal proceedings in the host State's domestic courts remains, but this may not always be in the interests of the host State (see Section 1.3). Further, when evaluating other dispute resolution fora, host States should consider the potential interactions between investment arbitration and the other dispute resolution forum. More specifically, it may be that a decision in the other forum will not be recognised in investment arbitration. To illustrate, if a host State is successful against the foreign investor in another forum, and an arbitral tribunal does not recognise this decision, the host State may have to bring evidence to the arbitral tribunal to prove the same point, which may or may not be accepted by the arbitral tribunal in the investment dispute. Therefore, host States will need to be strategic to ensure that any findings of foreign investor misconduct are recognised in investment arbitration if they form a key aspect of the investment dispute. Finally, relying on a different dispute resolution forum is likely to reinforce the fragmentation that exists between IIL and other fields of international law. Some host States may seek to challenge investment arbitration's specialist focus by highlighting its shortcomings using a counterclaim. It is unlikely that many host States will prioritise this factor, but if no alternative dispute resolution forum can meet the host State's needs, host States could seek to draw attention to the inability of investment arbitration to resolve counterclaims based on international law as a means of trying to reform investment arbitration.

Host States need to additionally consider what outcome they want from the claim against the foreign investor. If a host State is seeking a remedy to counter any liability for breaches of an IIA, it is likely that investment arbitration is the only forum that can award the appropriate levels of compensation (see Section 1.3). If seeking financial compensation, a host State will find it easier to enforce an investment award than a judgment from a domestic court in a foreign jurisdiction.[139] A host State may also want to dissuade foreign investors from breaching international law and may wish to use investment arbitration to draw attention to a foreign investor's misconduct. Alternatively, if the host State is seeking non-compensatory remedies, domestic courts may be better placed to award and enforce these types of remedy. As a result, host States should consider what they wish to achieve by challenging foreign investor misconduct and to find the best forum that can achieve this aim.

In short, host States cannot guarantee that arbitral tribunals will apply law sourced from beyond IIL as expected when resolving counterclaims based on international law. Hence, host States must consider whether alternative dispute resolution fora are better placed to address foreign investor misconduct. When making this decision, host States should consider a variety of factors on a claim-by-claim basis before deciding whether to commence a counterclaim based on international law in investment arbitration. In some instances, other dispute resolution fora may not be able to replicate what investment arbitration offers, whereas in other cases, the risk of using investment arbitration will be too great. Consequently, until investment arbitration refines how it addresses counterclaims based on international law in investment arbitration, host States will need to decide how best to address foreign investor misconduct.

139 Gustavo Laborde, 'The Case for Host State Claims in Investment Arbitration' (2010) 1 Journal of International Dispute Settlement 97, 101. See August Reinisch, 'Enforcement of Investment Treaty Awards' in Katia Yannaca-Small (ed), *Arbitration Under International Investment Agreements: A Guide to the Key Issues* (2nd edn, Oxford University Press 2018).

6.6 Preliminary Conclusions

At the merits stage of a counterclaim, there is the risk that arbitral tribunals may interpret law sourced from beyond IIL inconsistently. An arbitral tribunal's interpretation may conflict with how the legal principle is understood to function in its original legal regime, with another arbitral tribunal's interpretation of the same law, or it may conflict with both. Arbitral practice that has addressed counterclaims based on international law illustrate that arbitral tribunals have reached conflicting interpretations that could be caused by the fragmentation of international law. Further, arbitral tribunals have reached opposite conclusions when they have been presented with party-appointed expert evidence on unfamiliar legal systems. Conflicting interpretations of the law create unpredictable outcomes that can create risks for host States when they present a counterclaim, which may erode host State trust in investment arbitration and harm investment arbitration's legitimacy. To manage this risk, host States could rely on provisions that provide interpretative guidance to arbitral tribunals. However, interpretative guidance is insufficient to overcome a lack of familiarity with substantive law or address the structural issues in international law and investment arbitration that contribute to conflicting interpretations of the law. Therefore, arbitral tribunals should enhance investment arbitration's legitimacy by appointing legal experts to assist them with interpreting law sourced from beyond IIL. The use of tribunal-appointed legal experts complicates the dispute resolution process and presents challenges for arbitral tribunals and the disputing parties. Nonetheless, if tribunal-appointed legal experts are employed carefully, they can provide evidence that reduces the risk of conflicting interpretations of law sourced from beyond IIL. Despite the benefits of expert evidence, there is no guarantee that arbitral tribunals will be able or willing to appoint independent experts. Thus, host States will need to evaluate the risks of presenting counterclaims based on international law in investment arbitration when seeking redress for foreign investor misconduct.

CHAPTER 7

The 'Magic' of Counterclaims

7.1 Introduction

Counterclaims in investment arbitration are not currently used to their full potential. However, by utilising State practice and litigation strategies, host States can steer arbitral practice to maximise the promise of counterclaims in investment arbitration. Greater use of counterclaims would enable host States to rebalance the asymmetry of investment arbitration and to counter the privileging of foreign investors. Host States can then use counterclaims (when appropriate) based on principles of international law to challenge foreign investor misconduct. Hence, counterclaims based on international law have the potential to fundamentally alter the dynamics of investment arbitration. Despite the ability of counterclaims to create these changes, it is recognised that counterclaims based on international law cannot solve all problems related to foreign investor misconduct. Therefore, it is necessary to contextualise what counterclaims based on international law can modify in investment arbitration. Counterclaims based on international law perform a specific function in investment disputes. Yet, their proposed use may have wider repercussions in international law. Thus, it is important to additionally consider how using counterclaims based on international law in investment arbitration could adjust how non-State actors are regulated by international law.

This chapter examines the impact that counterclaims based on international law can have in investment arbitration and how they might influence international law more generally. It argues that counterclaims can be used more effectively in investment arbitration, which would permit counterclaims based on international law to deal with foreign investor misconduct (Section 7.2). However, counterclaims based on international law cannot solve all the legal challenges associated with foreign investor misconduct. Hence, counterclaims based on international law should be viewed as a significant aspect of the solution to foreign investor misconduct rather than as a panacea. Nevertheless, the proposed use of counterclaims based on international law disrupts how international law has traditionally conceptualised non-State actors and could influence wider practices in international law (Section 7.3). The chapter then presents concluding observations (Section 7.4).

 | DOI:10.1163/9789004420953_008

7.2 Counterclaims in Investment Arbitration

Investment arbitration practice evidences that counterclaims are rarely invoked and have low rates of success (see Section 1.2). These findings might explain why host States are reluctant to employ counterclaims in investment arbitration to address foreign investor misconduct. Yet, host States often struggle to successfully challenge foreign investor misconduct using other litigation strategies in investment arbitration (see Section 1.2). This book argues that, when State practice is altered and different litigation strategies are employed, counterclaims do possess the necessary attributes to enable host States to use international law to challenge foreign investor misconduct. Host States can then decide when it is appropriate to employ counterclaims for this purpose. Nonetheless, even when applied as envisaged, counterclaims based on international law cannot provide a comprehensive solution for all issues associated with foreign investor misconduct. Therefore, it is important to identify what role counterclaims based on international law can play in investment arbitration and where additional solutions will be required. Hence, this section illustrates how counterclaims can be used more effectively in investment arbitration to give greater powers to host States to challenge foreign investor misconduct using international law. Nonetheless, it also acknowledges that counterclaims based on international law have limitations and will need to form part of a wider solution to combat the problem of foreign investor misconduct.

The structure of IIL and investment arbitration make it difficult for host States to effectively challenge foreign investor misconduct. IIL privileges foreign investors with investment protection standards that only bind host States.[1] The asymmetry found in these obligations is enhanced by the general position that foreign investors do not inherently possess international legal personality,[2] meaning that foreign investors are not duty bearers in international law.

1 James Gathii and Sergio Puig, 'Introduction to the Symposium on Investor Responsibility: The Next Frontier in International Investment Law' (2019) 113 AJIL Unbound 1, 1; Martin Jarrett, *Contributory Fault and Investor Misconduct in Investment Arbitration* (Cambridge University Press 2019) 1–2; Ivar Alvik, 'The Justification of Privilege in International Investment Law: Preferential Treatment of Foreign Investors as a Problem of Legitimacy' (2020) 31 European Journal of International Law 289, 290; see also Jürgen Kurtz, 'On Foreign Investor "Privilege" and the Limits of the Law: A Reply to Ivar Alvik' (2020) 31 European Journal of International Law 313, 313–314.

2 Patrick Dumberry and Èrik Labelle-Eastaugh, 'Non-state actors in international investment law: The legal personality of corporations and NGOs in the context of investor-state arbitration' in Jean d'Aspremont (ed), *Participants in the International Legal System: Multiple Perspectives on Non-State Actors in International Law* (Routledge 2011) 365.

Further, existing procedures in investment arbitration fail to counter these attributes and, as a result, do not provide the means by which host States can challenge foreign investor misconduct (see Section 1.2). Counterclaims based on international law can allow host States to address foreign investor misconduct by overcoming these deficiencies. However, host States need to alter their State practice and litigation strategies in the following ways if counterclaims based on international law are to fulfil this aim.

1. *Host States should expressly consent to counterclaims – but not in terms that could expand an arbitral tribunal's jurisdiction and expose host States to more originating claims.* To be successful, counterclaims must initially fall within the jurisdiction of the arbitral tribunal. Consequently, counterclaims must align with any requirements set out in the applicable arbitration rules and fall within the scope of party consent. Host States can dictate the terms of party consent using standing offers set out in IIAs and domestic foreign investment legislation. Nonetheless, arbitral practice evidences that host States are not using party consent in a sufficiently nuanced manner. More specifically, host States are not appropriately balancing the risk of being exposed to originating claims with the ability to present a counterclaim. Host State consent drafted in broad terms means that an arbitral tribunal's jurisdiction includes counterclaims, but it also potentially exposes host States to a wide variety of originating claims. Drafting party consent in narrow terms limits originating claims but excludes counterclaims. Investment arbitrators seek to give effect to counterclaims where possible, but they are bound by the terms of party consent. Therefore, when party consent is drafted in wide or narrow terms, investment arbitrators have limited options. Hence, host States need to recalibrate how they consent to investment arbitration by using tailored clauses that create consent to counterclaims independently from originating claims. Drafting consent to counterclaims in this way ensures that arbitral tribunals can establish jurisdiction over counterclaims whilst minimising host State exposure to a wide range of claims being made by a foreign investor. This practice is achievable given that this type of clause is evident in some Model BITs and IIAs, but it needs to become more widespread to permit counterclaims to be used more frequently.
2. *Host States should use legal provisions to set out how a connection between originating claims and counterclaims can be established. Host States should supplement these legal provisions with legal argumentation that refers to the good administration of justice to encourage arbitral tribunals to adopt a wider understanding of what amounts to a connection.* A counterclaim

must display a connection to the originating claim to give effect to the good administration of justice. The good administration of justice seeks to ensure that related claims are heard together and that unrelated claims are heard in separate fora to ensure that dispute resolution remains efficient. Whether a counterclaim is deemed to be connected to an originating claim is dependent on how an arbitral tribunal defines the scope of a dispute. To give effect to the good administration of justice, arbitral practice has focused on identifying legal connections between the originating claim and the counterclaim. The dominant trend in arbitral practice has been that a legal connection must be established based on reciprocal obligations found in the same legal source. This does not assist counterclaims based on international law because obligations that directly bind foreign investors will not usually be found in an IIA. Legal obligations sourced in domestic legislation do not usually meet the need for a connection when establishing a counterclaim. Hence, counterclaims based on international obligations that indirectly bind foreign investors are also excluded. Finally, there is an emerging practice that factual connections can support a counterclaim. Whilst this practice does support counterclaims based on international law, there is limited arbitral practice that has adopted this stance. As a result, arbitral tribunals frame disputes, and the good administration of justice, in narrow terms.

Host States can seek to alter arbitral practice by including provisions in IIAs and in foreign investment legislation that require arbitral tribunals to consider a diverse range of connections. To increase the chances of a counterclaim meeting the nexus requirement, host States should additionally rely on legal argumentation that gives effect to a broader understanding of the good administration of justice. In many instances, host States can seek to convince an arbitral tribunal that a connection exists by adopting a wider understanding of what amounts to a dispute (which encompasses foreign investor obligations) and highlighting the efficiency of hearing the originating claim and the counterclaim together. As these arguments have not been fully developed in arbitral practice to date, there is scope to increase the type of counterclaims that can be addressed in investment arbitration to include those based on international law.

3. *Host States should draft applicable law clauses to increase the likelihood that an arbitral tribunal will apply international law to a counterclaim.* The substantive legal obligation that underpins a counterclaim must fall within the applicable law. Therefore, to establish a counterclaim based on international law, the applicable law must extend to principles of

international law sourced from beyond IIL. The applicable law is determined by party consent and the arbitration rules, however, many host States do not exercise party consent in the context of the applicable law. Consequently, arbitral tribunals are required to apply the applicable arbitration rules to identify the applicable law. Arbitration rules guide arbitral tribunals to select appropriate domestic laws as the applicable law, and in some instances, confer arbitral tribunals with the opportunity to decide whether to apply international law to a claim. Hence, whilst arbitration rules do not exclude the application of international law, they do not ensure that international law will form part of the applicable law. Thus, by relying on the arbitration rules, host States take the risk that arbitral tribunals will not be able to consider principles of international law sourced from beyond IIL when resolving a counterclaim. Yet, by making use of party consent in the form of an applicable law clause, host States can then ensure that an arbitral tribunal can apply principles of international law in support of counterclaims. To ensure that counterclaims based on international law can be heard, host States should include applicable law clauses in IIAs or foreign investment legislation that specify which principles of international law are included in the applicable law and how they should be applied by an arbitral tribunal.

4. *Host States can establish counterclaims based on international law by relying on certain sources of international law but should further enhance the precision of foreign investor obligations to provide a more secure foundation for a counterclaim.* A host State must substantiate a counterclaim based on a law that binds a foreign investor and that generates obligations to the host State. These laws must also be sufficiently precise to ensure that they are enforceable against a foreign investor. Although foreign investors do not possess inherent international legal personality, express provisions in IIAs, domestic law that implements international obligations and investment contracts have the potential to generate foreign investor obligations that can form the foundation of a counterclaim. Host States may be able to inform the interpretation of obligations found in these sources with reference to soft law obligations. While obligations from these sources of law can meet the minimum threshold to establish a counterclaim, there is scope for greater precision by introducing foreign investor obligations that are tailored to counterclaims and that provide even clearer obligations for arbitral tribunals to apply.

5. *Host States should encourage arbitral tribunals to appoint independent experts to guide them on the content of international law sourced from beyond IIL to prevent conflicting interpretations of the law and to*

enhance investment arbitration's legitimacy. However, as there is no guarantee that independent experts will be appointed, host States should also consider whether alternative dispute resolution fora are better placed to address foreign investor misconduct on a claim-by claim basis. Once the legal foundation of a counterclaim has been identified, an arbitral tribunal must interpret foreign investor obligations. Given international law's fragmented structure and investment arbitration's decentralised decision-making processes, there is the risk of inconsistent decision-making. Inconsistency may arise when arbitral tribunals interpret law sourced from beyond IIL differently to how it is interpreted in its original legal regime. Further, arbitral tribunals may reach opposing conclusions when addressing similar claims. Significantly, both forms of conflicting interpretation can undermine investment arbitration's legitimacy. Host States could rely on provisions that provide interpretative guidance to arbitral tribunals. Yet, arbitral practice indicates that interpretative guidance may not prevent conflicting interpretations of the law. While host States cannot dictate how arbitral tribunals reach their conclusions, they can encourage arbitral tribunals to refer to independent experts when addressing legal obligations beyond IIL. Host States can foster this practice by arguing that the use of experts will lead to correct legal interpretations, which in turn will encourage the use of counterclaims in investment arbitration and enhance investment arbitration's legitimacy. Nonetheless, there will be circumstances in which arbitral tribunals cannot or will not appoint experts. Consequently, host States will need to evaluate the risks of presenting counterclaims based on international law in investment arbitration when seeking redress for foreign investor misconduct and decide on a case-by-case basis whether investment arbitration is the best forum for their claim.

By altering State practice and litigation strategies in the ways suggested, host States can respond to arbitral practice that limits the use of counterclaims at each stage of the adjudicative process. When these actions are taken collectively, host States can overcome the inherent limitations that are currently found in IIL and investment arbitration, and counterclaims based on international law can become mainstream within investment arbitration. Host States can then decide when it is appropriate to employ counterclaims based on international law to challenge foreign investor misconduct in investment arbitration.

Despite the promise of what counterclaims based on international law might be able to achieve, they cannot comprehensively remedy all the issues associated with foreign investor misconduct. There are two key limitations regarding what counterclaims based on international law can achieve. First, counterclaims based on international law have a limited reach. Counterclaims can only be invoked by host States when a foreign investor has commenced an investment claim.[3] Investment claims will not be invoked by foreign investors in all instances of foreign investor misconduct. Thus, counterclaims based on international law will not capture all instances of foreign investor misconduct. Further, even if a host State can commence a counterclaim based on international law, not all counterclaims will be successful. Therefore, counterclaims based on international will only generate foreign investor liability in some investment disputes that involve foreign investor misconduct. Consequently, counterclaims based on international law have a confined scope of application.

Second, counterclaims based on international law cannot be used by local communities that have been affected by foreign investor misconduct to seek redress.[4] Investment arbitration only accommodates foreign investors and host States as disputing parties.[5] Thus, local communities are unable to be directly involved in the arbitration proceedings[6] and an arbitral tribunal cannot provide remedies for any violations of international law to a local community. Hence, the extent to which local communities are remedied for foreign investor misconduct is left to the host State.[7] As a result, counterclaims based on international law do not provide remedies for all the parties affected by foreign investor misconduct.

3 Anna De Luca, 'UNCITRAL Working Group III: Counterclaims in ISDS – Challenges and Prospects in Light of the UNCITRAL Reform Process' (*Kluwer Arbitration Blog*, 28 March 2020) <http://arbitrationblog.kluwerarbitration.com/2020/03/28/uncitral-working-group-iii-counterclaims-in-isds-challenges-and-prospects-in-light-of-the-uncitral-reform-process/> accessed 13 May 2021; Tomoko Ishikawa, *Corporate Environmental Responsibility in Investor-State Dispute Settlement: The Unexhausted Potential of Current Mechanisms* (Cambridge University Press 2022) 201.

4 See Tomoko Ishikawa, 'Counterclaims and the Rule of Law in Investment Arbitration' (2019) 113 AJIL Unbound 33, 35; Ishikawa, *Corporate Environmental Responsibility in Investor-State Dispute Settlement: The Unexhausted Potential of Current Mechanisms* (n 3) 12; Nicolás M Perrone, 'The "Invisible" Local Communities: Foreign Investor Obligations, Inclusiveness, and the International Investment Regime' (2019) 113 AJIL Unbound 16, 16.

5 Kristen Boon, 'Theorizing Responsibility in the Investor State Dispute Resolution System' (2021) 95 St John's Law Review 253, 253.

6 Although local communities may be able to file non-disputing party submissions.

7 Perrone (n 4) 18, 20; Lorenzo Cotula and Nicolás M Perrone, 'Investors' International Law and its Asymmetries: the Case of Local Communities' in Jean Ho and Mavluda Sattarova (eds), *Investors' International Law* (Hart Publishing 2021). See also Tomoko Ishikawa, 'Counterclaims in Investment Arbitration: Is the Host State the Right Claimant?' in Jean Ho and Mavluda Sattarova (eds), *Investors' International Law* (Hart Publishing 2021).

The limitations of counterclaims based on international law highlight that measures are needed beyond the specific context of investment arbitration if foreign investor misconduct is to be comprehensively addressed. Tools that seek to prevent foreign investor misconduct are needed when investment claims are unlikely to arise or when counterclaims are unlikely to be successful. Further, local communities need a means of being able to obtain a remedy when foreign investor misconduct has caused detrimental impacts to their community. Counterclaims based on international law are not intended to fill these gaps and cannot provide solutions to these problems. Therefore, counterclaims based on international law are not a panacea. Nonetheless, this does not detract from what counterclaims can achieve. Compared to the lack of procedural options that are currently available to host States, counterclaims based on international law provide a viable procedure by which host States can address foreign investor misconduct. Consequently, counterclaims based on international law should be viewed as part of a larger toolbox and should be understood as having the specific role of challenging foreign investor misconduct in investment arbitration.

In summary, counterclaims are not currently used by host States to challenge foreign investor misconduct. However, by altering State practice and litigation strategies, host States can maximise the potential of counterclaims in investment arbitration and decide when to challenge foreign investor misconduct by presenting counterclaims based on international law. Not all counterclaims based on international law will be successful and counterclaims do not provide local communities with a remedy. As a result, counterclaims based on international law do not provide a complete solution to foreign investor misconduct. Nonetheless, counterclaims based on international law can fill a large gap in the existing procedural framework in investment arbitration and can contribute to the reduction of foreign investor misconduct.

7.3 Wider Implications

This book explores the role of counterclaims based on international law as a means of challenging foreign investor misconduct in investment arbitration. Although the book focuses on investment arbitration, IIL is a specialist branch of international law and the proposed use of counterclaims relies on principles of international law sourced from beyond IIL. Consequently, it is not possible to discuss the book's findings in isolation from the broader international legal framework. Therefore, this section situates counterclaims based on international law in debates that discuss the role of non-State actors in international law. It argues that the proposed use of counterclaims based on international law enhances the position of foreign investors as subjects of international law, which has the potential to further integrate foreign investors on the international plane. In addition, the arbitral practice that results from the proposed use of counterclaims based on international law could influence how international law deals with non-State actors more generally.

Actors in international law were traditionally categorised as subjects or objects of international law. Subjects of international law possess rights and obligations under international law and have the power to bring, and be subjected to, international claims.[8] Given their full capacity to perform these functions, States are the primary subjects of international law.[9] Conversely, those actors that do not display these attributes are classified as objects of international law.[10] Thus, objects of international law include non-State actors such as individuals and corporations. The utility of framing actors in terms of whether they are a subject or an object of international law has come under scrutiny given that the subject/object dichotomy fails to capture the varying degrees to which actors may possess subjectivity in international law.[11] In response, varied conceptualisations of subjectivity in international law have been formulated to try and evaluate (and accommodate) the role of non-State actors in international law.[12] As a result, there is ongoing debate regarding non-State actors and what amounts to subjectivity in international law.[13]

Foreign investors are non-State actors for the purposes of international law. However, foreign investors are frequently deemed to possess partial subjectivity in IIL because they have the ability to commence investment claims against a host State for breaches of investment protection standards on the

---

8 James Crawford, *Brownlie's Principles of Public International Law* (9th edn, Oxford University Press 2019) 105.

9 ibid 105.

10 ibid 116.

11 See for example, Rosalyn Higgins, *Problems and Processes: International Law and How We Use It* (Clarendon Press 1994) 49; Theodor Meron, *Human Rights in International Law: Legal and Policy Issues* (Clarenden Press 1992); Andrew Clapham, *Human Rights Obligations of Non-State Actors* (Oxford University Press 2006) 78–80; Jose E Alvarez, 'Are Corporations Subjects of International Law?' (2011) 9 Santa Clara Journal of International Law 7.

12 For a summary of these positions, see Alessandro Suppa, 'UN Treaty on Business and Human Rights or Investor-State Arbitration? A Sober Answer for the Better Protection of Human Rights' (2022) 22 International and Comparative Law Review 152, 153–160.

13 See for example, Andrés Felipe López Latorre, 'In Defence of Direct Obligations for Businesses Under International Human Rights Law' (2020) 5 Business and Human Rights Journal 56; Ishikawa, *Corporate Environmental Responsibility in Investor-State Dispute Settlement: The Unexhausted Potential of Current Mechanisms* (n 3) 30–31.

international plane.[14] This is usually explained by reference to States granting this power to a foreign investor as an exception to the general principle that only States can invoke dispute resolution procedures in international law.[15] Consequently, foreign investors are an example of a non-State actor that displays limited subjectivity in international law and challenges the subject/object dichotomy.

Although foreign investors can already be understood to be partial subjects of international law, the proposed use of counterclaims based on international law in investment arbitration confers foreign investors with greater levels of subjectivity in international law. The proposed use of counterclaims alters how foreign investors are perceived to function as subjects of international law in two ways. First, counterclaims based on international law require that a foreign investor owes an obligation to the host State that is sourced from international law. As a result, this type of counterclaim requires foreign investors to bear duties in international law. The extent to which foreign investors bear duties in international law depends on whether the principles that form the foundation of the counterclaim directly or indirectly bind the foreign investor. Foreign investors are bound by host State laws by virtue of being in the host State's jurisdiction.[16] Therefore, when international law indirectly binds foreign investors through the host State's domestic law, foreign investor obligations reflect the existing legal framework. Yet, when a foreign investor is directly bound by international law, foreign investors bear obligations on the international plane, which is an attribute associated with subjectivity in international law. Hence, the proposed use of counterclaims based on international law confers foreign investors with greater subjectivity in international law because host States may be able to espouse claims based on foreign investor obligations sourced from the international plane.

The second modification brought about by the proposed use of counterclaims based on international law is that investment arbitration provides a forum for host States to enforce foreign investors' duties in international law.

---

14 See Ole Spiermann, 'Individual Rights, State Interests and the Power to Waive ICSID Jurisdiction Under Bilateral Investment Treaties' (2004) 20 Arbitration International 179, 185.

15 Merja Pentikäinen, 'Changing International "Subjectivity" and Rights and Obligations under International Law – Status of Corporations' (2012) 8 Utrecht Law Review 145, 146–147; Ishikawa, *Corporate Environmental Responsibility in Investor-State Dispute Settlement: The Unexhausted Potential of Current Mechanisms* (n 3) 32.

16 Monique Sasson, *Substantive Law in Investment Treaty Arbitration: The Unsettled Relationship Between International Law and Municipal Law* (Kluwer Law International 2010) 200.

Non-State actors do not usually possess standing in international dispute resolution fora.[17] Hence, in the absence of investment arbitration, it would be difficult for a host State to bring a claim against a foreign investor as a duty bearer on the international plane. An arbitral tribunal can have jurisdiction to hear a counterclaim against a foreign investor and can hold foreign investors accountable for breaches of their duties in international law through enforcement mechanisms.[18] Consequently, not only can foreign investors possess obligations in international law, but they can also be subject to claims in an international dispute resolution forum and be subject to enforcement proceedings. Thus, the proposed use of counterclaims based on international law arguably conveys foreign investors with expanded subjectivity in international law and brings foreign investors closer to possessing the characteristics of a State in investment arbitration. In so doing, counterclaim procedures can further integrate foreign investors in the international arena.

If counterclaims based on international law are employed by host States in the manner proposed, investment arbitration practice could be instructive in highlighting how non-State actors navigate international law. When addressing counterclaims based on international law, arbitral tribunals will have to consider how international law is applied to non-State actors. For example, arbitral tribunals will probably have to acknowledge that corporations owe obligations under international law. Thus, the acceptance of foreign investors as duty bearers in international law could fundamentally alter how corporations are understood within international law. In practical terms, arbitral practice could provide a foundation for establishing corporate liability in the field of business and human rights.[19] Arbitral tribunals will also potentially have to transpose legal obligations intended for States to non-State actors. Depending

17 Fergus Green, 'Fragmentation in Two Dimensions: The ICJ's Flawed Approach to Non-State Actors and International Legal Personality' (2008) 9 Melbourne Journal of International Law 47, 69.

18 ICSID Convention Article 54(1) creates a recognition and enforcement mechanism for pecuniary obligations which applies to both host States and foreign investors. For investment disputes conducted in accordance with the ICSID AF Arbitration Rules, or the UNCITRAL Arbitration Rules, host States will need to rely on the Convention on the Recognition and Enforcement of Foreign Arbitral Awards (adopted 10 June 1958, entered into force 7 June 1959) 330 UNTS 3 to enforce an investment award against a foreign investor.

19 See Lee McConnell, 'Assessing the Feasiblity of a Business and Human Rights Treaty' (2017) 66 International and Comparative Law Quarterly 143; Nicolás M Perrone, 'Bridging the Gap between Foreign Investor Rights and Obligations: Towards Reimaging the International Law on Foreign Investment' (2022) 7 Business and Human Rights Journal 375.

on the scope of the obligation involved, arbitral tribunals may have to address issues of whether States or non-State actors possess the power to ensure compliance with international law and how States and non-State actors allocate responsibility for a breach of international law in cases of shared responsibility. Arbitral tribunal determinations on issues of attribution and responsibility may impact how general principles of international law (such as those relating to State responsibility) are conceptualised.[20] Finally, the outcome of arbitral practice could shift perceptions regarding the nature of the relationship between States and non-State actors in international law. By acknowledging the role and influence of non-State actors in international law, the international legal system may be understood to be less State-focused and more transnational in nature. While the exact impact of counterclaims based on international law is difficult to predict, the legal framework that they create has the potential to contribute to the development of international law more generally.

In short, the proposed use of counterclaims based on international law would enhance the subjectivity of foreign investors in international law. Counterclaims based on international law require foreign investors to be duty bearers in international law and can subject foreign investors to claims on the international plane. By conferring foreign investors with these attributes, counterclaims based on international law could result in foreign investors becoming more integrated in the international arena. In turn, investment arbitration practice stemming from the use of counterclaims based on international law could influence how international law addresses non-State actors more generally.

7.4 Concluding Observations

Counterclaims are not widely used in investment arbitration. However, counterclaims permit host States to address the asymmetrical nature of investment protection standards that privilege foreign investors. By changing State practice and employing new litigation strategies, host States can maximise the potential of counterclaims in investment arbitration to permit counterclaims based on international law. International law regulates many forms foreign investor misconduct. Thus, counterclaims based on international law provide a means of addressing foreign investor misconduct in investment arbitration.

20 See Ishikawa, *Corporate Environmental Responsibility in Investor-State Dispute Settlement: The Unexhausted Potential of Current Mechanisms* (n 3) 140–142.

Although their impact is limited to this context, the use of counterclaims in this way is significant given the absence of any other procedural means of generating foreign investor liability in investment arbitration. Therefore, counterclaims based on international law can act as an important tool in combating foreign investor misconduct. Yet, the impact of counterclaims based on international law is not limited to investment arbitration. The proposed use of counterclaims based on international law requires foreign investors to be duty bearers in international law. Further, host States could use investment arbitration as a forum to enforce foreign investor obligations. As a result, the proposed use of counterclaims based on international law could enhance foreign investors' subjectivity in international law and increase their participation on the international plane. In turn, investment arbitration practice flowing from the proposed use of counterclaims based on international law could influence how international law governs non-State actors more generally. Consequently, counterclaims based on international law in investment arbitration enable host States to hold foreign investors accountable for violations of international law but could also exert a broader influence in international law.

Bibliography

Books

Amerasinghe CF, *International Arbitral Jurisdiction* (Brill 2011).

Begic T, *Applicable Law in International Investment Disputes* (Eleven International Publishing 2005).

Broches A, *Selected Essays: World Bank, ICSID and Other Subjects of Public and Private International Law* (Martinus Nijhoff 1995).

Caron DD and Caplan L, *The UNCITRAL Arbitration Rules: A Commentary* (Oxford University Press 2013).

Chernykh Y, *Contract Interpretation in Investment Treaty Arbitration: A Theory of the Incidental Issue* (Brill 2022).

Clapham A, *Human Rights Obligations of Non-State Actors* (Oxford University Press 2006).

Crawford J, *The International Law Commission's Articles on State Responsibility: Introduction, Text and Commentaries* (Cambridge University Press 2002).

Crawford J, *Brownlie's Principles of Public International Law* (9th edn, Oxford University Press 2019).

Croft C, Kee C and Waincymer J, *A Guide to the UNCITRAL Arbitration Rules* (Cambridge University Press 2013).

De Brabandere E, *Investment Treaty Arbitration as Public International Law: procedural aspects and implications* (Cambridge University Press 2014).

De Schutter O, *International Human Rights Law* (Cambridge University Press 2010).

Diel-Gligor K, *Towards Consistency in International Investment Jurisprudence: A Preliminary Ruling System for ICSID Arbitration* (Brill 2017).

Douglas Z, *The International Law of Investment Claims* (Cambridge University Press 2009).

Hernández G, *International Law* (2nd edn, Oxford University Press 2022).

Higgins R, *Problems and Processes: International Law and How We Use It* (Clarendon Press 1994).

Ishikawa T, *Corporate Environmental Responsibility in Investor-State Dispute Settlement: The Unexhausted Potential of Current Mechanisms* (Cambridge University Press 2022).

Jarrett M, *Contributory Fault and Investor Misconduct in Investment Arbitration* (Cambridge University Press 2019).

Kjeldgaard-Pedersen A, *The International Legal Personality of the Individual* (Oxford University Press 2018).

Kjos HE, *Applicable Law in Investor-State Arbitration: The Interplay between National and International Law* (Oxford University Press 2013).

Klager R, *'Fair and Equitable Treatment' in International Investment Law* (Cambridge University Pres 2011).

Kozyokova A, *Foreign Investor Misconduct in International Investment Law* (Springer 2021).

Kryvoi Y, *International Centre for Settlement of Investment Disputes* (Kluwer Law International 2010).

McBeth A, *International Economic Actors and Human Rights* (Routledge 2010).

Meron T, *Human Rights in International Law: Legal and Policy Issues* (Clarenden Press 1992).

Organisation for Economic Co-operation and Development, *International Investment Law: Understanding Concepts and Tracking Innovations* (Organisation for Economic Co-operation and Development Publishing 2008).

Parlett K, *The Individual in the International Legal System: continuity and change in international law* (Cambridge University Press 2011).

Paulsson J and Petrochilos G, *UNCITRAL Arbitration* (Kluwer Law International 2018).

Portmann R, *Legal Personality in International Law* (Cambridge University Press 2010).

Radović R, *Beyond Consent: Revisiting Jurisdiction in Investment Treaty Arbitration* (Brill 2021).

Reed L, Paulsson J and Blackaby N, *Guide to ICSID Arbitration* (2nd edn, Kluwer Law International 2011).

Sasson M, *Substantive Law in Investment Treaty Arbitration: The Unsettled Relationship Between International Law and Municipal Law* (Kluwer Law International 2010).

Saul B, Kinley D and Mowbray J, *The International Covenant on Economic, Social and Cultural Rights: Commentary, Cases and Materials* (Oxford University Press 2014).

Schreuer C, *The ICSID Convention: A Commentary* (Cambridge University Press 2001).

Steingruber A, *Consent in International Arbitration* (Oxford University Press 2012).

Tomuschat C, *Human Rights Between Idealism and Realism* (Oxford University Press 2014).

Weeramantry R, *Treaty Interpretation in Investment Arbitration* (Oxford University Press 2012).

Zerk JA, *Multinationals and Corporate Social Responsibility: Limitations and Opportunities in International Law* (Cambridge University Press 2006).

Book Chapters

Alvik I, 'The Hybrid Nature of Investment Treaty Arbitration – Straddling the National/International Divide' in Erikson C and Emberland M (eds), *The New International Law – An Anthology* (Martinus Nijhoff Publishers 2010).

Banifatemi Y, 'The Law Applicable in Investment Treaty Arbitration' in Yannaca-Small K (ed), *Arbitration under International Investment Agreements: A Guide to the Key Issues* (Oxford University Press 2010).

Banifatemi Y, 'Consistency in the interpretation of substantive investment rules: is it achievable?' in Echandi R and Sauvé P (eds), *Prospects in International Investment Law and Policy* (Cambridge University Press 2013).

Bjorklund AK, 'Applicable law in International Investment Disputes' in Giorgetti C (ed), *Litigating International Investment Disputes: A practitioner's guide* (Brill 2014).

Bjorklund AK and Vanhonnaeker L, 'Article 42' in Fouret J, Gerbay R and Alvarez GM (eds), *The ICSID Convention, Regulations and Rules: A Practical Commentary* (Edward Elgar Publishing 2019).

Bodansky D, Brunnée J and Hey E, 'International Environmental Law: Mapping the Field' in Bodansky D, Brunnée J and Hey E (eds), *The Oxford Handbook of International Environmental Law* (Oxford University Press 2008).

Brown C, 'Inherent Powers in International Adjudication' in Romano CPR, Alter K and Shany Y (eds), *The Oxford Handbook of International Adjudication* (Oxford University Press 2013).

Brubowski H, 'Balancing IIA Arbitration Through the Use of Counterclaims' in De Mestral A and Levesque C (eds), *Improving International Investment Agreements* (Taylor and Francis 2013).

Cappiello B, 'Applicable Law in Investment Arbitration' in Chaisse J, Choukroune L and Jusoh S (eds), *Handbook of International Investment Law and Policy* (Springer 2021).

Cazala J, 'Good Administration of Justice' in *Max Planck Encyclopedia of International Procedural Law* (2019).

Choudhury B, 'Human Rights Provisions in International Investment Treaties and Investor-State Contracts' in Scheu J and others (eds), *Investment Protection, Human Rights, and International Arbitration in Extraordinary Times* (Nomos 2022).

Cotula L and Perrone NM, 'Investors' International Law and its Asymmetries: the Case of Local Communities' in Ho J and Sattarova M (eds), *Investors' International Law* (Hart Publishing 2021).

Daly BW and Poon F, 'Technical and Legal Experts in International Investment Disputes' in Giorgetti C (ed), *Litigating International Investment Disputes: a practitioner's guide* (Brill 2014).

De Berti G, 'Experts and Expert Witnesses in International Arbitration: Adviser, Advocate or Adjudicator?' in Klausegger C and others (eds), *Austrian Yearbook of International Law* (C.H. Bec 2010).

Delaney J and Barstow Magraw D, 'Procedural Transparency' in Muchlinski PT, Ortino F and Schreuer C (eds), *The Oxford Handbook of International Investment Law* (Oxford University Press 2008).

Douglas Z, 'The enforcement of environmental norms in investment treaty arbitration' in Dupuy P-M and Viñuales JE (eds), *Harnessing Foreign Investment to Promote Environmental Protection: Incentives and Safeguards* (Cambridge University Press 2013).

Dudas S, 'Treaty Counterclaims under the ICSID Convention' in Baltag C (ed), *ICSID Convention after 50 Years: Unsetttled Issues* (Kluwer Law International 2017).

Dumberry P and Labelle-Eastaugh È, 'Non-state actors in international investment law: The legal personality of corporations and NGOs in the context of investor-state arbitration' in d'Aspremont J (ed), *Participants in the International Legal System: Multiple Perspectives on Non-State Actors in International Law* (Routledge 2011).

Hoffman AK, 'Chapter 36: Counterclaims' in Kinnear M and others (eds), *Building International Investment Law: The First 50 Years of ICSID* (Kluwer Law International 2015).

Ishikawa T, 'Counterclaims in Investment Arbitration: Is the Host State the Right Claimant?' in Ho J and Sattarova M (eds), *Investors' International Law* (Hart Publishing 2021).

Kaufmann-Kohler G and Potestà M, 'The Interplay Between Investor-State Arbitration and Domestic Courts in the Existing IIA Framework' in *The European Yearbook of International Economic Law* (Springer International Publishing 2020).

Kostadinova M, 'Aspects of Procedure for Institution of Proceedings and Establishment of Tribunals in Investment Treaty Arbitration' in Yannaca-Small K (ed), *Arbitration under International Investment Agreements: A Guide to the Key Issues* (2nd edn, Oxford University Press 2018).

Kriendler RH, 'The Law Applicable to International Investment Disputes' in Horn N (ed), *Arbitrating Foreign Investment Disputes: Procedural and Substantive Legal Aspects* (Kluwer Law International 2004).

Legum B, 'An Overview of Procedure in an Investment Treaty Arbitration' in Yannaca-Small K (ed), *Arbitration under International Investment Agreements: A Guide to the Key Issues* (2nd edn, Oxford University Press 2018).

Mégret F, 'Nature of Obligations' in Moeckli D, Shah S and Sivakumaran S (eds), *International Human Rights Law* (Oxford University Press 2010).

Methymaki E and Tzanakopolous A, 'Masters of Puppets? Reassertion of Control through Joint Investment Treaty Interpretation' in Kulick A (ed), *Reassertion of Control Over the Investment Treaty Regime* (Cambridge University Press 2017).

Petersmann E-U, 'Human Rights in International Investment Law and Adjudication: Legal Methodology Questions' in Chaisse J, Choukroune L and Jusoh S (eds), *Handbook of International Investment Law and Policy* (Springer 2021).

Redgwell C, 'International Environmental Law' in Evans MD (ed), *International Law.* (5th edn, Oxford University Press 2018).

Reiner C and Schreuer C, 'Human Rights and International Investment Arbitration' in Dupuy P-M, Francioni F and Petersmann E-U (eds), *Human Rights in International Investment Law and Arbitration* (Oxford University Press 2009).

Reinisch A, 'The challenge of fostering greater coherence in international investment law' in Echandi R and Sauvé P (eds), *Prospects in International Investment Law and Policy* (Cambridge University Press 2013).

Reinisch A, 'Enforcement of Investment Treaty Awards' in Yannaca-Small K (ed), *Arbitration Under International Investment Agreements: A Guide to the Key Issues* (2nd edn, Oxford University Press, 2018).

Reisman WM and Arsanjani MJ, 'Applicable Law under the ICSID Convention: The Tortured History of the Interpretion of Article 42' in Kinnear M and others (eds), *Building International Investment Law: The First 50 Years of ICSID* (Kluwer Law International, 2015).

Rigo Sureda A, 'Precedent in Investment Treaty Arbitration' in Binder C and others (eds), *International Investment Law for the 21st Century: Essay in Honour of Christophe Schreuer* (Oxford University Press 2009).

Rivas JA, 'ICSID Treaty Counterclaims: Case Law and Treaty Evolution' in Kalicki JE and Joubin-Bret A (eds), *Reshaping the Investor-State Dispute Settlement System: Journeys for the 21st Century* (Brill 2015).

Sasson M, 'The Applicable Law and the ICSID Convention' in Baltag C (ed), *ICSID Convention after 50 Years: Unsettled Issues* (Kluwer Law International 2017).

Sattarova M and Vytiaganets O, 'Learning from Investment Treaty Law and Arbitration: Developing States and Power Inequalities' in Behn D, Fauchald OK and Langford M (eds), *Legitimacy of Investment Arbitration* (Cambridge University Press 2021).

Schreuer C, 'Diversity and Harmonisation of Treaty Interpretation in Investment Arbitration' in Fitzmaurice M, Elias O and Merkouris P (eds), *Treaty Interpretation and the Vienna Convention on the Law of Treaties: 30 Years On* (Brill 2010).

Schreuer C, 'Coherence and Consistency in international investment law' in Echandi R and Sauvé P (eds), *Prospects in International Investment Law and Policy* (Cambridge University Press 2013).

Schreuer C, 'Investment Arbitration' in Romano CP, Alter KJ and Shany Y (eds), *The Oxford Handbook of International Adjudication* (Oxford University Press 2014).

Schultz T, 'Against Consistency in Investment Arbitration' in Douglas Z, Pauwelyn J and Viñuales JE (eds), *The Foundations of International Investment Law: Bringing Theory into Practice* (Oxford University Press 2014).

Sharpe J, 'From Delegation to Prescription: Interpretative Authority in International Investment Agreements' in Brower CD and others (eds), *By Peaceful Means: International Adjudication and Arbitration* (Oxford University Press 2024).

Shelton D, 'Commentary and Conclusions' in Shelton D (ed), *Commitment and Compliance: The Role of Non-Binding Norms in the International Legal System* (Oxford University Press 2000).

Sheppard A and Crockett A, 'Are Stabilization Clauses a Threat to Sustainable Development?' in Cordonier Segger M-C, Gehring MW and Newcombe A (eds), *Sustainable Development in World Investment Law* (Kluwer Law International 2011).

Shihata IFJ, 'Regulation of Foreign Investment' in Maniruzzaman A and others (eds), *International Sustainable Development Law Vol II* (Eolss 2010).

Spears S, 'Making Way for the Public Interest in International Investment Agreements' in Brown C and Miles K (eds), *Evolution in Investment Treaty Law and Arbitration* (Cambridge University Press 2011).

Veenstra-Kjos HE, 'Counter-claims by Host States in Investment Dispute Arbitration "without Privity"' in Khan P and Wälde T (eds), *New Aspects of International Investment Law* (Nijhof 2007).

Waibel M, 'International Investment Law and Treaty Interpretation' in Hofmann R and Tams C (eds), *International Investment Law and General International Law – From Clinical Isolation to Systemic Integration?* (Nomos 2011).

Weeramantry R, 'Treaty Interpretation, the ICSID Convention and Investment Treaties' in Baltag C (ed), *ICSID Convention after 50 Years: Unsettled Issues* (Kluwer Law International 2017).

Wehland H, 'Jurisdiction and Admissibility in Proceedings under the ICSID Convention and the Additional Facility Rules' in Baltag C (ed), *ICSID Convention After 50 Years: Unsetttled Issues* (Kluwer Law International 2017).

Yannaca-Small K, 'The Umbrella Clause: Is the Umbrella Closing?' in Yannaca-Small K (ed), *Arbitration under International Investment Agreements: A Guide to the Key Issues* (2nd edn, Oxford University Press 2018).

Zeiler G, 'Jurisdiction, Competence and Admissibility of Claims in ICSID Arbitral Proceedings' in Binder C and others (eds), *International Investment Law for the 21st Century: Essays in Honour of Christoph Schreuer* (Oxford University Press 2009).

Journal Articles

Abedian H and Eftekhar R, 'Consent to Investor-State Arbitration in the Second Largest International Investment Protection Agreement: The Correct Interpretive Approach to Article 17 of the OIC Investment Agreement' (2018) 35 Journal of International Arbitration 59.

Abel P, 'Counterclaims Based on International Human Rights Obligations of Investors in International Investment Arbitration: Fallacies and Potentials of the 2016 ICSID *Urbaser v. Argentina* Award' (2018) 1 Brill Open Law 61.

Allee T and Peinhardt C, 'Evaluating Three Explanations for the Design of Bilateral Investment Treaties' (2014) 66 World Politics 47.

Alvarez JE, 'Are Corporations Subjects of International Law?' (2011) 9 Santa Clara Journal of International Law 7.

Alvik I, 'The Justification of Privilege in International Investment Law: Preferential Treatment of Foreign Investors as a Problem of Legitimacy' (2020) 31 European Journal of International Law 289.

Andreeva Y, 'Interpreting Consent to Arbitration as a Unilateral Act of State: A Case Against Conventions' (2011) 27 Arbitration International 129.

Arato J, Brown C and Ortino F, 'Parsing and Managing Inconsistency in Investor-State Dispute Settlement' (2020) 21 Journal of World Investment and Trade 336.

Atanasova D, 'Applicable Law Provisions in Investment Treaties' (2019) 10 Journal of International Dispute Settlement 396.

Atanasova D, Benoit AM and Ostřanský J, 'The Legal Framework for Counterclaims in Investment Treaty Arbitration' (2014) 31 Journal of International Arbitration 357.

Benedettelli MV, 'Determining the Applicable Law in Commercial and Investment Arbitration: Two Intertwined Road Maps for Conflicts-Solving' (2022) 37 ICSID Review – Foreign Investment Law Journal 687.

Bianchi A, 'Human Rights and the Magic of *Jus Cogens*' (2008) 19 European Journal of International Law 491.

Bjorklund AK, 'The Role of Counterclaims in Rebalancing Investment Law' (2013) 17 Lewis and Clark Law Review 461.

Blackaby N and Wilbraham A, 'Practical Issues Relating to the Use of Expert Evidence in Investment Treaty Arbitration' (2016) 31 ICSID Review – Foreign Investment Law Journal 655.

Blyschak PM, 'State Consent, Investor Interests and the Future of Investment Arbitration: Reanalyzing the Jurisdiction of Investor-State Tribunals in Hard Cases' (2009) 9 Asper Review of International Business and Trade Law 99.

Boisson de Chazournes L, 'The Blurring of the Line Between Contract-Based and Treaty-Based Investment Arbitration' (2019) 1 ITA in Review 94.

Boon K, 'Theorizing Responsibility in the Investor State Dispute Resolution System' (2021) 95 St John's Law Review 253.

Bose D, '*David R Aven v Costa Rica*: The Confluence of Corporations, Public International Law and International Investment Law' (2020) 35 ICSID Review – Foreign Investment Law Journal 20.

Brandi C, Blümer D and Morin J-F, 'When Do International Treaties Matter for Domestic Environmental Legislation?' (2019) 19 Global Environmental Politics 14.

Brower C and Kumar SP, 'Investomercial Arbitration: Whence Cometh It? What Is It? Whither Goeth It?' (2015) 30 ICSID Review – Foreign Investment Law Journal 35.

Carlevaris A, 'The Conformity of Investments with the Law of the Host State and the Jurisdiction of International Tribunals' (2008) 9 Journal of World Investment and Trade 35.

Cate IMT, 'The Costs of Consistency: Precedent in Investment Treaty Arbitration' (2013) 51 Columbia Journal of Transnational Law 418.

Choudhury B, 'Investor Obligations for Human Rights' (2020) 35 ICSID Review – Foreign Investment Law Journal 82.

Chukwumerije O, 'International Law and Article 42 of the ICSID Convention' (1997) 14 Journal of International Arbitration 79.

Crawford J, 'Treaty and Contract in Investment Arbitration' (2008) 24 Arbitration International 351.

Crow K and Escobar LL, 'International Corporate Obligations, Human Rights and the *Urbaser* Standard: Breaking New Ground' (2018) 36 Boston University International Law Journal 87.

Cunningham AJ, 'The European Convention on Human Rights, Customary International Law and the Constitution' (1994) 43 International and Comparative Law Quarterly 537.

de Nanteuil A, 'Counterclaims in Investment Arbitration: Old Questions, New Answers' (2018) 17 Law and Practice of International Courts and Tribunals 374.

Demirkol B, 'Non-treaty Claims in Investment Treaty Arbitration' (2018) 31 Leiden Journal of International Law 59.

Douglas Z, 'The Hybrid Foundations of Investment Treaty Arbitration' (2003) 74 British Yearbook of International Law 151.

Dubois D, 'The Authority of Peremptory Norms in International Law: State Consent or Natural Law?' (2009) 78 Nordic Journal of International Law 133.

Ejims O, 'The 2016 Morocco-Nigeria Bilateral Investment Treaty: More Practical Reality in Providing a Balanced Investment Treaty?' (2019) 34 ICSID Review – Foreign Investment Law Journal 62.

Fahner JH and Happold M, 'The Human Rights Defence in International Investment Arbitration: Exploring the Limits of Systemic Integration' (2019) 68 International and Comparative Law Quarterly 741.

Focarelli C, 'Promotional *Jus Cogens*: A Critical Appraisal of *Jus Cogens*' Legal Effects' (2008) 77 Nordic Journal of International Law 429.

Francioni F, 'Access to Justice, Denial of Justice and International Investment Law' (2009) 20 European Journal of International Law 729.

Franck SD, 'The Legitimacy Crisis in Investment Treaty Arbitration: Privatizing Public International Law Through Inconsistent Decisions' (2005) 73 Fordham Law Review 1521.

Gaillard E and Banifatemi Y, 'The Meaning of "and" in Article 42(1), Second Sentence, of the Washington Convention: The Role of International Law in the ICSID Choice of Law Process' (2003) 18 ICSID Review – Foreign Investment Law Journal 375.

Garcia-Bolivar OE, 'Foreign Investment Disputes under ICSID: A Review of its Decisions on Jurisdiction' (2004) 5 Journal of World Investment and Trade 187.

Gathii J and Puig S, 'Introduction to the Symposium on Investor Responsibility: The Next Frontier in International Investment Law' (2019) 113 AJIL Unbound 1.

Giardina A, 'International Investment Arbitration: Recent Developments as to the Applicable Law and Unilateral Recourse' (2006) 5 The Law and Practice of International Courts and Tribunals 29.

Green F, 'Fragmentation in Two Dimensions: The ICJ's Flawed Approach to Non-State Actors and International Legal Personality' (2008) 9 Melbourne Journal of International Law 47.

Grusic U, 'The Evolving Jurisdiction of the International Centre for Settlement of Investment Disputes' (2009) 10 Journal of World Investment and Trade 69.

Guntrip E, 'Private Actors, Public Goods and Responsibility for the Right to Water in International Investment Law: An Analysis of *Urbaser v Argentina*' (2018) 1 Brill Open Law 37.

Hamida WB, 'L'arbitrage Etat-investisseur cherche son quilibre perdu: Dans quelle mesure l'Etat peut introduire des demandes reconventionnelles contre l'investisseur priv?' (2005) 7 International Law Forum du droit international 261.

Hanessian G and Duggal K, ' The Final 2015 Indian Model BIT: Is This the Change the World Wishes to See?' (2017) 32 ICSID Review – Foreign Investment Law Journal 216.

Hannum H, 'The Status of the Universal Declaration of Human Rights in National and International Law' (1995/1996) 25 Georgia Journal of International and Comparative Law 287.

Hansen R, 'The International Legal Personality of Multinational Enterprises: Treaty, Custom and the Governance Gap' (2010) 10 Global Jurist 1.

Harrison J, 'Environmental Counterclaims in Investor-State Arbitration' (2016) 17 Journal of World Investment and Trade 479.

Heiskanen V, 'Ménage à trois? Jurisdiction, Admissibility and Competence in Investment Treaty Arbitration' (2014) 29 ICSID Review – Foreign Investment Law Journal 231.

Hepburn J, 'Domestic Investment Statutes in International Law' (2018) 112 American Journal of International Law 658.

Hessbruegge JA, 'Human Rights Violations Arising from Conduct of Non-State Actors' (2005) 11 Buffalo Human Rights Law Review 21.

Ho J, 'The Creation of Elusive Investor Responsibility' (2019) 113 AJIL Unbound 10.

Hodgson M and Stewart M, 'Experts in Investor-State Arbitration: The Tribunal as Gatekeeper' (2018) 9 Journal of International Dispute Settlement 453.

Hoffman A, 'Counterclaims in Investment Arbitration' (2013) 28 ICSID Review – Foreign Investment Law Journal 438.

Igbokwe VC, 'Determination, Interpretation and Application of Substantive Law in Foreign Investment Treaty Arbitrations' (2006) 23 Journal of International Arbitration 267.

Ishikawa T, '*Marco Gavazzi and Stefano Gavazzi v Romania*: A New Approach to Determining Jurisdiction over Counterclaims in ICSID Arbitration?' (2017) 32 ICSID Review – Foreign Investment Law Journal 721.

Ishikawa T, 'Counterclaims and the Rule of Law in Investment Arbitration' (2019) 113 AJIL Unbound 33.

Jain AG, 'Consent to Counterclaims in Investor-State Arbitration: a post-Roussalis analysis' (2013) 16 International Arbitration Law Review 135.

Jones D, 'Choosing the Law or Rules of Law to Govern the Substantive Rights of the Parties' (2014) 26 Singapore Academy of Law Journal 911.

Karpoff JM, Lott Jr. JR and Wehrly EW, 'The Reputational Penalties for Environmental Violations: Empirical Evidence' (2005) 48 The Journal of Law and Economics 653.

Kendra T, 'State Counterclaims in Investment Arbitration – A New Lease of Life?' (2013) 29 Arbitration International 575.

Kinley D and Tadaki J, 'From Talk to Walk: The Emergence of Human Rights Responsibilities for Corporations at International Law' (2004) 44 Virginia Journal of International Law 931.

Kjos HE, 'Counterclaims by Host States in Investment Treaty Arbitration' (2007) 4 Transnational Dispute Management 1.

Krajewski M, 'A Nightmare or a Noble Dream? Establishing Investor Obligations Through Treaty-Making and Treaty-Application' (2020) 5 Business and Human Rights Journal 105.

Kriebaum U, 'Human Rights of the Population of the Host State in International Investment Arbitration' (2009) 10 Journal of World Investment and Trade 653.

Kryvoi Y, 'Counterclaims in Investor-State Arbitration' (2012) 21 Minnesota Journal of International Law 216.

Kurtz J, 'On Foreign Investor "Privilege" and the Limits of the Law: A Reply to Ivar Alvik' (2020) 31 European Journal of International Law 313.

Laborde G, 'The Case for Host State Claims in Investment Arbitration' (2010) 1 Journal of International Dispute Settlement 97.

Lalive P and Halonen L, 'On the Availability of Counterclaims in Investment Treaty Arbitration' (2011) II Czech Yearbook of International Law 141.

Leeks A, 'The Relationship Between Bilateral Investment Treaty Arbitration and the Wider Corpus of International Law: The ICSID Approach' (2007) 65 University of Toronto Faculty of Law Review 1.

Levashova Y, 'The Accountability and Corporate Social Responsibility of Multinational Corporations for Transgression in Host States through International Investment Law' (2018) 14 Utrecht Law Review 40.

Ling A, 'Adjudicating State Counterclaims in ICSID Investor-State Arbitration' (2021) 57 Texas International Law Journal 103.

López Latorre AF, 'In Defence of Direct Obligations for Businesses Under International Human Rights Law' (2020) 5 Business and Human Rights Journal 56.

Maniruzzaman A, 'International Commercial Arbitration: The Conflict of Laws Issues in Determining the Applicable Substantive Law in the Context of Investment Agreements' (1993) 40 Netherlands International Law Review 201.

Marcoux J-M and Bjorkland A, 'Foreign Investors' Responsibilities and Contributory Fault in Investment Arbitration' (2020) 69 International and Comparative Law Quarterly 877.

Mbengue MM, 'Africa's Voice in the Formation, Shaping and Redesign of International Investment Law' (2019) 34 ICSID Review – Foreign Investment Law Journal 455.

Mbengue MM and Schacherer S, 'The 'Africanization' of International Investment Law: The Pan-African Investment Code and the Reform of the International Investment Regime' (2017) 18 The Journal of World Investment and Trade 414.

McConnell L, 'Assessing the Feasiblity of a Business and Human Rights Treaty' (2017) 66 International and Comparative Law Quarterly 143.

McLachlan C, 'The Principle of Systemic Integration and Article 31(3)(c) of the Vienna Convention' (2005) 54 International and Comparative Law Quarterly 279.

Menaker AJ, 'The Determinative Impact of Fraud and Corruption on Investment Arbitrations' (2010) 25 ICSID Review – Foreign Investment Law Journal 67.

Mezgravis AA, 'The Standard of Interpretation Applicable to Consent and its Revocation in Investment Arbitration' (2011) 8 Transnational Dispute Management 1.

Moloo R and Khachaturian A, 'The Compliance with the Law Requirement in International Investment Law' (2011) 43 Fordham International Law Journal 1473.

Moss GC, 'Arbitration and Private International Law' (2008) 11 International Arbitration Law Review 153.

Muchlinski PT, '"Caveat Investor"? The Relevance of the Conduct of the Investor under the Fair and Equitable Treatment Standard' (2006) 55 International and Comparative Law Quarterly 527.

Muchlinski PT, 'Can International Investment Law Punish Investor's Human Rights Violations? Copper Mesa, Contributory Fault and its Alternatives' (2022) 37 ICSID Review – Foreign Investment Law Journal 359.

Niemoj A, 'The Limitations on Article 43 ICSID Convention: An (Un)limited Instrument of the Tribunal?' (2019) 34 ICSID Review – Foreign Investment Law Journal 697.

Nilsson A and Englesson O, 'Inconsistent Awards in Investment Treaty Arbitration: Is an Appeals Court Needed?' (2013) 30 Journal of International Arbitration 561.

Ordonez M, 'States' Counterclaims: How Hard Is it to Counterattack in International Investment Arbitration?' (2019) 22 International Arbitration Law Review 27.

Palevičienė S, 'Consent to Arbitration and the Legacy of the *SPP v. Egypt* Case' (2014) 7 Baltic Journal of Law & Politics 149.

Palombino FM, 'Judicial Economy and Limitation of the Scope of the Decision in International Adjudication' (2010) 23 Leiden Journal of International Law 909.

Paparinskis M, 'A Case Against Crippling Compensation in International Law of State Responsibility' (2020) 83 Modern Law Review 1246.

Parlett K, 'Claims under Customary International Law in ICSID Arbitration' (2016) 31 ICSID Review – Foreign Investment Law Journal 439.

Parra AR, 'Applicable Substantive Law in ICSID Arbitrations Initiated Under Investment Treaties' (2001) 16 ICSID Review – Foreign Investment Law Journal 20.

Paulsson J, 'Arbitration Without Privity' (1995) 10 ICSID Review – Foreign Investment Law Journal 232.

Paust JJ, 'The Other Side of Right: Private Duties under Human Rights Law' (1993) 5 Harvard Human Rights Journal 51.

Pentikäinen M, 'Changing International "Subjectivity" and Rights and Obligations under International Law – Status of Corporations' (2012) 8 Utrecht Law Review 145.

Perrone NM, 'The "Invisible" Local Communities: Foreign Investor Obligations, Inclusiveness, and the International Investment Regime' (2019) 113 AJIL Unbound 16.

Perrone NM, 'Bridging the Gap between Foreign Investor Rights and Obligations: Towards Reimaging the International Law on Foreign Investment' (2022) 7 Business and Human Rights Journal 375.

Peters A, 'Corruption as a Violation of International Human Rights' (2018) 29 European Journal of International Law 1251.

Popova IC and Poon F, 'From Perpetual Respondent to Aspiring Counterclaimant? State Counterclaims in the New Wave of Investment Treaties' (2015) 2 BCDR International Arbitration Review 223.

Potestà M, 'The Interpretation of Consent to ICSID Arbitration Contained in Domestic Investment Laws' (2011) 27 Arbitration International 149.

Puig S, 'Social Capital in the Arbitration Market' (2014) 25 European Journal of International Law 387.

Reisman WM, 'The Regime for Lacunae in the ICSID Choice of Law Provision and the Question of Its Threshold' (2000) 15 ICSID Review – Foreign Investment Law Journal 362.

Renteln AD, 'Encountering Counterclaims' (1987) 15 Denver Journal of International Law and Policy 379.

Roberts A, 'Power and Persuasion in Investment Treaty Interpretation: The Dual Role of States' (2010) 104 American Journal of International Law 179.

Rudall J, 'The Tribunal with a Toolbox: On *Perenco v Ecuador*, Black Gold and Shades of Green' (2020) 11 Journal of International Dispute Settlement 485.

Ruiz Fabri H, 'Enhancing the Rhetoric of *Jus Cogens*' (2012) 23 European Journal of International Law 1049.

Sattorova M, 'Denial of Justice Disguised? Investment Arbitration and the Protection of Foreign Investors from Judicial Misconduct' (2012) 61 International and Comparative Law Quarterly 223.

Sattorova M, 'Investor Responsibilities From a Host State Perspective: Qualitative Data and Proposals for Treaty Reform' (2019) 113 AJIL Unbound 22.

Schill SW, 'Illegal Investments in Investment Treaty Arbitration' (2012) 11 The Law and Practice of International Courts and Tribunals 281.

Schreuer C, 'Do We Need Investment Arbitration?' (2014) 1 Transnational Dispute Management 1.

Shao X, 'Environmental and Human Rights Counterclaims in International Investment Arbitration: at the Crossroads of Domestic and International Law' (2021) 24 Journal of International Economic Law 157.

Shelton D, 'Normative Hierarchy in International Law' (2006) 100 The American Journal of International Law 291.

Shihata IFJ and Parra AR, 'Applicable Substantive Law in Disputes Between States and Private Foreign Parties: The Case of Arbitration under the ICSID Convention' (1994) 9 ICSID Review – Foreign Investment Law Journal 183.

Shihata IFJ and Parra AR, 'The Experience of the International Centre for Settlement of Investment Dispute' (1999) 14 ICSID Review – Foreign Investment Law Journal 299.

Sohn L, 'The Human Rights Law of the Charter' (1977) 12 Texas International Law Journal 129.

Spiermann O, 'Individual Rights, State Interests and the Power to Waive ICSID Jurisdiction Under Bilateral Investment Treaties' (2004) 20 Arbitration International 179.

Steingruber A, 'Counterclaims: a Critical Analysis of Article 6 of the 2019 The Hague Resolution of the Institut de Droit International on the "Equality of Parties before International Investment Tribunals"' (2020) 35 ICSID Review – Foreign Investment Law Journal 595.

Suppa A, 'UN Treaty on Business and Human Rights or Investor-State Arbitration? A Sober Answer for the Better Protection of Human Rights' (2022) 22 International and Comparative Law Review 152.

Swinehart MW, 'Reliability of Expert Evidence in International Disputes' (2017) 38 Michigan Journal of International Law 287.

Trinel PE, 'Counterclaims and Legitimacy in Investment Treaty Arbitration' (2022) 38 Arbitration International 59.

Van Harten G, 'Five Justifications for Investment Treaties: A Critical Discussion' (2010) 2 Trade, Law and Development 19.

Vázquez CM, 'Direct vs. Indirect Obligations of Corporations Under International Law' (2005) 43 Colombia Journal of Transnational Law 927.

Veenstra-Kjos HE, 'Counterclaims by Host States in Investment Treaty Arbitration' (2007) 4 Transnational Dispute Management 1.

Viñuales JE, 'Investor Diligence in Investment Arbitration: Sources and Arguments' (2017) 32 ICSID Review – Foreign Investment Law Journal 346.

Vohryzek-Griest A, 'State Counterclaims in Investor-State Disputes: A History of 30 Years of Failure' (2009) 15 International Law, Revista Colombian de Derecho Internacional 83.

Von Papp K, 'Biting the Bullet or Redefining Consent in Investor-State Arbitration: Pre-Arbitration Requirements After *BG Group v Argentina*' (2015) 16 Journal of World Investment and Trade 695.

Wang G, 'Consent in Investor-State Arbitration: A Critical Analysis' (2014) 13 Chinese Journal of International Law 335.

Wehland H, 'Domestic Courts and Investment Treaty Tribunals: The Effect of Local Recourse Against Administrative Measures on the Breach of Investment Protection Standards' (2019) 36 Journal of International Arbitration 207.

Weil P, 'Towards Relative Normativity in International Law' (1983) 77 The American Journal of International Law 413.

Weisburd AM, 'The Effect of Treaties and Other Formal International Acts on the Customary Law of Human Rights' (1995/1996) 25 Georgia Journal of International and Comparative Law 99.

Yamamoto H, Ramesh S and Seelmann-Eggebert S, '*Perenco Ecuador v Republic of Ecuador Lessons from Perenco*: Tribunal-Appointed Experts and Avoiding Double Recovery' (2020) 35 ICSID Review – Foreign Investment Law Journal 459.

Zarra G, 'The Issue of Incoherence in Investment Arbitration: Is There Need for a Systemic Reform?' (2018) 17 Chinese Journal of International Law 137.

Zou H and others, 'How Do Environmental Violations Harm Corporate Reputation?' (2015) 24 Business Strategy and the Environment 836.

Zugliani N, 'Human Rights in International Investment Law: The 2016 Morroco-Nigeria Bilateral Investment Treaty' (2019) 68 International and Comparative Law Quarterly 761.

Websites and Blogs

Aatreya S, '"Private" Breaches of International Law: Lessons from Domestic Courts for International Investment Law' (*OpinioJuris*, 4 March 2020) <http://opiniojuris.org/2020/03/04/private-breaches-of-international-law-lessons-from-domestic-courts-for-international-investment-law/> accessed 5 April 2023.

De Luca A, 'UNCITRAL Working Group III: Counterclaims in ISDS – Challenges and Prospects in Light of the UNCITRAL Reform Process' (*Kluwer Arbitration Blog*, 28

March 2020) <http://arbitrationblog.kluwerarbitration.com/2020/03/28/uncitral-working-group-iii-counterclaims-in-isds-challenges-and-prospects-in-light-of-the-uncitral-reform-process/> accessed 13 May 2021.

Guntrip E, '*Urbaser v Argentina*: The Origins of a Host State Human Rights Counterclaim in ICSID Arbitration?' (*EJIL:Talk!*, 10 February 2017) <https://www.ejiltalk.org/urbaser-v-argentina-the-origins-of-a-host-state-human-rights-counterclaim-in-icsid-arbitration/> accessed 17 January 2023.

International Labour Organization, 'Introduction to International Labour Standards: Conventions and Recommendations' (5 April 2023) <https://www.ilo.org/global/standards/introduction-to-international-labour-standards/conventions-and-recommendations/lang--en/index.htm> accessed 5 April 2023.

Mbengue MM, 'Consent to Arbitration Through National Investment Legislation' (*Investment Treaty News*, 19 July, 2012) <https://www.iisd.org/itn/en/2012/07/19/consent-to-arbitration-through-national-investment-legislation/> accessed 12 July 2020.

Office of the High Commissioner of Human Rights, 'Guiding principles on business and human rights: implementing the United Nations "Protect, Respect and Remedy" framework (UNGPS) (2011) <https://www.ohchr.org/sites/default/files/documents/publications/guidingprinciplesbusinesshr_en.pdf> accessed 5 April 2023.

Office of the High Commissioner of Human Rights, 'Instruments and Mechanisms: International Human Rights Law'. <https://www.ohchr.org/en/instruments-and-mechanisms/international-human-rights-law> accessed 5 April 2023.

Schill SW, 'Access to Justice in Investment Dispute Settlement' (*Kluwer Arbitration Blog*, 2020) <http://arbitrationblog.kluwerarbitration.com/2020/02/10/access-to-justice-in-investment-dispute-settlement/> accessed 12 May 2021.

Southern African Development Community, 'SADC Model Bilateral Investment Treaty Template with Commentary' <https://www.iisd.org/itn/wp-content/uploads/2012/10/sadc-model-bit-template-final.pdf> accessed 5 April 2023.

Ünüvar G and Küçüksu A, 'From Protection to Governance of Foreign Investment: Vulnerability Theory as a Paradigm Shift in International Investment Law' (*EJIL: Talk!*, 27 December 2019) <https://www.ejiltalk.org/from-protection-to-governance-of-foreign-investment-vulnerability-theory-as-a-paradigm-shift-in-international-investment-law/> accessed 11 May 2021.

Yilmaz-Vastardis A, 'Is International Investment Law Moving the Ball Forward on IHRL Obligations for Business Enterprises?' (*EJIL: Talk!*, 15 May 2017) <https://www.ejiltalk.org/is-international-investment-law-moving-the-ball-forward-on-ihrl-obligations-for-business-enterprises/> accessed 13 May 2021.

Reports

Atanasova D, Martínez CA and Ostřanský J, *Counterclaims in Investor-State Dispute Settlement (ISDS) under International Investment Agreements (IIAs)* (Trade and Investment Law Clinic Papers, 2012).

Berge TL and Stiansen Ø, 'Negotiating BITS with Models: The Power of Expertise' (10th Annual Conference on the Political Economy of International Organizations, University of Bern, Switzerland, January 12–14, 2017).

de Mestral A and Vanhonnaeker L, *Reforming Investor-State Arbitration by Recourse to the Domestic Courts of Host States* (Centre for International Governance Innovation, Policy Brief 156, 2019).

Jarrett M, Puig S and Ratner SR, *Investor Accountability: Indirect Actions, Direct Actions by States, and Direct Actions by Individuals* (Academic Forum on ISDS Concept Paper 2021/1, 10 June 2021).

Nowrot K, *The Other Side of Rights in the Processes of Constitutionalizing International Investment Law: Addressing Investors' Obligations as a New Regulatory Experiment* (Heft 21 Rechtswissenschaftliche Beiträge der Hamburger Sozialökonomie, 2018).

Oman C, *Policy Competition for Foreign Direct Investment* (Organisation for Economic Co-operation and Development, 2000).

Tams CJ, *An Appealing Option? The Debate about an ICSID Appellate Structure* (Essays in Transnational Economic Law No 57, 2006).

Waibel M and Rylatt J, *Counterclaims in International Law* (Legal Studies Research Paper Series, University of Cambridge, Faculty of Law, Paper No 66/2014, 2014).

Index